# IN THE STEPS OF PAUL

We want to hear from you. Please send your comments about this book to us in care of zreview@zondervan.com. Thank you.

*In the Steps of Paul*


Requests for information should be addressed to:

Zondervan, *Grand Rapids, Michigan 49530*

ISBN 978-0-310-29065-0



*Typeset in 9/12 Century Schoolbook*

*Printed and bound in Hong Kong*

08 09 10 11 12 13 14 • 23 22 21 20 19 18 17 16 15 14 13 12 11 10 9 8 7 6 5 4 3 2 1

# IN THE STEPS OF PAUL

## AN ILLUSTRATED GUIDE TO THE APOSTLE'S LIFE AND JOURNEYS

PETER WALKER

ZONDERVAN®

For Ralph,
a fellow traveller on this 'journey of faith,'
with thanks for your generous support.

And for my mother, who in her teenage years loved to study Paul's journeys, and in her latter years travelled with me 'in his steps.'

And with grateful memories of all those who have been my hosts and companions around the Middle East, including:
Michael and Stephanie (Cyprus); Louis and Jane (Malta);
Tom, Hugh, and Tim (Greece); Bruce, Mark, and Nick (Turkey);
Chris (Syria); Georgie, Hannah, and Jonathan (Rome);
as well as those associated with McCabe Travel (London).

# Contents

# Introduction



Saul of Tarsus – known to many as Saint Paul – is a figure from ancient history who, after nearly 2,000 years, continues to provoke controversy. There are those who see him as a great hero, and others who see him as something of a villain. For some, he is the person, perhaps more than any other single individual, who must be credited with successfully exporting the Christian message about Jesus to the world beyond Jesus' native Palestine. For others, he is the person who, because of his own agendas or perhaps an unhealed personality, distorted that message out of all recognition – turning a message of simple love into one of complex theology, or transforming Jesus' kingdom, seemingly open to all, into an exclusive organization, now known as the church.

In writing this book, I have continued to meet both kinds of people, whether in their writings or in personal conversations: those who cannot speak of Paul without an evident trace of annoyance, even anger, and those who cannot speak of him without being moved to tears, brimming with sheer admiration for this remarkable man. In his own day, Paul seems to have provoked a similar polarization of viewpoints. His gutsy determination and dogged persistence, his sharpness of mind and ability to 'fight his corner', were qualities that people could admire, but also resent. What no one could doubt, however, was the way this brilliant, academically able, Jerusalem-trained rabbi had been utterly transformed by the conviction that, contrary to his own earlier beliefs, Jesus was the true Messiah of Israel. That conviction – instilled deep within him, so he claimed, through an encounter with Jesus himself after his crucifixion – was what drove him through the rest of his life and what propelled him far away from Tarsus and Jerusalem into the various far-flung places we will discover in this book.

To follow 'in the steps of Paul', then, is to be taken on a wide-ranging tour around the lands of the Mediterranean. In contrast to Jesus, whose public ministry was effectively confined to an area not more than 150 miles (240 km) in size, with Paul we are looking at an area extending (at its greatest extent, say, from Jerusalem to Rome) of some 1,400 miles (2,250 km) – with a host of places in between. Paul himself clearly had a good sense of geography: on one occasion, writing to the church in Rome (Romans 15:19), he described his ministry as having been conducted in an arc 'from Jerusalem *all the way around* to Illyricum' (modern Albania). So in this book we will find ourselves effectively following that 'arc', travelling around the northern shores of the Mediterranean and tracing the trajectory Paul had set himself – from Jerusalem to Rome.

*'Three times I was shipwrecked, I spent a night and a day in the open sea, I have been constantly on the move. I have been in danger from rivers, in danger from bandits… in danger in the city, in the country, in danger at sea…'*

**2 Corinthians 11:25–26**

And as we do so, it will be hard – whatever our personal attitudes towards this strange figure of the ancient past – not to be moved at least to an admiration, even if a slightly begrudging one, of this man who was prepared to travel so far – on foot, by boat or on a mule – for this cause in which he so passionately believed.

Thus, to pass through the rugged 'Cilician Gates' in southern Turkey today, or to look out over the bleak expanses of ancient Galatia, to visit the market place of Corinth

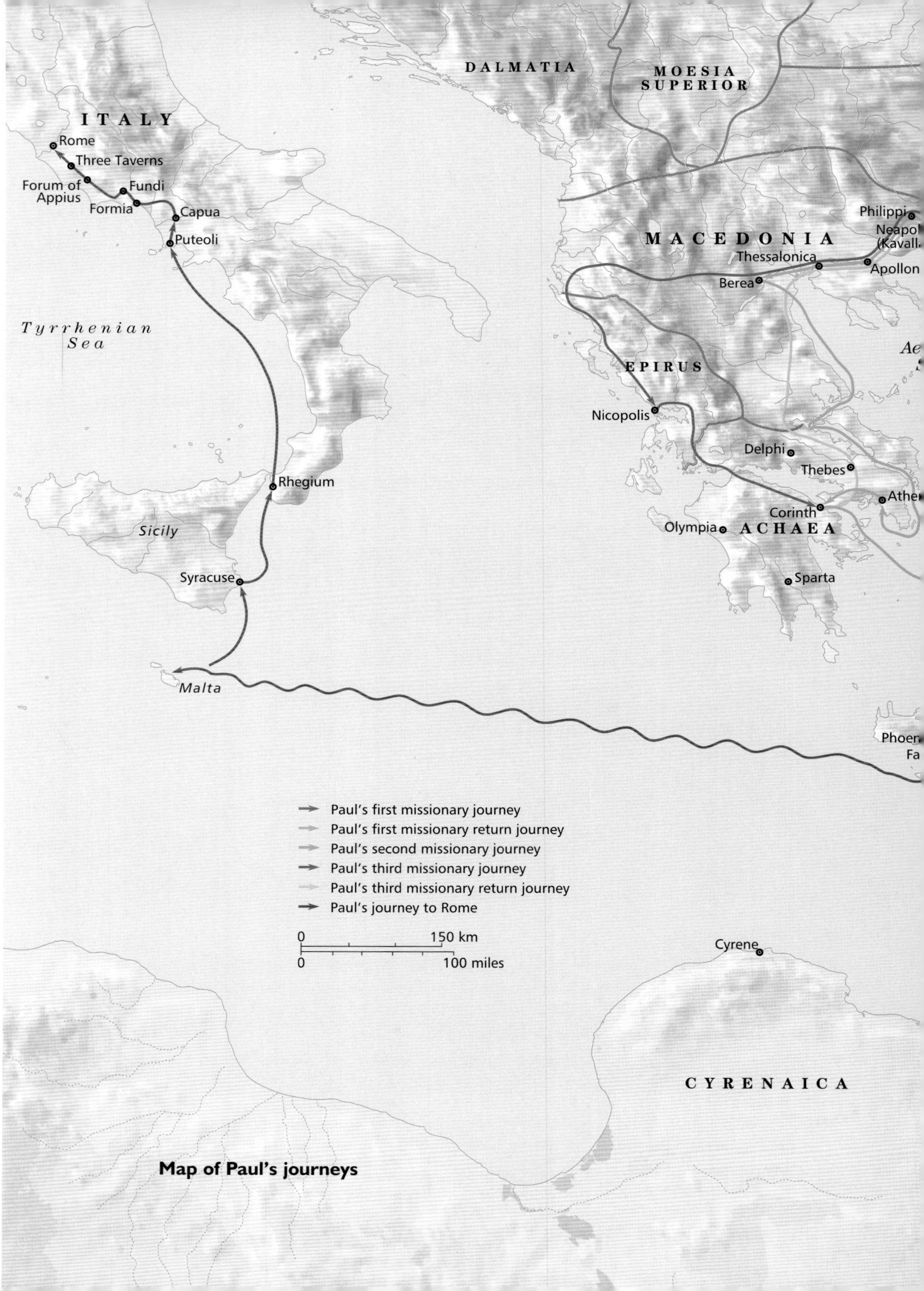

Map of Paul's journeys

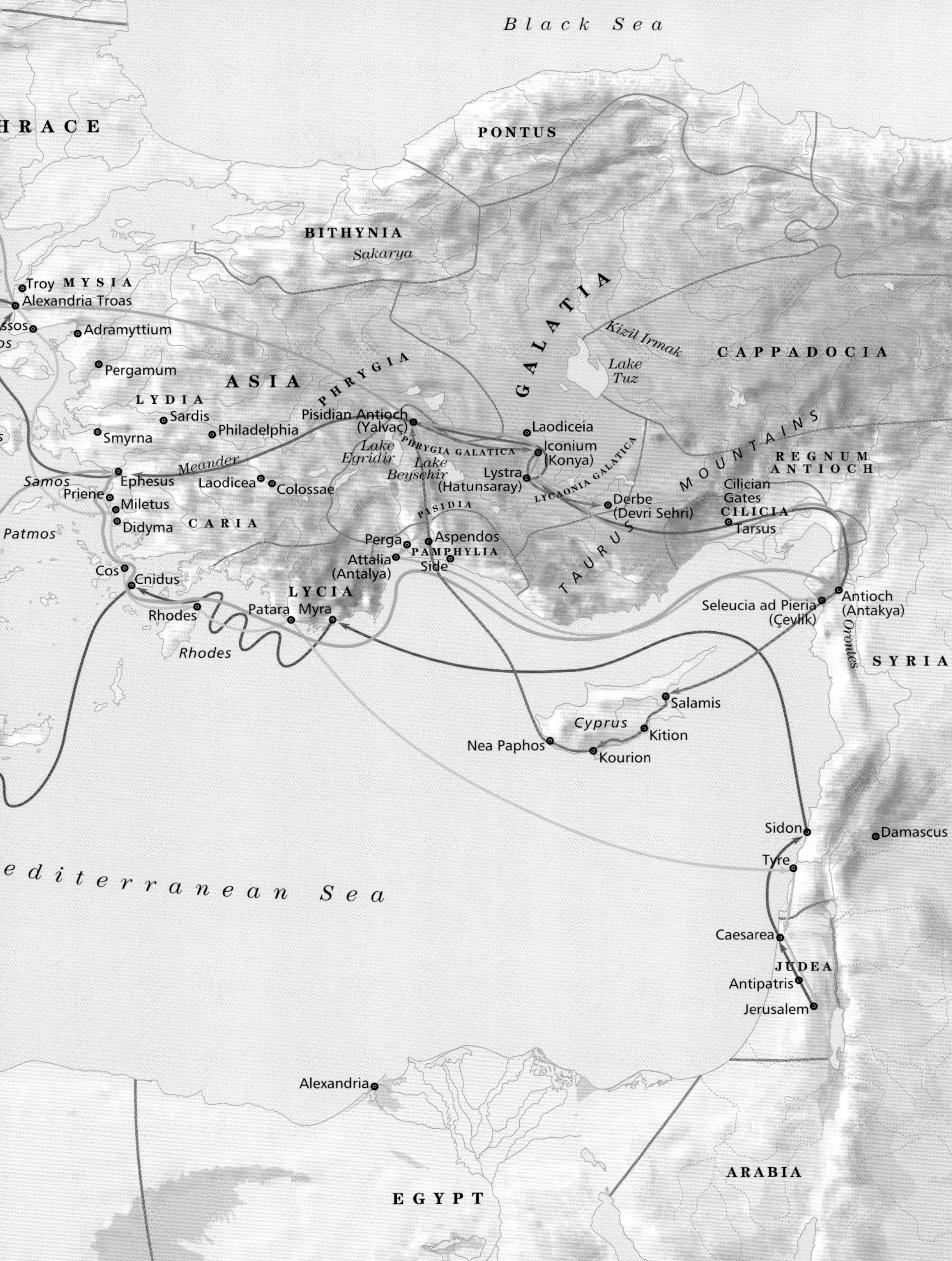
Black Sea
HRACE
PONTUS
BITHYNIA
Sakarya
Troy
MYSIA
Alexandria Troas
Assos
Adramyttium
Pergamum
ASIA
LYDIA
Sardis
Philadelphia
Smyrna
PHRYGIA
GALATIA
Kizil Irmak
CAPPADOCIA
Lake Tuz
Pisidian Antioch (Yalvaç)
Laodiceia
Iconium (Konya)
Lake Egridir
Lake Beysehir
PHRYGIA GALATICA
Lystra (Hatunsaray)
LYCAONIA GALATICA
Derbe (Devri Sehri)
MOUNTAINS
TAURUS
REGNUM ANTIOCH
Cilician Gates
CILICIA
Tarsus
Samos
Ephesus
Meander
Laodicea
Colossae
Priene
Miletus
Didyma
CARIA
Patmos
PISIDIA
Perga
Aspendos
Attalia (Antalya)
PAMPHYLIA
Side
Cos
Cnidus
LYCIA
Rhodes
Patara
Myra
Rhodes
Seleucia ad Pieria (Çevlik)
Antioch (Antakya)
Orontes
SYRIA
Salamis
Cyprus
Kition
Nea Paphos
Kourion
Sidon
Damascus
Tyre
Mediterranean Sea
Caesarea
JUDEA
Antipatris
Jerusalem
Alexandria
EGYPT
ARABIA

The unexcavated mound of ancient Colossae: the city, which lay at the meeting of three rivers, was destroyed by earthquake soon after Paul wrote Colossians.

or Athens or Ephesus, or to stand on the wintry, wind-swept shores of Malta – as I have done in bringing this book to you – all these can be profoundly moving experiences. For these were the places where, without any of the benefits of modern travel, this man – often virtually on his own – was prepared to travel, simply in order to bring people what he believed was good news, the truth of God for their lives. He went way beyond his preferred 'comfort zone'. As a result, one is entitled to believe that he may have been wrong, even mad; but one can hardly claim that he did not love people, or that he was something of a wimp.

Speaking personally, to follow in Paul's physical steps has been an enormously enjoyable enterprise, going back many years. I have been to all the places discussed in this book (apart from two small sites, which you can try to detect!). My journeys to the Mediterranean began in 1977. Five years later, still only twenty years old, I found myself wandering through Turkish cotton fields, trying to discover the then hard-to-find mound of Ancient Colossae. Carrying my two plastic bags and calling out '*harabe?*' (the Turkish for 'ruin?'), I must have made for an interesting sight! Yet I was determined to be one of the few English-speaking people who had stood on this ancient biblical site. In recent years, a tarmac road has been built, making access much easier.

Since then the journey has continued. There were ten years during which, almost without interruption, I was able to celebrate Orthodox Easter somewhere in the Middle East. I was able to lead tours to various countries with McCabe Travel: Greece and Turkey (1993), Turkey (1995), Jordan and Syria (1997), Rome (2002), Turkey (2006). During the 1980s I was privileged to teach various courses at St George's College, Jerusalem. And in 2006/07, thanks to a study grant for this particular project, I was able to make research visits to Cyprus, Malta and Rome. My many thanks to those who made these visits possible, or who made them such good fun as well as so informative (some of whom find themselves mentioned as dedicatees). Repeatedly I have found being in these Pauline areas a source of spiritual encouragement, yielding many fresh

## Key dates: The Roman world

|  |  |
|---|---|
| 218–201 BC | Rome's Second Punic War against Carthage (and Hannibal). |
| 168 BC | Rome's victory in Macedonian War. |
| 149–146 BC | Carthage destroyed in Third Punic War. |
| 146 BC | Rome annexes the Greek mainland. |
| 71 BC | Spartacus' slave revolt crushed by Crassus and Pompey. |
| 60–50 BC | Triumvirate of rulers: Julius Caesar, Crassus and Pompey. |
| 51 BC | Julius Caesar conquers Gaul. |
| 44 BC | Murder of Julius Caesar by Brutus and Cassius (15 March). |
| 42 BC | Octavian defeats Brutus and Cassius at Battle of Philippi. |
| 31 BC | Octavian beats Mark Antony at Battle of Actium. |
| 27 BC–AD 14 | Augustus as emperor. |
| AD 14–37 | Reign of Tiberius. |
| AD 37–41 | Reign of Caligula. |
| AD 41–54 | Claudius as emperor. |
| AD 54–68 | Nero as emperor. |
| AD 64 | Great fire in Rome. |
| AD 68 | The 'year of the four emperors'. |
| AD 69–79 | Vespasian as emperor. |
| AD 79–81 | Titus as emperor. |
| AD 81–96 | Domitian as emperor. |
| AD 96–98 | Nerva as emperor. |
| AD 98–117 | Trajan as emperor. |
| AD 117–38 | Hadrian as emperor. |
| AD 138–61 | Antoninus Pius as emperor. |
| AD 161–80 | Marcus Aurelius as emperor. |
| AD 284 | Empire divided into East and West. |
| AD 312 | Constantine I's victory at Milvian Bridge brings him to power in the West. |
| AD 324 | Constantine I's victory at Adrianople brings him to power in the East. |
| AD 380 | Emperor Theodosius makes Christianity the religion of the Roman empire. |
| AD 410 | First sack of Rome by Alaric and the Goths. |
| AD 475 | Fall of western Roman empire; transfer of power to Byzantium. |





insights into Paul's life and ministry (none of which would have been brought about through sitting in an Oxford study!). The task of regularly teaching students from Paul's letters and also preaching from his words Sunday by Sunday may also have helped narrow any gaps between his era and ours, re-igniting a sense of admiration for this profound theologian and follower of Christ.

So the following pages are an invitation to you now to join in something of Paul's journey, to follow his movements, and to learn from him on the road. They are also an invitation to travel with an open mind, reserving final judgment on this ancient character until we have gone the whole distance and – even if only in our mind's eye or perhaps even in the comfort of our armchair – to follow respectfully 'in his steps'.

## Luke's story of Jesus, then Paul

This volume is intended as a sequel to *In the Steps of Jesus* (Lion Hudson, 2006). This means, for example, that the chapter on Jerusalem – the one significant place visited by *both* Jesus and Paul – deliberately passes over the many places around Jerusalem associated with the life of Jesus, which are covered in the previous volume. It also means we will be following the same format within each chapter: an opening section telling the story of Paul within that location; a final section looking at that site as a visitor might encounter it today (with key features highlighted in bold text to guide readers to places of special interest); and, in between, a list of 'key dates' which gives

## Paul's letters: date and location

The dating of Paul's letters is a subject of great debate. Indeed, it is frequently questioned whether several of them authentically come from Paul himself: might some of them have been written by a follower of Paul? This applies especially to the so-called 'pastoral epistles' (1 and 2 Timothy, Titus) and, to a lesser extent, to Ephesians and Colossians. The charge is made that these letters contain theology, interests or a style that appears inconsistent with the known Pauline letters; there are also perceived issues as to how we may reconcile them with Acts.

This issue cannot be discussed in detail, but a good case can be made for the authenticity of them all. Even from c. AD 100 the Pauline corpus has always included all thirteen letters (that is, there is no record of them being separated from one another). Moreover, 'pseud-epigraphy' (writing under someone else's name 'falsely') was probably not as acceptable a genre in that period as has been argued (especially for what purport to be personal letters by a recently deceased person, rather than impersonal statements of theology or apocalyptic visions imputed to a writer of the ancient past).

Then again, differences in language may be explained in part by the fact that all Paul's letters were actually penned by an *amanuensis* (or scribe) – all, that is, except for the pastoral epistles (which may, paradoxically, reflect Paul's own personal style more accurately than the so-called 'indubitably Pauline' letters). And there is inevitably something rather circular about using the content of these assuredly Pauline letters as a touchstone for judging – 2,000 years after the event – what Paul could have written in his other letters. Far better to take in all the available evidence and let that dictate back to us what is or is not 'Pauline'.

As for dating, one critical issue focuses on Galatians. Because Augustus' new province of 'Galatia' covered a vast area in the central landmass of Asia Minor (and crossed over many regional boundaries), it has been questioned whether Paul's visit to Iconium, Lystra and Derbe (Acts 14) can be seen, strictly, as a visit to Galatia. If not, then Paul's letter must have been written after a different, later visit to the more well-known, northern part of Galatia (probably in AD 50: see Acts 16:6).

Yet, ever since the work of Sir William Mitchell Ramsay (see p. 40), there has been good evidence that Paul could justifiably refer to his converts in this more southern area as 'Galatians' (Galatians 3:1). If Galatians is Paul's first letter, it then contains the opening verses of the entire New Testament – focused remarkably on the divinity of Jesus (Galatians 1:1).

Paul's Corinthian correspondence is also quite complex. Paul probably wrote up to five letters: a short letter, 'A', from Ephesus, warning about immorality (1 Corinthians 5:9–11); after receiving further worrying news, a much longer letter, 'B' (what we know as 1 Corinthians); then, after himself making a brief 'painful visit', a shorter, stronger letter, 'C', sent with Titus (2 Corinthians 2:1–3); next, after meeting up with Titus (in Philippi?), who spoke of receiving a positive welcome from the Corinthians, another longer letter, 'D' (what we now call 2 Corinthians 1–9); and finally, perhaps soon afterwards, a final postscript, 'E' (what we now know as 2 Corinthians 10–13), which takes a rather different tone – perhaps caused by news of disturbances by false teachers.

The greatest disputes relate to the three pastoral epistles. If received as genuinely Pauline, they are dated to the middle 60s AD, presuming that Paul was released from prison and continued further work around the Aegean. There is no independent evidence for this, however, and those (both ancient and modern) who propose this season of ministry only suggest it to find a possible setting for these letters. The position adopted here is that each letter can be located successfully within an earlier period in Paul's ministry.

Luke's words in Acts 20:2–3 suggest there was an extended period (perhaps fifteen to eighteen months between late AD 55 and early AD 57) when Paul was in Macedonia: 'Paul set out for Macedonia [from Ephesus]; he travelled through that area... and *finally* arrived in Greece.' So Paul would have been travelling westwards into Illyricum (which he has visited by the time he writes Romans 15:19 in early AD 57). To this period we can assign 1 Timothy and Titus, both being memos to his key assistants now facing major challenges of their own. Timothy he has just reassigned to Ephesus (1 Timothy 1:3), while Titus (after his visit to Corinth) he has assigned to Crete (Titus 1:5). He then hopes Titus will soon rejoin him for the winter in Nicopolis (Titus 3:12) – which fits well with this suggested reconstruction, since Nicopolis is on the west coast of Greece, a main town through which Paul would have travelled en route to Corinth.

If this reconstruction is correct, then Paul's practical concerns in these two letters (such as arranging widows' rotas) are not signs of Paul having lost his evangelistic edge, but of an experienced church planter who knows that young churches need strong, practical management. And the language he uses (while travelling in remote locations) is the more blunt short-hand one uses in private 'business memos' to trusted colleagues.

Paul's second letter to Timothy breathes a very different air, clearly being written from prison and at some distance in time from 1 Timothy. Written from Rome (2 Timothy 1:17), it is normally assumed to be Paul's last letter, because of Paul's tone as he approaches death. As suggested later (p. 191), however, it could be Paul's *first* letter after arriving in Rome. Timothy's arrival from Ephesus then cheers his spirits and, with Timothy, he writes Colossians and Philemon, and also a more general letter to the churches in Asia (Ephesians). This would leave Philippians to be Paul's last extant letter.

Although some have argued that several of these 'prison epistles' might date to Paul's earlier confinements (in Ephesus or, especially, in Caesarea), the majority favour this Roman location. If so, Paul's final words from Rome are very suitable: 'Rejoice in the Lord always... my God will meet all your needs... The grace of the Lord Jesus be with your spirit. Amen' (Philippians 4:4, 19, 23).

| | ACTS REFERENCE | LETTER | LOCATION | DATE |
|---|---|---|---|---|
| **A. After first journey** | (Acts 13–14) | Galatians | Antioch | Late AD 48 |
| **Apostolic council** | (Acts 15:1–35) | | | AD 49 |
| **B. During second journey** | (Acts 15:36 – 18:22) | 1 Thessalonians | Corinth | AD 51 |
| | | 2 Thessalonians | Corinth | AD 52 |
| **C. During third journey** | (Acts 19:1–21:17) | 1 Corinthians | Ephesus | AD 53/54 |
| | | 2 Corinthians (1–9) | Philippi? | AD 55 |
| | | 2 Corinthians (10–13) | Western Macedonia | AD 56 |
| | | 1 Timothy | Illyricum | AD 56 |
| | | Titus | Illyricum | AD 56 |
| | | Romans | Corinth | AD 57 |
| **Arrival in Jerusalem** | | | | May AD 57 |
| **Caesarean imprisonment** | | | | AD 57–59 |
| **Final journey to Rome** | (Acts 21:17 – 28:29) | | | AD 59 |
| **D. During Roman imprisonment** | (Acts 28:30–31) | | | AD 60–?64 |
| | | 2 Timothy | Rome | Early AD 60 |
| | | Colossians | Rome | AD 61/62 |
| | | Philemon | Rome | AD 61/62 |
| | | Ephesians | Rome | AD 61/62 |
| | | Philippians | Rome | AD 62/63 |

Relief of Paul's martyrdom on a Roman sarcophagus (fourth century AD).

Greek Orthodox Christians celebrate the message of Jesus' resurrection in an Easter Vigil service at the church of Panagista, on the island of Aegina in the Saronic Gulf near Athens.

the reader at a glance an overview of all the significant events associated with that place – both before and since the time of Paul.

We will also continue to be guided in our travels by Luke. In the previous volume we followed the life of Jesus by looking at fourteen sites from Luke's Gospel; here, there are fourteen sites from Luke's sequel volume, the book of Acts. As with Jesus, some of these places were, of course, places Paul visited more than once. Inevitably this means that the main sequential storyline gets broken up a little – for example, when we need to look at *all* Paul's dealings with Antioch, both *before* and *after* his visits to Jerusalem. Yet the main trajectory of Luke's account is still preserved. Thus we begin in Damascus (followed by a 'recap' back to Tarsus), then follow Paul on his first and second 'missionary journeys', then return to Palestine for his final visits to Jerusalem and Caesarea, and eventually (after a detour to Malta) arrive in Rome.

Luke himself, when constructing the book of Acts, seems to have had in mind a fairly clear geographical scheme. Taking his cue from Jesus' command to his followers to bear witness to him 'in Jerusalem, and in all Judea and Samaria, and to the ends of the earth' (Acts 1:8), he then tells the story of the early church as one of expanding concentric circles. Thus Acts chapters 1 to 7 are focused exclusively on Jerusalem (from the first preaching about Jesus through to the death of Stephen, the first martyr). With chapter 8 we move north to Samaria, as many believers in response to persecution are 'scattered throughout Judea and Samaria' (Acts 8:1); indeed we find the message of Jesus spreading out westwards as well – along the road to Gaza (Acts 8:26), and to the coastal city of Caesarea (Acts 10:1 – 11:18). And then, after a final story in chapter 12 relating to Jerusalem (Peter's escape from prison), we begin to leave Palestine altogether as Luke recounts Paul's first 'missionary journey' (from Antioch to Cyprus, Pamphylia and Galatia).

So, despite Paul's fairly frequent returns to his 'sending church' in Antioch as well as to the 'mother-church' in Jerusalem, the overall direction of both Paul's travels and Luke's recounting of them is persistently outwards – going out to the 'ends of the earth'. The first reference explicitly to Rome comes quite early (in Acts 19:21), and





## Key dates: Luke and Paul

Many of these dates must remain conjectural due to lack of evidence. Fortunately independent Roman records allow us to establish two 'fixed points': the procurator Festus arrived in Judea during AD 59; and Gallio served as proconsul in Achaia during the 26th year of Claudius' emperorship (AD 52), so his period of office probably started on 1 July, AD 51.

For Paul's early years as a Christian we need to interpret the combined evidence of Luke's account in Acts and Paul's own letter to Galatians, in which Paul mentions two visits to Jerusalem after his conversion – one 'after three years', the other 'after fourteen years' (Galatians 1:18; 2:1). These references are probably to be read *concurrently* (i.e. with the gap between visits therefore being *eleven* years). Assuming that the second visit is to be identified with that recorded in Acts 11:30, the date for Paul's conversion must fall within the first couple of years after Jesus' crucifixion.

What precisely happens after Luke and Paul reach Rome is also unclear, with many suggesting later dates for the deaths of Paul and (especially) Luke: for further discussion, see pp. 192–95.

| | |
|---|---|
| C. AD 5? | Birth of Paul (in Tarsus) and Luke (in Philippi?). |
| C. AD 20 | Paul sent to Jerusalem for his education under Gamaliel II (rejoining members of his wider family?). |
| AD 30 | Probable date of crucifixion (Friday, 7 April). An alternative possible date is Friday, 4 April, AD 33. |
| AD 31/32 | Paul's conversion on road to Damascus (Acts 9:1–19). |
| AD 34/35 | Paul's brief return to Jerusalem and then home to Tarsus (Acts 9:26–30; Galatians 1:18–20). |
| C. AD 40 | Paul summonsed by Barnabas to work in Antioch (Acts 11:25–26). |
| AD 45 | Paul and Barnabas visit Jerusalem to offer famine relief (Acts 11:27–30; Galatians 2:1). |
| AD 46 | Paul and Barnabas' first 'missionary journey' to Cyprus, Pamphylia and Galatia (Acts 13–14). |
| AD 49 | Urgent apostolic council in Jerusalem (Acts 15). |
| AD 50 | Paul's second 'missionary journey', travelling into Macedonia and Athens (Acts 15:41–17:33). Luke first meets Paul in Troas (Acts 16:8–10) and stays on in Philippi. |
| AD 50–52 | Paul stays eighteen months in Corinth and appears before Gallio (proconsul of Achaia). |
| AD 52–55 | Paul based in Ephesus for three years (Acts 19:1 – 20:1). |
| AD 55–56 | Paul travels for up to eighteen months through Macedonia, Illyricum and western Greece (Acts 20:1–2). |
| AD 57 | Paul spends three months in Corinth (Jan–Mar) and then reconnoitres with Luke in Philippi, travelling with him and other Gentile converts up to Jerusalem in time for Pentecost (late May). |
| AD 57–59 | Paul imprisoned in Caesarea Maritima for two years under governor Felix (Acts 23:34 – 24:27); Luke travels round Palestine. When Festus arrives as governor, Paul appeals to Caesar (Acts 25:11). |
| AD 59 (autumn) | Paul and Luke sail from Palestine and are shipwrecked, landing eventually on Malta (Acts 27). |
| AD 60 (spring) | Paul and Luke arrive in Rome (Acts 28:14). |
| AD 62/63? | Earliest possible date for death of Luke in Rome. |
| AD 63/64 | Paul martyred in Rome under Nero (beheaded near Ostian Way), probably some time prior to the great fire in Rome (14 July, AD 64). |

thereafter the final third of Luke's volume is effectively the story of how Paul, by some circuitous routes, eventually arrived in Rome. 'And so we came to Rome' (Acts 28:14) may thus be a tiny sentence, but it serves as a powerful climax to Luke's account. So, although the overall story of the book of Acts is that of the early church's message going out from Jerusalem 'to the ends of the earth', within that there is a major sub-plot, which is the story of how *one man*, Paul, himself came eventually to *Rome*.

For obvious reasons, in this volume the focus is squarely upon that sub-plot; so comparatively little attention will be given to the parts of Acts that do not relate directly to Paul. Even so, I hope this book will be a useful accompaniment to the book of Acts (offering something of an illustrated commentary) and serve as a useful window, not just onto the world of Paul, but also onto the world of Luke.

## Luke's two worlds

Luke was a man who lived in two worlds. Probably a native of Philippi on the Aegean, his natural world was Greco-Roman. At some point, however, he seems to have become a 'God-fearer', standing at the edge of the Jewish synagogue, looking in respectfully on the alternative world of Judaism.

Then, when he came to faith in Jesus as the Jewish Messiah, a strange thing happened. For, in one sense, he was thereby ushered into the very centre of that Jewish world. That is why in his Gospel he takes such great pains to help his readers (perhaps originally Gentiles like him) to travel back into the Jewish world of Jesus – so that they can better understand Jesus when set truly in *his* native world. In the book of Acts, however, Luke at last has the opportunity to travel in the opposite direction, coming back into the Greco-Roman world, but this time with the good news of Jesus. And his account in Acts then tells the story of how these two different worlds began to collide, jostling with one another, as the message about Jesus – if you like, the *Jewish* king set paradoxically over the *whole world* – began to make its journey out from Jerusalem.

So, as we travel with Paul and learn the very different histories of the places that he visited, we can begin to sense too something of this clash of cultures – a clash that his own visits brought dramatically to a head. We can also sense some of the reasons why Paul might have been so unpopular: going out as a Jew into the 'pagan' world, he was now neither straightforwardly Jewish, nor straightforwardly Gentile, but something in between – something bizarrely new. No wonder people on both sides sometimes reacted against him. And no wonder, too, that the Christian communities he founded sometimes experienced a 'rocky ride' as they tried to navigate successfully between these two well-established, but competing, worlds.

## Finding Paul's heart

Finally, a word about trying to reconstruct Paul's life from this distance in time (for a proposed chronology, see pp. 12–13, 15). From a historian's point of view, we are fortunate to have not just Luke's account in Acts but also Paul's own letters. We should be so grateful that Paul actually wrote something down in black and white – unlike Jesus! Paul's 'epistles' therefore give us the possibility of a further window into Paul's world, giving us key insights into his inner character and his detailed responses to various situations. In fact, Paul often writes in touchingly personal ways with his 'heart on his sleeve', which means we can come to know him more intimately perhaps than any other figure from ancient history.

There continues, of course, to be scholarly debate about the authenticity of some of Paul's letters and also about the reliability of Luke's account in Acts. The view adopted here, however, is that all this first-century evidence is to be highly valued and respected. Moreover, the various pieces of evidence, through using a bit of common sense and human intuition, can quite reasonably be brought together to provide a reliable, indeed three-dimensional, portrait of Paul.

In what follows, then, I have tried to take you inside something of Paul's mind and heart, as gleaned from his own writings. In the previous volume, which focused on Jesus, that was not possible – for all kinds of reasons. With Paul, however, this attempt can be made. So, although our title means we need only follow in Paul's *steps*, it remains possible that on this journey we may also, hopefully, come to find and follow something of his heart.

CHAPTER

# Damascus

*[Saul] went to the high priest and asked him for letters to the synagogues in Damascus, so that if he found any there who belonged to the Way… he might take them as prisoners to Jerusalem. As he neared Damascus on his journey, suddenly a light from heaven flashed around him. He fell to the ground and heard a voice say to him, 'Saul, Saul, why do you persecute me?' 'Who are you, Lord?' Saul asked. 'I am Jesus, whom you are persecuting,' he replied. 'Now get up and go into the city, and you will be told what you must do.' So [his companions] led him by the hand into Damascus. For three days he was blind, and did not eat or drink anything.*

*In Damascus there was a disciple named Ananias. The Lord called to him in a vision, 'Ananias!… Go to the house of Judas on Straight Street and ask for a man from Tarsus named Saul.'*

**Acts 9:2–6, 8–11**

## Drama on the road

A young, bearded man, perhaps in his late twenties, is making his way to a foreign city. He is a man with an agenda – right now he is planning what to do once inside the city's gates. Some people there will regret the day he arrived, but that doesn't matter. They should have thought of that before joining this new 'messianic' sect – this wretched so-called 'Way'!

This earnest Law student, plotting his strategy under his breath, is approaching the end of an arduous, 150-mile- (240-km-) long journey, which began in Jerusalem nearly a week ago. He set out with several companions, and ever since they've been riding their mules by day and camping under the stars at night. Some of them are soldiers, ready to help him take some prisoners, and he's asked one of them to carry the all-important 'extradition warrants'.

The day before yesterday they were beside Lake Galilee, travelling along the *Via Maris* through a tiny village called Capernaum. But now, after making their way over the bleak, volcanic hills of Gaulanitis, they are at last travelling downhill. The massif of Mount Hermon is now behind them away to their left, but there in front of them, less than 10 miles (15 km) towards the north-east, set in a plain amid some low hills, is their destination – the capital of Israel's ancient Syrian enemies, the trading city of Damascus.

The oasis city certainly looks attractive in the piercing heat of the noon-day sun. He's never been to this 'pagan' city of commerce before, but this pernicious teaching about Jesus of Nazareth must be 'nipped in the bud' before it spreads any further. In a strange, sinister way he is rather looking forward to this assignment. Perhaps even by bedtime tonight he will have caught red-handed some followers of this dangerous 'Way'.

Success here will surely not go unnoticed by the bosses back home.

But what happens next is something totally unexpected and undesired, something that turns his tiny world upside down and inside out. He is encountered, so Luke asserts, by the risen Jesus. The very person whose followers he is going to arrest now appears to him and speaks directly to him by name. Almost speechless with fear, dreading the truth that this might indeed be that impostor Jesus, he falls to the ground before the one whose name he has hated, the object of his righteous anger and zeal.

We are witnessing here the 'conversion' of Saul, the Jew from Tarsus – known to later history and to us as the 'apostle Paul'. (From this point on we shall refer to him by his Greek name, 'Paul'.)





## Christ on the road

It is a powerful story. A 'Damascus road experience' is a phrase used in many different contexts – political or religious – to describe a sudden change in a person's beliefs or direction. But for Luke (the event's narrator in Acts) this was a change that the individual concerned neither desired nor effected. It was done *to* him; it came from outside.

A satellite view over the Bible Lands (Israel, Jordan, Lebanon and Syria), showing (from the south) the Dead Sea, Lake Galilee, the snows on Mount Hermon and the anti-Lebanon Mountains, and the Mediterranean coast near Sidon. Damascus, marked by the red dot, is only 50 miles (80 km) from Capernaum, Jesus' base of operations near Lake Galilee.

It was also, for Luke, yet another instance of something strange happening on a 'road' outside a capital city. The climax of Luke's first volume (his Gospel) was the account of the risen Jesus appearing to some of his followers on the Emmaus road outside Jerusalem. Now, as Luke launches what will become the major focus of his second volume (the adventures and mission of Paul), he is compelled by the facts to begin in the same way: *the risen Christ appeared to Paul*. We won't begin to understand Paul, says Luke, if we don't reckon seriously with this surprising idea – the resurrection of Jesus from the dead. No risen Christ, no Paul. The story of Paul, then, more deeply, is the story of the risen Jesus at work through his servant. In following the 'steps of Paul', if you like, we find ourselves once again tracing the 'steps of Jesus' – but in a different mode.

So this road outside Damascus is where we too have to begin as we follow *In the Steps of Saint Paul*. Paul's earlier life had taken him from Tarsus to Jerusalem (see pp. 34–35), but Paul would have seen those earlier days as no true life at all: 'whatever was to my profit', he wrote many years later, 'I now consider loss for the sake of Christ' (Philippians 3:7). If we wish to understand what made him tick, we have to start here – nowhere else – on the trade route approaching Damascus. It is indeed a strange place, but then Paul himself would have been the first to agree!

## Paul's conversion in later Christian thought

Paul's experience on the Damascus road has almost always been referred to as his 'conversion' – even though this term is not used by either Luke or Paul himself – and has often been held up as the definitive version of genuine 'conversion'. Such dramatic 'conversions' do occur; many people, however, go through a process far less dramatic or sudden.

The New Testament writers are clear that there is a vital distinction between belief and non-belief; they are far less prescriptive about how any one individual may cross over that line. Their refusal to use Paul's experience as the necessary paradigm can then bring reassurance to many who can be troubled that they have never themselves had such a 'Damascus road experience'; seeing a 'blinding light' is not the only way people meet with Christ by faith.

### A unique event

The New Testament refuses to use Paul's conversion in this way precisely because it was unique. Paul claimed it was the last of the never-to-be-repeated resurrection appearances granted by the risen Jesus to his apostles (1 Corinthians 15:8). Although it occurred in a different time and place from those other appearances, there is evidence that the other apostles recognized it as such (Acts 9:27; 1 Corinthians 9:1). Moreover, in this event Paul received a unique calling – to be the 'apostle to the Gentiles' (Romans 15:16).

There are other ways in which Paul's conversion was highly unusual. These have more to do with the fact that Paul himself had become such a unique individual – a learned Pharisee, zealous to the point of extremism, now suddenly brought to his knees. The Jewish persecutor becomes the Christian apostle. It is a story, then, which speaks of other major themes: the triumph of divine grace; the vanquishing of a human will; the conquering of human pride.

### Paul's prior problems?

In recent years Pauline scholars have asked whether Paul's conversion also speaks about the way a tortured, questioning soul finds a sudden resolution to its seemingly hopeless problem. Two of the church's greatest theologians, Augustine (AD 354–430) and Luther (1483–1546), both experienced years of self-questioning before they had a life-changing encounter with the truth of Christ. Was this what Paul also went through?

Many have thought so, suggesting that Paul was secretly anxious about his spiritual state, perhaps despairing of his sins and becoming disillusioned with the Torah as a means of solving this inner conflict. They see Paul as beset by a 'plight' which then found a glorious 'solution' in Christ – hence his delight in the message of God's forgiveness and his (sometimes strong) criticisms of the Law (Romans 3:20). Did Paul criticize the Law because of his own earlier struggles, finding that it could not make him righteous but only revealed to him his sin?

Intriguingly, however, Paul's own references to his former life speak strongly against this reconstruction. 'As for legalistic righteousness,' he says, he was 'faultless' (Philippians 3:6); 'I was once a blasphemer, a persecutor and a violent man' (1 Timothy 1:13). These phrases suggest someone who had a robust conscience, with little awareness that anything was amiss. If so, Paul's inner life was not secretly unravelling; there were no feelings of inner turmoil or desperation that might have been propelling him towards Christ, finding in him their resolution; on the contrary, he was moving 'full steam ahead' in the opposite direction.

If you like, then, it was not until he was confronted by the 'solution' offered by Christ that he realized the 'plight' he was in. And this 'plight' was not just his own total 'ignorance and unbelief' (1 Timothy 1:13), but also the plight of the nation of Israel (in danger of missing her messiah, using the Law wrongly and failing to see God's purposes for the Gentiles). If God's covenant purposes entailed the crucifixion of Israel's messiah, then evidently something had gone radically amiss; and he, despite his great learning, had evidently totally 'missed the plot' as revealed in the Hebrew Scriptures. Paul was thus sent back by Christ to re-evaluate everything from scratch.

Yet, not everything was therefore dismissed. A further reason why the word 'conversion' can be misleading is that it might imply that Paul therefore jettisoned *everything* he had previously believed. In fact, of course, his fundamental framework never changed. He was always an ardent believer in Israel's covenant God and radically opposed to idolatry. What was new was the *content* within this framework – it had been filled with the realities of God's Spirit and the risen Jesus. In this sense Paul's 'conversion' might better be called a 'transformation'.

### The long-term view

Surprisingly, neither Augustine nor Luther was tempted to see Paul's conversion as a mirror of his own. Instead, throughout most of the church's history, Paul's conversion has been seen primarily as a demonstration of God's power and grace overcoming a proud, human will, not as the calming of an excessively introspective conscience. In fact, this theme was only promoted by the Puritans (noting how individuals are 'prepared' to encounter God's grace) and then by post-Enlightenment scholars (trying to find a less 'supernatural' and more psychological explanation).

These latter attempts often led to some fanciful reconstructions: was Paul an epileptic under seizure, or perhaps suffering from a fever and then confused by a strike of lightning over Mount Hermon? By contrast, the book of Acts on three separate occasions goes to great length to insist that Paul truly was met by the risen Christ. And, though there may be questions about precise details, the radical new direction of Paul's life confirms for many that what occurred on the Damascus road was indeed nothing other than what he claimed – a dramatic encounter with Christ.

## Damascus' biblical background

Damascus was a city with a long history, going back nearly two millennia. Endowed with two main rivers (the Abana and the Pharpar), which brought water down from the 'anti-Lebanon' mountain range to the north-west, it was indeed a welcome oasis. Anyone travelling towards the Mediterranean from the Fertile Crescent to the East would, almost of necessity, pass through Damascus. It was the natural gateway for anyone taking trade to the coast or down to Egypt. Meanwhile, for those coming from the land of Israel, Damascus was the natural goal of the *Via Maris* (the 'Way of the Sea') – the first city you encountered as you travelled over what we now know as the 'Golan Heights'.

Of all the places we shall visit, Damascus is the only one that has any real significance within previous biblical history, being mentioned in episodes associated with Abraham, David, Solomon and kings of the northern kingdom of Israel such as Ahab and Ahaz (see p. 24). For our purposes, however, perhaps the most intriguing biblical story associated with Damascus is that of Naaman, a Syrian army commander in the era of the prophet Elisha, who suffered from leprosy and travelled in the hope of finding a cure. When told by Elisha (not directly, but via some messengers) to wash seven times in the River Jordan, he was affronted, thinking he could have saved all this travel by washing instead in the much better Abana and Pharpar rivers back in Damascus. But, persuaded by his servant (who recognized his master was reacting in pride), Naaman did what Elisha had instructed: washed himself in the Jordan and was healed. His skin, we read, 'was restored and became clean like that of a young boy' (2 Kings 5:14).

The story has parallels with Paul's: against his wishes, a proud man is humbled by the gracious act of Israel's God, and then receives physical healing; and this all happens, humiliatingly, under the gaze of 'servants' who witness what their leader goes through. In Paul's case, however, he was not a Gentile person travelling *towards* Israel, but instead an Israelite going *out* to a foreign nation.

*'I consider everything a loss compared to the surpassing greatness of knowing Christ Jesus my Lord, for whose sake I have lost all things. I consider them rubbish, that I may gain Christ…'*

**Philippians 3:8**

## The colony in a foreign land

By the first century AD, Damascus would have been home not just to people of Syrian background but also to many Greeks and Jews. There was a substantial Jewish colony here in the first century AD – the nearest such colony outside the borders of historic 'Israel'. As such, it was a natural first choice both for Jesus' first followers (wishing to spread their message) and for Paul (desiring to rein in this contagious new sect).

Some suggest that Paul's journey to Damascus (recounted by Luke in Acts 9) may have taken place up to seven years after Jesus' resurrection (itself probably in AD 30). It is more likely that it occurred in the first couple of years (c. AD 32). There is no real reason why the events mentioned in Luke's previous chapters (Acts 5–8) could not have occurred in the first year or two of the church's life. Regardless of the precise date, however, what is remarkable is that the message about Jesus had already been taken to Damascus (with news of this then being reported back to Jerusalem). There was clearly something sufficiently sensational about Jesus that people wanted to share with others far and wide. This rapid spread of the message about Jesus (going out beyond the historic borders of Israel) then becomes further evidence for Jesus' resurrection. For a message about a merely crucified (and therefore failed) messiah would have offered little to anyone happily settled in Damascus' Jewish colony. If Jesus was simply a holy man and a great teacher, so what? It was only the resurrection that suddenly lifted Jesus' messiahship onto a whole new level – with implications for people far away from Jerusalem.

## Detecting motives: Paul and the high priest

*'… a Hebrew of Hebrews; in regard to the law, a Pharisee; as for zeal, persecuting the church; as for legalistic righteousness, faultless.'*
**Philippians 3:5–6**

We can only speculate as to what exactly Paul was doing in Jerusalem at this time (see p. 35) and why he was entrusted with this delicate task by the chief priests. Was he the most capable Torah student in the city, or the most nationalistic? Paul may have been, as we say, 'ahead of his class'; but in two later descriptions of his 'previous way of life' he twice highlights his 'zeal'. Within a few years the name 'Zealot' would be coined to describe those ardent Jewish nationalists who wanted to take God's law into their own hands and take up arms against the Roman overlords to fulfil God's prophesied purposes for Israel. Perhaps, then, Paul's Pharisaism was deeply coloured by this nationalistic agenda.

There were two main schools of Pharisaism: the strict Shammaites and the more moderate Hillelites. What, then, if the young Paul in his zeal identified with the Shammaite school? And what if that strand of Pharisaism was fiercely nationalistic – zealous for political independence? This would fit well with the wording of some of Paul's later speeches when, for example, he states that he 'lived as a Pharisee, according to the strictest sect of our religion' (Acts 26:5). So Paul's particular brand of Pharisaism may have played its part in making him something of a hot-head – both in religious terms and in more overtly 'political' ones.

*'For you have heard of my previous way of life in Judaism, how intensely I persecuted the church of God and tried to destroy it. I was advancing in Judaism beyond many Jews of my own age and was extremely zealous for the traditions of my fathers.'*
**Galatians 1:14**

This might then only have made his anger at this new messianic movement all the more heated. For not only were the first followers of Jesus being almost blasphemous in their exaltation of Jesus as 'Messiah'; they were also effectively undermining this all-important nationalistic cause. In effect, they were saying that Israel should be grateful for being sent a non-political messiah. Quite possibly, too, they may already have begun welcoming Gentiles into their new messianic movement, thus compromising the political boundary lines of Israel. Paul himself was probably quite keen on Gentile 'proselytism' – that is, bringing people into the nation of Israel. But this would have involved their being circumcised. What he could never have countenanced was a movement that brought people in as *un*circumcised Gentiles. No wonder, in Luke's memorable phrase, he was 'breathing out murderous threats' against any followers of this Jesus (Acts 9:1).

And why was the high priest getting himself involved? All becomes clear if this was Caiaphas (the chief priest who, a few years earlier, had put Jesus on trial). For his determination to root out this Jesus 'heresy' would be fuelled by personal anger – that Jesus' followers were saying that he, Caiaphas, had been involved in the execution of Israel's Messiah. In any event, this despatching of Paul comes across as a fairly desperate strategy, showing the evident threat that this new sect was posing. For it probably represented a significant overplaying of his prerogatives. After all, Damascus was a foreign city under the authority of King Aretas IV; so it was highly unusual – perhaps even quite a risk – to be extraditing some of the king's citizens.

## The moment of revelation

Luke then gives us three fascinating accounts of what happened next, as Paul drew close to Damascus (Acts 9; Acts 22:5–11; Acts 26:11–18). These accounts provide a key into understanding Paul's subsequent life and work. And in each of them we find the same nugget at the heart of the story. The voice says, 'Saul, Saul, why are you persecuting me?' Paul asks, 'Who are you, Lord?' And Jesus replies, 'I am Jesus whom you are persecuting.'

This interchange would be branded on Paul's memory for the rest of his life. Just as Moses had encountered Israel's God, who gave himself the name 'I AM', at the burning bush (Exodus 3), so now Paul under the noon-day sun encounters him – but in the form of Jesus ('*I AM* Jesus'). And just as Moses had thereby been given a new commission (to rescue God's persecuted people and bring them to freedom), so now Paul finds himself with a new task, as relayed to him by Ananias a few days later in Damascus: Paul learns he is to be God's 'chosen instrument' to carry his name 'before the Gentiles' (Acts 9:15).

Paul learns from this that he must stop playing the role of the arch-persecutor (as Pharaoh had in the past); that it is *Jesus'* people who are now truly God's people; and that, if people everywhere are to experience true freedom, it will come about through his proclaiming this message about Jesus.

*'God, who set me apart from birth and called me by his grace, was pleased to reveal his Son in me so that I might preach him among the Gentiles.'*

**Galatians 1:15–16**

## The lessons Paul learnt

The event marked Paul for life. Not surprisingly, soon afterwards he went off on his own into the deserts of Arabia to begin the task of processing it all (Galatians 1:17) – a process that continued once back home in Tarsus (see pp. 36–39). For now we note what this event may have meant for Paul himself.

Because of the encounter on the Damascus road Paul became convinced that God's surprising purposes included a distinct role for him as an individual. All the accounts in Acts indicate that Paul's role as an apostle to the Gentiles was a vital ingredient within this encounter. This man, a 'Hebrews of Hebrews', would have the paradoxical role of taking this radical new message out to the Gentiles – perhaps precisely because only someone so steeped in the Jewish faith would have the theological agility and necessary authority to declare that this was God's appointed time for Gentiles to be included.

At a more personal level, Paul learnt this: that he could be massively wrong. His religious 'zeal' had been misplaced; his devotion to the Law had misled him; he was more of a sinner than he knew; and to follow Jesus was now to be his supreme goal. He was broken and then remade; he was humbled and then lifted up. The whole thing spoke of undeserved, unexpected 'grace', as seen in the way Paul spoke of this event in later life:

*Even though I was once a blasphemer and a persecutor and a violent man, I was shown mercy because I acted in ignorance and unbelief. The grace of our Lord was poured out on me abundantly... Christ Jesus came into the world to save sinners – of whom I am the worst.*

**1 Timothy 1:13–15**

*'For I am the least of the apostles, because I persecuted the church of God. But by the grace of God I am what I am.'*

**1 Corinthians 15:9–10**

## Away from Damascus

Paul's life had been turned upside down in an instant: going 'full steam ahead' in one direction, the next moment he had hit a brick wall and was being propelled in completely the opposite direction. We can imagine Paul lying on his bed in Damascus the next day, temporarily blinded, trying to make sense of it all. We are told, not surprisingly, that he was 'praying' (Acts 9:11). He was trying to take it all in.

Then a few days later, Ananias bravely came to where Paul was staying somewhere 'on Straight Street' (the main street in Damascus' walled city). Paul's sight was restored, he received God's Spirit and was soon 'preaching in the synagogues' (Acts 9:18–22). This understandably provoked a heated reaction – the very reaction he himself would have had a few weeks earlier – and some even desired to kill him. 'But his followers took him by night and lowered him in a basket through an opening in the wall' (Acts 9:25).

### Key dates: Damascus

|  |  |
|---|---|
| 2400–2250 BC | Clay tablets in Ebla refer to the city of 'Dimashqi'. |
| 2000–1800 BC | Abraham rescues Lot from his captors in a battle near Damascus (Genesis 14:15–16) and fears that 'Eliezer of Damascus' will become his heir (Genesis 15:2). |
| 1400s BC | An inscription attributed to the Egyptian pharaoh, Thutmose III, refers to a 'Timasqu', now under Egyptian control. |
| 1300s BC | The Amarna letters refer to 'Timaasghi'; Damascus occasionally under Hittite control. |
| c. 1250–c. 1000 BC | Damascus is under Aramaean control. |
| c. 1000–960 BC | David and then Solomon control the city (2 Samuel 8:5–6; 10:6–19). |
| 850–750 BC | Damascus' kings (Ben-Hadad I and II, Hazael etc) in frequent conflict with Israel's kings (1 Kings 15, 20, 22; 2 Kings 6–13). |
| 727 & 720 BC | Unsuccessful revolts in Damascus against the Assyrians. |
| 612 BC | Damascus ruled by the Babylonians; then by the Persians (from 539 BC); then by the Greeks (from 333 BC). |
| 274 BC | Damascus rescued from a brief spell of Egyptian control and brought within the Seleucid empire. |
| 85 BC | King Aretas III of Nabataea takes over control from the Seleucids. |
| 64 BC | The Roman general, Pompey, captures the city, now included in the Roman province of Syria; later Antony gives the city to Cleopatra, who in turn gives it to Octavian. |
| 40 BC | Brief marauding attack by the Parthians on both Damascus and Galilee. |
| 9 BC | Reign of the Nabataean king, Aretas IV. |
| c. AD 20s | The temple of Hadad-Rimmon (the storm god) is rebuilt as an imperial temple to Jupiter. |
| AD 31/32 | Paul's aborted visit to the Jewish colony in Damascus and his 'conversion' as he approaches the city; he later escapes in a basket through the city wall (Acts 9:1–25). |
| AD 34/35 | Paul (after some time in Arabia) returns to Damascus and then departs for Jerusalem (Galatians 1:17–18). |
| AD 40 | Death of the Nabataean ruler of Damascus, Aretas IV. |
| AD 67 | 18,000 Jews massacred in Damascus during the First Jewish War (Josephus, *War* 2.20.2). |
| AD 105 | Damascus and Nabataea brought within Roman province of Syria (ruled from Antioch). |
| AD 325 | Delegation from Damascus attends the Council of Nicaea. |
| AD 379 | Emperor Theodosius destroys the temple of Jupiter, replacing it with a church dedicated to John the Baptist. |
| AD 635–36 | Damascus falls to the Islamic armies, and is evacuated prior to the major Battle of Yarmuk; the city becomes the capital of the Caliphate of Mu'awiya. |
| c. AD 690 | The Christian theologian and hymn writer, John of Damascus, leaves for the Judean wilderness. |
| AD 708 | The church of St John the Baptist is gutted by Caliph Walid I and replaced with the Umayyad Mosque. |
| AD 750 | Baghdad is established as the capital; Damascus, now a provincial centre, changes hands several times over the next 400 years. |
| 1174 | Damascus is controlled briefly by Salah al-Din, then by the Mongols (under Genghis Khan), then by the Mamelukes. |
| 1516 | Ottoman Turks take control. |
| 1918 | Damascus brought within the French 'Mandate' after the First World War. |
| 1946 | Damascus becomes the capital of a free Syria. |

This event, which proved to be a lifeline, was also one that he saw, once again, as part of God's humbling him. Writing of it later, he lists some of the many insults he had borne in Christ's service. In the Roman army, there was a special accolade for the soldier who was the first one to storm an enemy's wall, but Paul's boast is of the exact opposite:

*In Damascus the governor under King Aretas had the city of the Damascenes guarded in order to arrest me. But I was lowered in a basket from a window in the wall and slipped through his hands.*

**2 Corinthians 11:32–33**

Paul would revisit Damascus briefly on his way back to Jerusalem 'three years' later (Galatians 1:18). Though never returning thereafter, Paul would no doubt have thought of Damascus often – as the unexpected place where he had been stopped abruptly in his steps by the full force of the risen Christ.

Historic photos of Damascus' Old City: the 'House of Ananias' (ABOVE) and the eastern end of 'Straight Street'.

# Damascus today

Damascus can lay claim to being the oldest continuously inhabited city in the world. Its location, as a fertile oasis on the edge of the desert, fed by streams from the 'anti-Lebanon' Mountains, made it an obvious place for early settlement. So, until the twentieth century, to approach Damascus from almost any direction would have meant being greeted by a welcome sight – its green texture replacing the brown monotony of the desert.

Now, however, the overriding impression is of concrete urban existence, with numerous breeze-block constructions and tall apartment blocks. Tree-lined meadows have been replaced by buildings and roads; the Berada River (formerly the Amana) now passes along the north of the Old City as a putrid, polluted stream. To gain any sense of Damascus as it was, you need to go up nearby Mount Kassioun, from where one or two orchards and parks can still be detected amid the urban sprawl.

Yet the city still works its magic. On a clear spring day the snows of Mount Hermon are clearly visible. And the Old City is truly impressive with its spice bazaars, its narrow streets, its places of historic worship and its ancient walls (complete with eight gates). The walls on the north-western side of the Old City were knocked down in the nineteenth century, allowing some limited vehicle access inside. And the main street within the Old City is still called 'Straight' – just as it was when Paul lodged in the 'house of Judas on Straight Street' (Acts 9:11). Inevitably this is where many visitors go soon after arriving in Damascus – though we must remember that the street level in the first century was about 15 feet (5 m) below the present city.

Damascus' **Straight Street** (or the *Via Recta*) was simply an example of the east–west street found in many ancient cities built on what is known as the

*'This "holy" Damascus... is a city of hidden palaces, of copses and gardens, and fountains and bubbling streams. The juice of her life is the gushing and ice-cold torrent that tumbles from the snowy sides of anti-Lebanon. Close along the river's edge through seven sweet miles of rustling boughs, the deepest shade, the city spreads out her whole length...'*

**Alexander Kinglake, *Eothen***

The lintel of one of the gates of Damascus, known as 'Paul's window'.

Hippodamian plan (named after the man who redesigned Athens' harbour-town of Piraeus in the 400s BC). Here in Damascus, this Straight Street has been recently refurbished as a splendid colonnaded thoroughfare, with a width of 27 yards (25 m) – something hard to imagine as you pass through the confined *souks* now constructed along this street at its western end.

After nearly 400 yards (365 m), the street eventually opens out as you pass a **Roman arch**. This arch, which only came to light in the early twentieth century during some demolition work and which was reconstructed here at ground level, would have covered the northern colonnade of the street. It was probably part of an impressive *tetrapylon* – a 'four-gated' edifice that often marked a city's central crossroads. To the south-east of the arch is the Jewish quarter, with the Christian quarter being in the north-east. So, immediately to the north of the arch is a **Greek Orthodox church**, dedicated to the Virgin Mary. There was probably a Byzantine church on this site; the present building is quite recent, however, erected after an arson attack had destroyed the previous church during a horrendous massacre of Christians in 1860.

Continuing down the ancient Straight Street (which now becomes Bab Sharqi Street), you eventually reach the gate of the same name. This Roman **'Gate of the Sun'** is the oldest surviving monument in Damascus (being built in the third century AD, or possibly earlier) and marks the end of Straight Street – a total length of nearly 1,420 yards (1,300 m). Looking back up the street, one senses how splendid this street would have been, with its porticoed pavements (in line with the two side-arches beside Bab Sharqi) supported by columns, some of which remain standing to this day. One wonders, too, where exactly was the **House of Judas**, in which Paul lay blinded, recovering from shock.

As you face the city, the first side-street on your right takes you, after about 200 yards (180 m) of shops, to the traditional **House of Ananias**. Going down some 15 feet (5 m)



*'The silent gardens blurred green with river mist, in whose setting shimmered the city, beautiful as ever, like a pearl in the morning sun...'*

T. E. Lawrence ('Lawrence of Arabia')

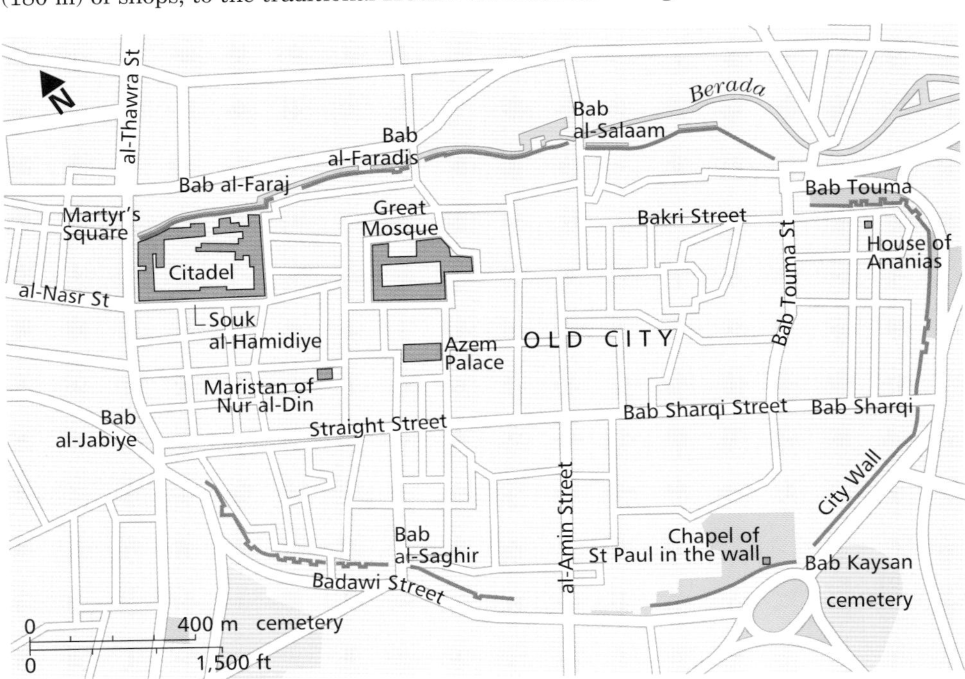


Plan of modern Damascus.

## Visiting modern Syria

Apart from Damascus itself, there are a host of major sites to be explored in Syria.

In the desert to the east of Damascus (some 150 miles or 240 km) stand the vast ruins of **Palmyra** (the 'place of palms'), which flourished in the first three centuries AD. Much further to the east is **Dura-Europos**, with its remains of the oldest 'house-church' in the world (c. AD 240).

To the north are three modern cities: **Homs** (ancient Emesa), **Hama** (with its distinctive wooden water wheels) and **Aleppo**, with its many atmospheric *souks* at the foot of its impressive citadel (built by Saladin's son Ghazi in the era of the Crusades). Near Aleppo are the beautiful ruins of **Qalaat Samaan** – the magnificent basilica built c. AD 480 in honour of Simeon Stylites, who had stood here on a pillar for 38 years until his death in AD 459. People flocked from all over the empire to see this man of prayer and, if possible, to hear some of his words of wisdom.

Close to the Mediterranean are the ruins of **Apamea** (a major Seleucid city), **Ras Shamra** (where Ugaritic script was discovered), and the Crusader castle at **Krak de Chevaliers** (described by T. E. Lawrence as the 'finest castle in the world').

Meanwhile, at the southern end of the country are the sparkling basalt ruins of **Bosra** (the capital of the Roman province of Arabia).

Christian visitors may also be interested in the villages and churches to the west of the Homs-Aleppo road, deserted by Byzantine Christians around AD 800 when their olive trade ended. Many enjoy going to **Maaloula**, to visit its monastery, the church of St Sergius and the convent at nearby **Seidnaya**, and to meet some of the local Syrian Christians, who still speak ancient Aramaic, the language that Jesus would have spoken. Visitors frequently will hear the Lord's Prayer recited in Jesus' mother tongue.

Syrian highlights (clockwise from top right): the stunning Crusader fortress of Krak des Chevaliers; the Roman ruins at Palmyra; the ruins of Qalaat Samaan (the basilica commemorating Simeon Stylites and his pillar); and the Syrian Christian monastery at Maaloula.

below street level, you enter a small chapel, which shows signs of inhabitation from the first century BC. Whether or not this is the exact spot, we are at the street level of ancient Damascus. Perhaps very near here was the place where Ananias received his challenging commission.

Back at Bab Sharqi gate, there is a nearby underpass where you can see an exposed section of the **Roman wall**. You are also not far from the place where Paul was lowered down the wall in a basket. Knowing the precise location of this night-time escapade is impossible, but it is traditionally remembered as happening near the next gate going clockwise (southwards), called **Bab Kaysan**. This is a Mameluke gate built on the site of the Roman 'Gate of Saturn' and close to an ancient cemetery. During the twentieth century the small **St Paul's Chapel** was built around this Mameluke gate. Its windows (together with windows of ordinary homes nearby, often with washing hanging out) act as a reminder of Paul's speedy exit. The lower sections of the wall along here do go back to Roman times; so some of them may be those touched by Paul's feet as he abseiled down the wall.

There are many other sites to detain the interested visitor – not least the many oriental shops and tempting bazaars. In the Old City, there is, of course, the **Umayyad or 'Great' Mosque**. This magnificent building intriguingly occupies the same area as a massive temple in honour of Jupiter (being constructed in the decades around the time

The Umayyad or 'Great' Mosque in Damascus.

of Paul's conversion) as well as a Byzantine cathedral dedicated to John the Baptist. Some of the Roman walls, columns and arches can still be seen by exploring the eastern side of the enclosure (near Bab al Nawfarah) and the neighbouring streets. Meanwhile, outside the Old City, a visit to the **National Museum** (with its many treasures from Ras Shamra, Palmyra, Dura Europos and so on) can give key insights into life in Roman times.

The road approaching Damascus from the Golan Desert.

Those interested in Paul, however, will also want to find the place that commemorates his conversion. Although there is an alternative site (in the cave grotto in the pleasant grounds of the St Paul's Convent near Bab Sharqi), the traditional location is a hill with a slight gradient known as **Kaukab Hill** some 6 miles (10 km) to the west of the Old City. The reasons for this choice are fairly clear, for from here the Old City walls would have been visible and temptingly close after a long journey; moreover, the hill is right on the edge of the Golan Desert, thus marking the place where at last one encounters the fertile gardens of Damascus (known as the *ghuta*).

Today the site is marked by an Orthodox Church which, despite its modern exterior, is no longer in use (and therefore is quite frequently closed). Instead visitors can find themselves standing nearby, perhaps reading the account of Paul's conversion in Acts, and looking round at the scenery. Over the brow to the south-west are the Golan Heights, to the north-west the impressive lower slopes of Mount Hermon, and to the east the bustling city of Damascus. Somewhere near here was where it all began – when Paul was stopped in his tracks, so he claimed, by an encounter with the risen Christ.

*'Your Kingdom, O Christ, is the kingdom of all ages and your rule is for all generations.'*

**Theodosius' inscription, based on Psalm 145:13, over the central portal in the south wall of the Umayyad Mosque**

2

CHAPTER

# Tarsus

*When [Paul] came to Jerusalem, he debated with the Grecian Jews, but they tried to kill him. When the brothers learned of this, they took him down to Caesarea and sent him off to Tarsus.*

**Acts 9:26, 29–30**

*Then Barnabas went to Tarsus to look for Saul, and when he found him, he brought him to Antioch.*

**Acts 11:25–26**

*'I am a Jew, from Tarsus in Cilicia, a citizen of no ordinary city... I am a Jew, born in Tarsus of Cilicia, but brought up in this city. Under Gamaliel I was thoroughly trained in the law of our fathers and was just as zealous for God as any of you are today.'*

**Acts 21:39, 22:3**

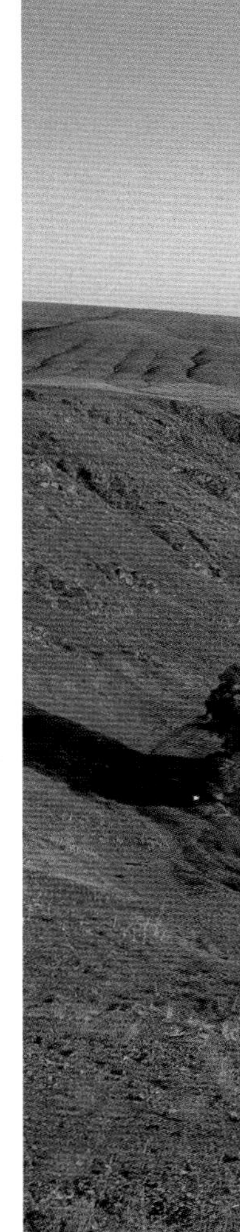

RIGHT: The more gentle scenery of Cilicia 'Pedia': here the Ceyhan River meanders slowly to the Mediterranean from the lower slopes of the steep Taurus Mountains near Adana.

## Reflections at home

Around three years after his conversion, Paul returned from Damascus to Jerusalem. This time he travelled not with the determination of a persecutor, but with the uneasy questions of a seeming defector. We can imagine him travelling up to Judaism's mother-city with a string of questions in his mind: 'How has the high priest been reacting to the news of my defection? Will my old teacher, Gamaliel, wish to meet me? Have Jesus' followers heard the news about me yet and how will they react to my arrival? How much does the risen Jesus want me now to witness to him in this difficult city, Jerusalem?'

*'Leave these men alone! Let them go! For if their activity is of human origin, it will fail. But if it is from God, you will not be able to stop them.'*

**The words of Gamaliel, Paul's former teacher, as recorded in Acts 5:38–39**

### A brief visit to Jerusalem

Luke gives us some of the answers in Acts 9. The Christian believers were understandably cautious until a man called Barnabas spoke up on Paul's behalf, introducing him to the apostles. But when Paul started preaching in the Greek-speaking synagogue, this caused a stir among the Jewish population, necessitating his speedy departure.

We never learn, however, of the responses of Caiaphas or Gamaliel.

Caiaphas' reaction is fairly predictable, but Gamaliel's might well have been more positive. A few years earlier, he had shown quite an open-minded approach to the apostles Peter and John. But who knows how he would have reacted when this new sect claimed the allegiance of his former star pupil?

Paul himself refers to this brief visit to Jerusalem on a couple of later occasions (Galatians 1:18–21; Acts 22:17–21). His comments clarify that it was indeed a short visit (only a fortnight), that Paul only met Peter and James (perhaps the other apostles had already left Jerusalem for other mission fields?), and that Paul *did* receive the necessary guidance from Jesus. For, while praying in the Temple and wondering whether his unique background might give him a special role to play in Jerusalem, he gets the answer: 'Leave Jerusalem immediately, because they will not accept your testimony about me' (Acts 22:18). If Paul was called to suffer in Jerusalem for Jesus' sake, it must wait for another season. So Paul is whisked away, down to Caesarea Maritima on the coast, there to take a boat (perhaps via Antioch?) destined for his home town of Tarsus.

# Tarsus: Paul's home city

Tarsus was a significant port on the southern coast of Asia Minor; it lay a few miles inland, beside the Cydnus River. If the references to 'Tarshish' in the Old Testament refer to somewhere else (see p. 38), then Paul's Tarsus does not feature at all in the previous biblical story. Yet it had a significant history of its own: it was a prominent city in the Seleucid empire, and then became the regional capital within the Roman province of Cilicia, visited by such figures as Alexander the Great, Julius Caesar, Mark Antony and Cleopatra.

The province of Cilicia covered the region of the coastal plain, which is quite narrow at points because of the imposing Taurus Mountains just to the north. Eastern Cilicia (Cilicia Pedia or 'flat Cilicia') was a fertile plain, but western Cilicia (Cilicia Trachaea or 'rugged Cilicia') was forested and quite mountainous. One of the few passes through these mountains was just to the north of Tarsus, and was known in ancient times as the 'Cilician Gates'. Tarsus was therefore a significant gateway for traders and travellers going inland.

The narrow pass of the Cilician Gates, cutting through the Taurus Mountains north of Tarsus, was a much-travelled but dangerous route.

The same was true for those travelling by sea along the coast. In fair weather some boats might risk the open seas and land on Cyprus, but many would dock along the Cilician coast. Not surprisingly, then, this busy coastline of Cilicia became famous for its piracy until this was dealt with by the Romans (including Cicero, the Roman governor here in 51 BC). Nearly a hundred years later, when Paul and Luke travelled the 'open sea off the coast of Cilicia' (Acts 27:5), the problem they faced was not pirates but the strong westerly winds.

With just a touch of civic pride, Paul describes Tarsus as 'no ordinary city' (Acts 21:39). Indeed the city was famous throughout the empire for its educated culture and university learning, with a reputation disproportionate to its size. Presumably Paul, when younger, had some access to this educational world – perhaps learning here some of the classical writings which he would later quote to good effect (see, for example, Acts 17:28; Titus 1:12). But his Jewish parents may also have placed some limits on their son's access to the secular city and its culture; so we can only guess how exactly the young Paul inhabited these two very different worlds.

*'The people of Tarsus have devoted themselves so eagerly – not only to philosophy, but also to the whole round of education in general – that they have surpassed Athens, Alexandria and other schools of philosophy.'*

**Strabo, the Greek historian and philosopher**

# The Roman 'citizen' leaving for Jerusalem

Paul's time in Tarsus leaves us with some questions. First, there is the issue of Paul's Roman citizenship. According to Luke, Paul expressly states that he was 'born' a Roman citizen (Acts 22:28), but how had his family first gained this coveted status? Quite possibly his parents received what was known as *manumission* – a practice whereby slaves, on being given their freedom by their Roman patron, automatically received Roman citizenship as well. This might then explain why Saul of Tarsus later adopted the Roman name 'Paul'. For manumitted slaves commonly took on a new *cognomen* (or 'third name') derived from the name of their former master. Conceivably, then, Paul's parents had been in the service of a man called 'Paulus'.

A further intriguing possibility is that Paul's parents, before their manumission, were not just slaves, but prisoners of war – perhaps taken captive in one of the Romans' campaigns in Judea and Galilee. For example, when quelling the uprising after the death of Herod the Great, General Varus had taken numerous captives. Were Paul's parents in that number?

If so, then this might explain two other parts of the jigsaw. First, if (as suggested on p. 22) Paul belonged to the more nationalistic wing of Pharisaism, then this might only be natural for one whose parents had fought in an uprising and experienced the humiliation of defeat. Their son might well be determined to 'put the record straight'.

Secondly, this might also explain why Paul's parents sent him off to Jerusalem. Was this simply a matter of wanting their intelligent son to experience the best of a Jewish education? Or was it, instead, because they were Jewish nationalists in exile who saw this as a means of getting their son back into the mainstream of the Jewish cause? Paul could become a trainee 'freedom-fighter'. And, to cap it all, there is the intriguing fact that Paul had a nephew living in Jerusalem (described explicitly as the 'son of Paul's *sister*' in Acts 23:16). Although this nephew may himself have travelled singly to Jerusalem for his education, it is also possible that he was there because *his* parents were Jerusalem residents. If so, we have to ask why Paul's married *sister* had been living in Jerusalem through all these years. Was she too sent to Jerusalem from Tarsus by eager parents, not primarily (as a girl) for educational possibilities, but because of these historic family roots embedded in the land of Israel?

We will never know. Yet the overall impression we gain is that Paul left Tarsus for Jerusalem at quite a young age. In Acts 22:3 Paul says that, though he was 'born in Tarsus of Cilicia', he was '*brought up* in this city [of Jerusalem]'. This would then match his later statement that the Jews in Jerusalem had known him 'for a long time' (Acts 26:5).

This ancient gate, known locally as Cleopatra's Gate or St Paul's Gate (see p. 41), is one of the few things surviving in Tarsus from antiquity; it was built long after Paul's time, however, around AD 300.

## Paul's return to Tarsus: the start of his tent-making?

So Paul may not have spent many years in Tarsus as a child. And when he returned there after the Damascus road experience, he probably stayed for no more than five years before being summonsed to Antioch.

What did Paul do during this later, 'hidden' period? Conceivably this is when he took up his trade of tent-making – especially if he left for Jerusalem at a young age before any apprenticeship from his parents was possible. Indeed he may have taken up this trade upon his return for a strictly practical reason: for what if his parents disinherited him when he returned home as a follower of this new messianic sect? If so, Paul would soon need to develop an independent form of income.

Initially this idea of Paul's taking up a new craft sits uneasily with our vision of the urgent missionary. Yet it may have been a brute necessity. And in later years Paul would stress the need for believers to work hard and would offer his own example of manual labour as a model, meaning that he was a not a financial 'burden' to people (1 Thessalonians 2:9; 2 Thessalonians 3:6–11). So Paul may have seen no inconsistency in starting this new trade. On the contrary, this trade, which was so easily transferred to other settings, would prove a key 'point of entry' for his later ministry.

## Early mission to Gentiles?

There is also the unanswered question of whether Paul, while in Tarsus, began to experiment in his task of reaching *Gentiles* with the message of Jesus. Acts (with its tidy ordering of material) gives the impression that it was others who first started speaking to Gentiles in Antioch (Acts 11:20); but had the message about Jesus been reaching Gentiles before this? Some scholars, going right back, suggest believers could have been spreading the message to Gentiles even in Damascus in the early 30s AD – thus triggering Paul's Pharisaic anger; others wonder if Paul himself used his few years in Arabia to speak about Jesus to non-Jews (Galatians 1:17). Perhaps the majority think it likely that Paul used this time in Tarsus for some Gentile mission. If so, Barnabas' decision to summons Paul may have been triggered by an awareness that Paul was 'piloting' such a work in his native Tarsus.

Some small support for this comes later in Acts 15 when the Jerusalem apostles send their letter affirming Gentile mission 'to the Gentile believers in Antioch, Syria and *Cilicia*' (Acts 15:23). For when had these Gentiles in Cilicia been told the message about Jesus? Although this *could* have happened only after Paul returned from his first 'missionary journey' – when Luke says he stayed in Antioch 'a long time' (Acts 14:28) – it is perhaps more likely that they heard about Jesus from Paul during those earlier years in Tarsus. Either way, we note how Paul decided to take the Jerusalem decree himself *in person* to the 'churches' in 'Syria and Cilicia' (Acts 15:41). This was his home territory and he wanted them to know this piece of brilliant news, which also gave the 'green light' to what he had been doing among the Gentiles.

## Personal growth and reflection

Paul's primary goal during those hidden years, however, may have been simply to think and pray more deeply, developing the personal and spiritual resources he would need for the critical journey ahead. Several biblical figures (such as Moses, and even Jesus himself) had experienced this time of waiting after their initial call, so Paul may have viewed this as a valuable season of preparation.

We only know for sure of one event during all those years in Tarsus – a mystical experience that Paul later describes in 2 Corinthians. Although he makes it sound anonymous, it fairly clearly refers to him and gives us a window into Paul's prayer life during those years:

*I know a man in Christ who fourteen years ago was caught up to the third heaven. Whether it was in the body or out of the body I do not know – God knows… [He was] caught up to paradise. He heard inexpressible things, things that no one is permitted to tell.*

**2 Corinthians 12:2–4**

Such an experience would have strengthened Paul's resolve for the future. So too would the greater clarity he would gradually have gained about what precisely he had been taught on the Damascus road. That had been a sudden, instantaneous event, containing in a nutshell all the important building-blocks for the shape of a new

Christ-centred worldview; yet processing that event would have taken time. By the time Barnabas summonsed him to Antioch, what were the key ideas that had grasped Paul's mind and heart? Below is a summary of the four key truths that must have been crystallising in Paul's mind during those years of suspense in Tarsus.

The interior of a church in Tarsus dedicated to St Paul.

## 1. God's Messiah

On the Damascus road Paul had encountered the risen Jesus. He had learnt that Jesus, far from being a failed messiah-king, was indeed God's appointed ruler of the world. Previously he may have thought that Jesus' death on a Roman cross was a sure sign that Jesus had been 'cursed' in God's sight (Deuteronomy 21:23). Now he believed that Israel's God had been at work in this strange event, that Jesus had taken upon himself the 'curse' that sinful humans deserve in order to set them free (Galatians 3:13). Paul learnt he had misread the Old Testament and missed the deeper magic of the prophecies in Isaiah that had predicted the coming of such a 'suffering servant' (see, for example, Isaiah 53).

He learnt too, in an unforgettable way, that this Jesus, raised from the dead, was powerfully and actively alive. When listing Jesus' post-resurrection appearances in 1 Corinthians 15, he therefore cites his Damascus road experience as being, strangely, on a par with those experienced by others in Jerusalem and Galilee. For Paul claimed he had truly been privileged to 'see Jesus our Lord' (1 Corinthians 9:1). From this he derived his conviction that the physical resurrection of Jesus was a non-negotiable part of the gospel (1 Corinthians 15:4) and that Jesus was unique – the risen 'Lord' and God's 'Son' (Acts 9:20).

*'Am I not free? Am I not an apostle? Have I not seen Jesus our Lord?'*

**1 Corinthians 9:1**

## Key dates: Tarsus

|  |  |
|---|---|
| Before 2000 BC | Fortified town on site of Tarsus. Later Hittite records refer to 'Tarsa' as a leading city in the region of 'Kizzuwatna' (later 'Cilicia'?). |
| c. 1200 BC | Destruction of Tarsus by the sea peoples (subsequently refounded by the Greeks). |
| c. 970 BC | King Solomon's 'royal merchants' import horses 'from Egypt and Kue' ('Kue' being a possible reference to later 'Cilicia': 1 Kings 10:28). |
| 832 BC | Anatolia brought under Assyrian control, but Tarsus remains independent. |
| 698 BC | The Assyrian king, Sennacherib, loots the city. |
| 500s BC | Area brought under Persian control. Biblical references to 'Tarshish' (Jonah 1:3; Jeremiah 10:9; Ezekiel 27:12) probably refer, not to Tarsus, but to Spain or North Africa. |
| 333 BC | Alexander the Great visits Tarsus, but becomes seriously ill after bathing in the cold waters of the River Cydnus. |
| 323 BC | Tarsus brought under the rule of the Seleucids, who rename it 'Antioch on the Cydnus'. |
| c. 170 BC | Tarsus and a neighbouring town revolt against Antiochus Epiphanes IV (2 Maccabees 4:30). |
| 67 BC | Tarsus becomes the capital of the Roman province of Cilicia. |
| 51–50 BC | Cicero serves as Roman proconsul of Cilicia, living in Tarsus and ensuring the end of piracy along the coast. |
| c. 50 BC | Athenodorus, from Tarsus' well-established and famous university, tutors the young Octavian (later Augustus). |
| 47 BC | Visit of Julius Caesar, in whose honour the city is renamed 'Juliopolis'. |
| 41 BC | Mark Antony rewards the city for its loyalty against his rival, Cassius; he also meets Cleopatra here, who arrives by barge. |
| c. AD 5? | Paul's birth in Tarsus to parents with Roman citizenship. |
| c. AD 20 | Paul leaves Tarsus to continue his education in Jerusalem, eventually studying under the famous Gamaliel (Acts 22:3; 26:4–5). |
| c. AD 35 | Paul returns to Tarsus from Damascus via Jerusalem and possibly Antioch (Acts 9:30; Galatians 1:21). |
| c. AD 40 | Barnabas collects Paul from Tarsus and brings him to teach in Antioch (Acts 11:25–26). |
| c. AD 44 | Cilicia incorporated into the province of Syria (under Antioch). |
| c. AD 47 | Possible brief return visit after his first 'missionary journey' (Acts 14:28). |
| AD 49/50 | Paul passes through Cilicia, carrying the 'apostolic decree' from the Jerusalem council (addressed to the 'churches of Syria and Cilicia'), en route for Galatia; he almost certainly travels through the 'Cilician Gates' (Acts 15:23, 40–41). |
| AD 260 | Tarsus falls to the Parthians, before being regained by the Romans. |
| AD 363 | The pagan emperor Julian the Apostate is buried in Tarsus. |
| c. AD 530 | Emperor Justinian moves the main course of the River Cydnus away from the city. |
| 1300s | Tarsus incorporated into the Ottoman empire. |

*When she first met Mark Antony,*
*She pursed up his heart, upon the river of Cydnus...*
*The barge she sat in, like a burnish'd throne,*
*Burn'd on the water: the poop was beaten gold;*
*Purple the sails, and so perfumed that*
*The winds were love-sick with them; the oars were silver,*
*Which to the tune of flutes kept stroke, and made*
*The water which they beat to follow faster,*
*As amorous of their strokes. For her own person,*
*It beggar'd all description: she did lie*
*In her pavilion – cloth-of-gold of tissue –*
*O'er-picturing that Venus where we see*
*The fancy outwork nature....*

**Shakespeare, *Antony and Cleopatra*, III, ii, describing Cleopatra's arrival in Tarsus by boat**

### 2. God's purposes

If Jesus was truly God's Messiah, this signalled the dawn of the long-awaited Messianic Age (the 'age to come' or the 'last days'). Yet if the age of fulfilment had been inaugurated, this also meant that it was time for those outside Israel (the Gentiles) to be brought into God's kingdom. God's purposes in calling Abraham had been to bless 'all nations', but until now it had been unclear how these universal purposes of God would be realized. However, now that Jesus had been revealed as the Lord of the world, this vision could all kick into motion. So any narrow nationalism that Paul had espoused previously (believing God's prime purpose was to vindicate Israel politically) could now be seen as a blind alley. God's purposes were now to bless the whole world through the message of King Jesus.

## 3. God's Law

Paul had been a devotee of the Jewish Law (the Torah). But now he believed that his interpretation of this had been wrong. It was not that God's standards or laws had changed, but rather that *the Law itself could not be the means of God's rescuing the world*. After all, look what obedience to the Law had brought about in his own case – it had led him to blaspheme God's Son! And Jesus' death showed that human sin evidently required something much more radical than what the Law could provide. From this Paul would begin to see that Christ, not the Law, was the centre of God's new purposes and that the key thing required of God's people was not obedience to the Law but rather faith – faith in the crucified Messiah.





## 4. God's people

All this affected Paul's understanding of who exactly were God's true people. The risen Jesus had so clearly identified himself with those who believed in him: in persecuting *them*, Paul was told, he was persecuting *Jesus* (Acts 9:5). Here were the first hints of what would later flower into Paul's understanding of the church as Christ's *own* 'body' (1 Corinthians 12:12–27) – such was the strong link between Jesus and his people. Yet this also meant that Paul needed to develop a whole new way of thinking about ethnic 'Israel'. If Jesus was forming a new people around himself – 'reconstituting' Israel, if you like – then the true 'Israel of God' from now on would be those who were joined by faith to Jesus, Israel's true Messiah (Romans 2:28–29; 9:6).

With these four major insights rooted in his mind and heart – pondered over time and again, and fuelled by prayer – Paul was ready to leave his home town and to set out, at last, into the unknown world in obedience to Jesus' commission. The world was about to witness what it meant for Jesus to have called a Jewish rabbi to be the 'apostle to the Gentiles'.

# Tarsus today

Ironically, Tarsus, though Paul's home town, helps the visitor very little to imagine how things looked in Paul's day. The modern city of Tarsus (with a population of over 350,000) has preserved the ancient city's name, but obliterated its contents. These now lie beneath more than 20 feet (6 m) of accumulated silt.

Located on a narrow coastal plain, Tarsus looks up to the steep Taurus Mountains behind, which are often covered in snow until May. These surroundings have given the city a continuing trade, for the long-haired mountain goats still provide local craftsmen with what they need to

St Paul's Well: an ancient well in the courtyard of a house associated in local tradition with Paul.

## Visitors to Asia Minor: past and present

The landmass of Anatolia or 'Asia Minor' (as it came to be called by the Romans) has always attracted interested visitors. This is true both of individuals and of major people groups: the Hittites (c. 1750 BC) arrived from the East; the peoples of its central plains (Galatia) came from Thrace in the third century BC; the Selcuk Turks came from the East in the eleventh century AD and the Ottoman Turks two centuries later. Meanwhile, its western shores were colonized by the Greek-speaking peoples of Ionia at the dawn of the classical age.

In addition to the many rulers and armies that marched through this land, famous visitors include: Cicero, sent from Rome as governor of Cilicia in 51 BC, who wrote back to his friends in Rome, describing the province; and Strabo, the geographer, who visited the area around 25 BC and described it as 'surpass[ing] Athens, Alexandria, or any other place that can be named where there have been schools and lectures of philosophers'. We also have some letters from Pliny the Younger who was the governor of Bithynia around AD 112, and the interesting story of Justin Martyr, a native of Palestine, being converted to Christianity while talking to an old man on a beach near Ephesus around AD 135 (*Dialogue with Trypho* 3). In due course it would become the most densely Christianized area of the world; Gregory of Nyssa, who lived in the beautiful central area of Cappadocia, returned from a visit to Palestine in the AD 380s and, frankly, was more impressed by what he found at home. The Holy Spirit was not confined to Jerusalem, he argued: 'one might more justly consider that He dwelt in the Cappadocian nation more than anywhere else; for how many altars there are there – one could hardly count so many in all the rest of the world' (*Epistle* 2).

Travel to Turkey effectively opened up for Western visitors only in the nineteenth century with the development of the new railway networks. Archaeologists began to recognize the treasures that lay buried in the Anatolian soil, largely ignored by a local population for whom these ruins were not part of their own history: Heinrich Schliemann worked at Troy (1871–90), John Turtle Wood laboured in Ephesus (1863–74). However, a key figure, especially for New Testament studies, was Sir William Mitchell Ramsay, Professor of Humanities at Aberdeen University from 1886 to 1911. His books included *Luke the Physician* (1908), *St Paul the Traveller and the Roman Citizen* (1898), and *Bishoprics of Phrygia* (1895). From this one can detect his wide historical interests, and the way he was seeking to set Luke and Paul within the framework of ancient history. He did much to challenge the radical, dismissive views of Luke's historical reliability (which were growing in that period): his work on the political boundaries in the first century brought clarity to the debate about Paul's letter to the Galatians (see p. 12); his maps, showing ancient roads and territories, have never been matched; and his photographs (many taken, it seems, by his

patient wife and daughter) will have given many of his readers their first-ever sighting of these biblical sites.

Something similar took place a generation later, only at a more popular level, with the publication of H.V. Morton's *In the Steps of Saint Paul* (1935). Like this present work, this was a sequel to a similar book on Jesus (*In the Steps of the Master*: 1933). Both books, however, focused more on the contemporary culture and that which an intrepid visitor might encounter. So his travel narrative is filled with colourful stories of local Turkish culture, scary taxi rides, chance encounters and memorable conversations. Sprinkled through it all, however, are key insights into Paul's travels – insights that only come to those who themselves travel to this historic, inspiring land.

There simply is nothing like visiting ancient Asia Minor – being surrounded by its hills, seeing the sites in location, perhaps struggling to work out the best routes from A to B – for gaining a realistic but intuitive grasp of what Paul was up against. Speaking personally, visiting Turkey has always been an incredible inspiration; if there are any fresh ideas about Paul pulsating through these pages, it is in large part because they were triggered by the places themselves.

The unusual landscape of ancient Cappadocia (near modern Goreme). Cappadocia was heavily Christianized in antiquity: it was home to three great theologians (the 'Cappadocian Fathers') in the late fourth century; and over the centuries numerous small churches were cut out of rock formations such as these.

weave their distinctive tent cloths. In the days when Paul was making his tents, this tough fabric was known as *cilicium*; the same fabric is still being made today – and the French word for such haircloth is still *cilice*.

Until recently the chief place to visit in Tarsus for Pauline visitors was **St Paul's Gate** in the centre of a roundabout on the road towards Mersin. In fact, this gate (known more frequently as 'Cleopatra's Gate') would not have been here in Paul's day. This monumental arch dates instead to around AD 300. Conceivably, however, it marks the site of one of the three main gates that Paul would have known. Nearby, to the north, there is also **St Paul's Well**, which in local tradition is associated with the home in which Paul lived. This is most unlikely historically. Yet this deep well does go back to the Roman period and, being an immoveable object, gives us an identifiable link with Paul's Tarsus.

Since 1993, however, archaeological interest has focused on the area some 175 yards (160 m) to the south-west of the well, where a stretch of an **ancient street** has been uncovered. Dating back to the second century BC, its large, black basalt stones give it a distinctive appearance. Underneath was a drainage system and then, some time after Paul, a colonnaded row of shops would have been built alongside. Further excavations are uncovering a series of houses, courtyards and mosaics – our first glimpse into the Tarsus Paul would have known as a child.

*'Tarsus – its feet resting on a great inland harbour and its head reaching up to the hills.'*

**Sir William Mitchell Ramsay, *The Historical Geography of Asia Minor***

The existence of certain Islamic legends means there are several mosques associated with figures from the Old Testament (especially Daniel), but otherwise there is little to detain a visitor further: the **Tarsus Museum** contains a number of local archaeological finds; there are some remains of a **Roman temple** from the second century AD (known locally as Donuktas); parts of an **ancient hippodrome** can be seen in the campus of

Tarsus American College and parts of a **theatre** in a primary school across the street.

Leaving the city, however, some may be interested in seeing either the area of **Lake Rhegma** (the site of Tarsus' harbour, now a silted lagoon) or the disused **triple-arched bridge** (built by Justinian) on the Adana–Ankara road. Perhaps of greatest interest, however, is the long section of an **ancient road** now visible some 10 miles (6 km) to the north of the city. Built by the Romans, this 10-foot- (3-m-) wide road would have been the main thoroughfare towards the Cilician Gates, some 20 miles (32 km) further to the north.

The **Cilician Gates** are an impressive natural cutting through the Taurus Mountains. In ancient times this land route was used by great conquerors (such as Xerxes and Alexander), but also by anyone travelling into central Anatolia. Almost certainly Paul came this way when he travelled overland from Antioch to Ephesus (Acts 18:23; 19:1). Possibly he had ventured through them as a child or, more likely, during his 'hidden years' in the late 30s AD (see p. 35). Although the railway (built in 1886) and the modern roads make the journey so much easier, one can well imagine the energy and caution required of ancient travellers. Paul spoke of the dangers he had experienced while 'on the move': 'in danger from rivers, in danger from bandits' (2 Corinthians 11:26). Perhaps, as he wrote those words, he pictured this narrow mountain pass near his childhood home, through which he had ventured forth for the sake of Christ.

# Antioch on the Orontes

3

CHAPTER

*Now those who had been scattered by the persecution… travelled as far as Phoenicia, Cyprus and Antioch, telling the message only to Jews. Some of them, however, men from Cyprus and Cyrene, went to Antioch and began to speak to Greeks also, telling them the good news about the Lord Jesus…*

*News of this reached the ears of the church at Jerusalem, and they sent Barnabas to Antioch. When he arrived and saw the grace of God, he was glad… Then Barnabas went to Tarsus to look for Saul, and brought him to Antioch. So for a whole year Barnabas and Saul taught great numbers of people. The disciples were called Christians first at Antioch.*

*Some prophets came down from Jerusalem to Antioch… [predicting] that a severe famine would spread over the entire Roman world… The disciples… decided to provide help for the believers living in Judea… sending their gift to the elders by Barnabas and Saul.*

**Acts 11:19–20, 22–23, 25–30**

## City of commissioning

Paul's waiting had ended: Barnabas found him in Tarsus and brought him to the large, cosmopolitan city of Antioch. The tent-maker had now been given a new job. There was the task of building up the church in Antioch, and especially of developing its mission and ministry among the Gentiles.

For the next few years Antioch became Paul's 'home church'. And in due course, it would also become his 'sending church' – the place that gave him prayerful support when he set out on his various travels (whether to Jerusalem, Cyprus, 'Syria and Cilicia' or finally, to Ephesus.) So, today when we speak of his 'missionary journeys', we are reflecting the fact that between all such journeys Paul regularly touched base with this sending church in Antioch. It was from *here* that he set out on his 'first', 'second' and 'third' journeys.

Antioch was the third largest city in the Roman empire (after Rome and Alexandria) with a population, some suggest, of over 500,000. Founded by Seleucus I on the banks of the River Orontes at the foot of Mount Silpius, this Antioch (one of fifteen of the same name founded by Seleucus in honour of his father) soon became known as 'Antioch on the Orontes' or, simply, the 'Great'.

Originally founded for Macedonian army veterans, it was also home to Syrians and Greeks. The Greek influence developed strongly during the Seleucid empire, but

A nineteenth-century view of Antioch, nestling under the impressive slopes of Mount Silpius.

Antioch was now firmly under Roman authority – with significant attention being given to it by Julius Caesar, Augustus, Tiberius and, most recently, Claudius. At its heart was a colonnaded street with porticoes (almost 2 miles or 3 km in length and with over 3,200 columns).

## Antioch, Judaism and Jerusalem

There were also Jewish settlers here, who by the Roman period made up at least a tenth of the city's population. Though not normally 'citizens', they lived as a distinctive minority in various areas in and around the city. Although there were occasional troubles (for example, under Antiochus IV during his campaign to 'Hellenize' the Jews in Jerusalem in the 160s BC), the Jews in Antioch had a reasonably secure status. Josephus expressly mentions the wealth of many of the Antiochene Jews (*War* 7.1.3).

But peace and harmony evaporated around the year AD 39/40. Triggered by Caligula's attempts to erect a statue of himself in the Jerusalem Temple, violent mob attacks broke out around Antioch's synagogues. Anti-Semitic feelings ran high, with repeated outbursts coming later in AD 48 and then during the First Jewish Revolt (AD 66–70), when Jewish leaders were burnt to death in the theatre for refusing to sacrifice to the Roman gods.

So the years from AD 40 to AD 70 were very volatile ones within Antioch, with Paul's ministry (like Jesus' before him) taking place under the clouds of a gathering storm – fuelled by the tension between Jewish nationalists and Rome. As Rome's gateway into the East (from where her armies set out), Antioch could not but be affected by the growing tensions reverberating from Jerusalem.

This connection between the two cities then helps to explain something of what we see happening in this early period of the church's life; for, when reading Acts and Galatians, we discover a sequence of frequent communications between them. Figures such as Barnabas, Peter and Agabus, along with representatives of the Jerusalem church, all came down to Antioch during this period (Acts 11:20–28; 15:1; Galatians 2:1–11); meanwhile, return visits were made by Barnabas and Paul (Acts 11:25–26; 15:2). Clearly what was going on in the other city really mattered. Just as Roman officials in Antioch watched out for any developments in Jerusalem (the Jewish capital), so too the Jerusalem church's leaders kept an eye on Antioch (effectively the Roman capital in the East). In particular, they were keen to know whether the new believers in Antioch were relating to the Gentiles in ways that they would disapprove of or that would make their own witness to Jesus more difficult in Judaism's mother-city.

There was something almost inevitable about Antioch being the location for the eruption of this controversial issue (of how Gentiles should be admitted into the church). Although there had been advance rumblings of this vexed matter, it naturally came to a head here in Antioch, where a sizeable Jewish community was set in a vast cosmopolitan city. Josephus expressly says that in Antioch there were a large number of Greek-speaking Gentiles who were attracted to Judaism (*War* 7.45). Such people, often known as 'God-fearers' (see p. 80), would have been a natural constituency in which the message about Jesus could find a hearing. So here in Antioch there could be no ducking of the issue: were Gentiles to be admitted to this new Jewish sect simply as *Gentiles* or effectively by first becoming *Jews*?

## Paul and Barnabas: visit to Jerusalem

For someone with a calling to be an 'apostle to the Gentiles', any time spent in Antioch would be critical – not only for learning how to build a new community of believers that included both Jews and Gentiles, but also for winning the necessary debate with the church back in Jerusalem.

Initially Paul was there for 'an entire year', teaching the believers alongside Barnabas. This would have been a fascinating time to learn from these two teachers, as they drew on their prayerful reading of the Old Testament Scriptures, as they enriched each other with the more detailed teachings of Jesus, and as they interacted with the believers, forging new understandings of what it meant to follow Christ. But then (some time in the period AD 40–42) they received a prophecy about a likely famine facing the believers in Jerusalem (which would reach its worst around AD 45). This prompted Paul and Barnabas to set out with a love-gift from the believers in Antioch.

*'Fourteen years later I went up again to Jerusalem, this time with Barnabas. I took Titus along also. I went in response to a revelation and set before them the gospel I preach to the Gentiles. But I did this privately to those who seemed to be leaders...'*

**Galatians 2:1–2**

Almost certainly this visit is that which Paul himself describes in Galatians 2:1–10 (see pp. 12–13). If so, they took along a Gentile called Titus and, once in Jerusalem, discussed their recent ministry at a private meeting with Peter, James and John (whom Paul describes as the three 'pillars' of the church). These prime leaders, recognizing that Paul had a ministry to the Gentiles, then gave their backing to his Gentile mission. 'All they asked was that we should continue to remember the poor, the very thing I was eager to do' (Galatians 2:10) – a promise that Paul would keep over a decade later.

## Permission to expand?

So Paul returned to Antioch, believing he had Jerusalem's full endorsement to press ahead with his mission to the Gentiles. The reality, however, was slightly different – not least because those in Jerusalem who had *not* been at this 'private' meeting disapproved. But Paul, believing he had received the 'green light', was eager to press on; and, to this end, he brought with him from Jerusalem a young man called John Mark, usually referred to as Mark (Acts 12:25), hoping he would prove to be a very useful younger colleague on his travels. Mark's family background in Jerusalem (Acts 12:12) and his good knowledge of the traditions about Jesus would be a strong resource. What happened next, once back in Antioch?

*Now in the church at Antioch there were prophets and teachers: Barnabas, Simeon who was called Niger, Lucius of Cyrene, Manaen a member of the court of Herod the tetrarch, and Saul. While they were worshipping the Lord and fasting, the Holy Spirit said, 'Set apart for me Barnabas and Saul for the work to which I have called them.' Then after fasting and praying they laid their hands on them and sent them off.*

**Acts 13:1–3**

The list of names is remarkably cosmopolitan, including a well-to-do court official who had been in Galilee with Herod Antipas (perhaps in Sepphoris) and two men probably from North Africa. As they prayed, God's will became clear to them. Though Paul and Barnabas had probably been discussing such a possibility beforehand, they now got the endorsement they had been seeking. The time had come, they deduced, to set out as a small team, heading west with the news about Jesus. The first 'missionary journey' was being launched.

## Problems back home

What happened on that historic journey is discussed in Chapters 4 to 6 of this book. What happened when they returned to Antioch, however, is told at the end of Acts 14:

*When they arrived, [Paul and Barnabas] gathered the church together and reported all that God had done through them, and how he had opened the door of faith to the Gentiles. And they stayed there a long time with the disciples. Certain individuals came down from Judea to Antioch and were teaching the believers, 'Unless you are circumcised, according to the custom taught by Moses, you cannot be saved.' This brought Paul and Barnabas into sharp dispute and debate with them; so… they went up to Jerusalem to see the apostles and the elders about this question.*

**Acts 14:27–15:2**

The rejoicing and homecoming proved quite short-lived. For the whole issue of how Gentiles should be brought within the church flared up again in their faces. From Paul's account in Galatians 2:11–21, we can reconstruct the events roughly as follows.

## Key dates: Antioch

|  |  |
|---|---|
| 333 BC | Alexander the Great defeats the Persians in a great battle in the Plain of Issus; a few years later, Seleucus I Nicator founds the cities of Seleucia and Antioch (the latter being named after his father, Antiochus). |
| 281 BC | After the assassination of Seleucus I, his son Antiochus I transfers the capital from Seleucia to Antioch. |
| 167 BC | Antiochus Epiphanes IV triggers the Maccabean revolt in Palestine, trying to bring Jerusalem under pagan control. |
| 64 BC | Pompey defeats Tigranes of Armenia (Antioch's previous ruler) and makes Antioch the capital of the new Roman province of Syria. |
| 47 BC | Visit of Julius Caesar, who commissions many new buildings. |
| C. 36 BC | Wedding of Mark Antony to Cleopatra takes place in Syria, probably at the sanctuary of Apollo in nearby Daphne. |
| C. AD 37 | Emperor Caligula sends money for the city's rebuilding after a severe earthquake. |
| AD 39/40 | Mob violence against the Jews, probably provoked by Caligula's intended insults to Jerusalem (Philo, *Legatio ad Gaium* 185–90). |
| C. AD 43 | Emperor Claudius re-establishes the city's 'Olympic' games on a five-yearly basis; his ruling in support of the Alexandrian Jews is communicated to the Syrian authorities too. |
| C. AD 45 | Severe famine in Judea during which believers send relief to Jerusalem with Paul and Barnabas (Acts 11:27–30); see Josephus, *Antiquities* 20.2.5. |
| C. AD 48 | Further mob violence 'in the eighth year of Claudius' (according to John Malalas, 247:5–10). |
| AD 66–70 | Violent unrest soon after Vespasian's arrival in Syria (Josephus, *War* 3.2.2) followed later by a great fire, blamed on the Jewish population. |
| C. AD 107 | Ignatius, bishop of Antioch, is arrested and taken to Rome for trial and martyrdom. |
| AD 115 | A major earthquake almost harms the emperor Trajan and Hadrian, both in the city at that time. |
| AD 231–33 | The mother of Emperor Severus Alexander, Julia Mammaea, invites the Christian scholar, Origen, to visit her in Antioch from Caesarea Maritima. |
| AD 268 | Paul of Samosata, bishop of Antioch, is condemned for heretical teaching (akin to later Arianism). |
| C. AD 303 | Severe persecution of Christians under Emperor Diocletian, including the death of the biblical scholar, Lucian. |
| AD 325 | Antioch named as one of the three leading 'patriarchates' in the Byzantine Church (together with Rome and Alexandria; later joined by Jerusalem and Constantinople). |
| C. AD 330 | Bishop Eustathius is deposed. |
| AD 341 | The 'Great' or 'Golden' church, commissioned by Constantine, is completed during the reign of his son, Constantius, with a dedication festival attended by 90 bishops. |
| AD 373 | Jerome is converted to faith in Christ through a visionary experience while in Antioch. |
| AD 386–97 | Ministry of John Chrysostom (the 'golden-mouthed' preacher), who later became bishop of Constantinople. |
| AD 458 | Further major earthquake in Antioch. |
| AD 459 | Simeon Stylites the Elder is buried in Antioch, having perched for 38 years on his pillar 30 miles (50 km) to the east of Antioch. |
| AD 526–28 | Devastating earthquake and after-tremors kills up to 250,000 people and levels most of the city (with only limited rebuilding under Emperor Justinian). |
| AD 540 | Further Persian sacking of the city. |
| AD 600s | Area under Arab control: the Mamluks from AD 600s and then the Ottomans from AD 1200s. |
| 1098–1268 | Crusaders' influence in the area. |
| 1919 | Area of Antioch transferred to Syria (under French control). |
| 1939 | Area incorporated into Turkey. |

First, Peter arrived in Antioch and initially seemed quite happy to eat with Gentile believers (thereby not observing strict Jewish food laws). But then some people came down from Jerusalem, claiming to come 'from James' (that is, the younger brother of Jesus, now the prime leader of the Jerusalem church). They disapproved of Peter's eating with Gentiles, so Peter changed his policy (perhaps genuinely unsure whether they truly had James' backing or were simply using his name for their own agenda). To Paul's amazement and disapproval, 'even Barnabas was led astray' by them and separated himself from the Gentile believers for a while.

## Paul's response

This led to Paul speaking out in no uncertain terms (Galatians 2:15–21). The true badge of membership in God's people, he insisted, was now faith in Jesus, not circumcision or the food laws. So *anyone* who had faith in Jesus, even supposedly Gentile 'sinners', should be welcome to sit together at table – as a clear sign that such aspects of the Law were now annulled by God's 'grace' in Jesus. Paul saw all this as a matter of ultimate first principle. No doubt he also feared that all he had done to bring Gentiles to faith was about to be undermined; moreover, that Jesus' death on the cross was similarly being discarded – for why had Jesus died, if it was not precisely to bring about salvation for those with repentant faith, and thus to break down the former barriers between Jew and Gentile?

*'I have been crucified with Christ and I no longer live, but Christ lives in me... I do not set aside the grace of God, for if righteousness could be gained through the Law, Christ died for nothing!'*
**Galatians 2:20–21**

This issue had to be resolved once and for all. People could not keep going round the Mediterranean claiming to have the support of James (or some other leader) and effectively wrecking the work that others were doing. The matter needed to be taken back to Jerusalem for resolution. However, things got even worse. Paul then received news that his Gentile converts in Galatia had been persuaded by some visitors (presumably from Jerusalem) that they must be circumcised (see p. 84). And then a further delegation arrived from Jerusalem, again demanding the absolute necessity of circumcision (Acts 15:1). This makes sense historically. For the same Jewish nationalism that had triggered the clashes in AD 48 (mentioned above) may have put pressure on the believers in Jerusalem – to ensure they were not associated with a movement that was so obviously compromising the borders of Judaism.

All this, however, was too much even for Barnabas, who now swung round to defend his Gentile mission (Acts 15:2). And Paul's response in Galatians is highly charged – his work was being undermined by others and he had to return to Jerusalem to argue his case once more. His life's work now hung in the balance. So, travelling with Barnabas, he made his way once more up to Jerusalem, but this time with hot passion, mixed with desperation and determination. This was 'make or break'.

## The apostles' ruling: good news for Antioch and beyond

This so-called 'apostolic council', which took place almost certainly in AD 49, is described by Luke in Acts 15. And the end result, for Paul, was brilliant. James, perhaps being made newly aware of how Paul and Barnabas had already 'risked their lives for the name of the Lord Jesus Christ' (Acts 15:26), gave a definitive ruling in Paul's favour. And the apostles issued a letter (or 'decree') which, while emphasizing that idolatry and sexual immorality must be avoided, also gave clear reassurances to Gentile converts that circumcision was *not* a requirement. The return to Antioch (joined by Judas and Silas, two Jerusalem church leaders) must have been sweet indeed. For when the believers in Antioch read the letter, we read that they were 'glad for its encouraging message' (Acts 15:31).

*'It is my judgement that we should not make it difficult for the Gentiles who are turning to God.'*
**James' decisive and brave words at the apostolic council (Acts 15:19)**

In fact this sounds like an understatement. This was the vital news that the Gentile believers had been waiting for! But this good news could not be kept in Antioch. Soon Paul wanted to be off again, especially to take this good news to the believers in Galatia. Barnabas wanted to take Mark again, but Paul was adamantly against this (because Mark had deserted them in Pamphylia: see p. 68). So they went their separate ways – Barnabas went back to his native Cyprus with Mark; Paul took Silas through 'Syria and Cilicia' en route for Galatia (Acts 15:36–41).

Paul would only return once more to Antioch, when he spent 'some time' there between his 'second' and 'third' missionary journeys (Acts 18:23). But his years there, interrupted by his various travels, had been formative and important. They had given him experience of being part of a large teaching team, set in congregations that were learning how to worship together as Jew and Gentile, united through faith in Christ. He had been well supported there – in prayer, encouragement and practical resources. And it had been the necessary 'holding ground' (near Jerusalem in one sense, but far removed from it in another) while his vision for mission among the Gentiles was being evaluated and then endorsed by the wider apostolic community. Now, at last, he was set free, unfettered, to break new ground in lands much further afield.



## Antioch: home for 'Christians'

Finally, it was in Antioch that 'the disciples were first called "Christians"' (Acts 11:26). Almost certainly this was a label first given to Jesus' followers by *others* (the name is similar in form to other 'nicknames'); people may soon have noticed this new grouping

Modern Antakya, looking across the River Orontes towards the slopes of Mount Silpius.

within Antioch's Jewish community (even as early as the anti-Semitic riots in AD 40?). And Jesus' followers were probably only too pleased, given this context of violent anti-Semitism and ardent Jewish nationalism, to try to distinguish themselves from the general ranks of Judaism.

For the national aspirations of their fellow Jews (which were fuelling the present crisis) were, to them, focused in the wrong direction. Now that the Jewish royal Messiah-King had come in Jesus, God's kingdom was clearly not going to be a political one, brought by the sword. This distinctive belief (in Jesus as Messiah or 'anointed' one) meant they could rightly be labelled 'messianics', or (in Greek) '*christianoi*'. To the Romans the nickname probably made little sense; after all, a similar nickname might be given to people who particularly enjoyed *anointing* themselves with oil after a hot bath! But for Jesus' followers it was a nickname they could live with – and, as history reveals, it was a name that stuck.

## Antioch after the New Testament

There were two major urban centres in the eastern half of the Roman empire: Antioch and Alexandria. Paul never visited Alexandria, though there is a tradition that the gospel was first taken there by his former assistant, John Mark (Eusebius, *Ecclesiastical History* 2.16). Alternatively (and perhaps more likely), the gospel reached Alexandria with Jewish believers travelling from Jerusalem – such that Apollos was already a Christian believer when he left Alexandria around AD 52 (Acts 18:24). Both Alexandria and Antioch would become key centres in the developing Christian world, being honoured in AD 325 as 'patriarchates' (along with Rome and then Constantinople).

Antioch's role in Christian history from Paul's time onwards is particularly interesting. Some scholars, for example, suggest that the Gospel of Matthew was written in and for the church in Antioch. Certainly there are many features that suggest this Gospel was written within an urban, rather than a rural, environment (hence its references to 'towns' rather than villages in chapters 10–13). Moreover, alone of the four Gospels, Matthew writes that 'news about Jesus spread all over *Syria*' (Matthew 4:24). This probably refers to the towns and village of northern Galilee and the Golan Heights towards Damascus (all within the Roman province of Syria-Palestina), but it certainly shows an interest in Syria – which would fit with a Gospel emanating from the provincial capital in Syrian Antioch.

More certain is the link with Ignatius, an early Christian martyred for his faith in Rome around AD 107. Ignatius had for some time been the bishop of the church in Antioch, but he was arrested and taken captive to Rome. While on this journey he wrote some fascinating short letters to various church communities en route, including several that would have been known to Paul and/or the writer of Revelation (Ephesus, Smyrna, Philadelphia, Philippi, Rome; also Magnesia and Tralles: see p. 147). In them we sense Ignatius' clear readiness to be a martyr and his passion for Jesus Christ, but we also gain a rare glimpse into the life of the early church: its developing pattern of church order; the importance of the local bishop as a figure of unity; the importance of the Eucharist as the 'medicine of immortality'; and the constant need to be wary of false teaching or division. For our purposes one of his most apt quotations concerns the 'saintly and renowned Paul of blessed memory': 'may I be found', he then adds, 'to have *walked in his footsteps* when I come to God!' (*Ephesians* 12).

Other colourful personalities would emerge among Antioch's later bishops. In the late third century, disputes flared up because of the teachings of its bishop, Paul of Samosata, who espoused views similar to those later held by Arius and ruled as heretical; at one point in this lively debate, backed by rival factions, there were no less than four bishops of Antioch holding the post simultaneously!

Antioch would naturally then find itself embroiled in the full-blown Arian controversy in the first half of the fourth century, being the scene for numerous debates and councils. One of these took place at the dedication festival for Antioch's magnificent 'golden church', commissioned by Constantine. Then, at the end of the century, Antioch's bishop for a short while was John Chrysostom ('John of the Golden Mouth'), whose preaching attracted large crowds and provoked some strong reactions before he was elevated to become bishop of Constantinople.

# Antioch today

Ancient Antioch, the third largest city in the Roman empire (after Rome and Alexandria), played a major part in early Christian history; so it is a pity that so little of it survives. Modern Antakya (population c. 175,000) covers the site. The main street today (Kurtulus Caddesi) runs along exactly the same line as the ancient 2-mile- (3-km-) long colonnaded street, but nothing remains to be seen. Ancient Antioch may now be up to 30 feet (10 m) below the present street level; and the only remains of the extensive fortifications run along the heights of nearby Mount Silpius (2,000 feet or 600 m above sea level).

Even so, it can be a powerful place to visit. Standing on a bridge over the wide River Orontes (now the River Asi), the modern visitor can easily imagine why this location proved ideal for a major city. And, in the light of Juvenal's famous quotation (when speaking out against excessive Oriental influences affecting Rome), to see the Orontes is to be reminded graphically of the influence that Antioch had throughout the Roman world. The city's location meant it was the conduit for everything that came from the Fertile Crescent; down the Orontes the exotic East flowed into a ravenous, enchanted Mediterranean world. Moreover, looking up towards Mount Silpius, one can easily imagine the ancient figures who passed through Antioch: powerful rulers (from Antiochus Epiphanes to Hadrian) and Christians (from Bishop Ignatius to John Chrysostom). This was the city, overlooked by these same hills, that played such a key part in their lives.

*'The Syrian Orontes flowed into the Tiber long ago, carrying with it its language and customs, its flute-players and slanting strings; its native timbrels, and the girls ordered to sell themselves at the circus.'*

**Juvenal, *Satires* 3.60–65**

Finding any connection with Paul is difficult in Antioch. There is a (not very reliable) tradition that Paul preached near the Pantheon, in a street known either as 'Singon' or 'Siagon' (the latter meaning 'jaw-bone'). But where was the Pantheon? Bishop John Chrysostom pointed out a mountain cave associated with Paul's preaching. But where exactly was it?

The Church of St Peter, built in the side of Mount Silpius: the façade (LEFT) was built by the Crusaders; inside (RIGHT) there is a large cave, associated with Christian worship from very early times.

Finding a connection with Peter appears a fraction easier. The Antiochene church, not surprisingly, soon claimed Peter as its apostolic founder (based on Galatians 2:11). So the one historic church is the **Church of St Peter**. This is located some 2 miles (3 km) north-east of the city on the side of Mount Staurin (a continuation of Mount Silpius). Effectively this is a church carved out from a natural cave in the hill-side, which seems to have been used for Christian worship since the fourth or fifth century AD. Although the façade was added by the Crusaders (and then substantially restored in the mid-nineteenth century), some of the floor mosaics do go back to that early Byzantine era. Is this a place that was visited by the apostle Peter?

The exhibition halls of the Hatay Archaeological Museum in Antakya, containing numerous mosaics: the detail is 'Summer' (from a depiction of the four seasons).

It is not impossible. However, as with other places in the Holy Land, so here the Byzantines probably focused on a natural cave, not because of any reliable tradition, but simply because they were reckoning that the first Christians must have used such 'safe' places for their worship. Such caves were also important because, as natural fixed points, they gave a tangible link to that now-distant apostolic era. Almost certainly, then, the tradition does not pre-date the third or fourth century.

Even so, this particular church has now become a historic place in Christian memory. Owned at different times by Armenians, Greek Orthodox and now the Catholic Capuchin Fathers, it does provide the only clear reminder in modern Antakya that this city played a key role in the apostolic era. Not surprisingly, therefore, it is much valued by the small Christian communities who continue to live in Antakya. They are also keen to point out that the very name of Mount Staurin is derived from the Greek word for the cross (*stauros*) – apparently because a cross appeared in the sky above this mountain during the devastating earthquakes in AD 526–28.

While on Mount Staurin, it is worth walking some 200 yards (180 m) to the north to see the carved **Charonion** relief – presumably named after Charon, the man in Greek mythology who ferried departed souls across the River Styx. According to ancient sources, this carving may date back to c. 170 BC, being intended as a talisman to ward off a vicious plague. The unfinished nature of the small, carved figure (on the main figure's right shoulder) is sometimes taken as a sign that the plague indeed halted.

Back in the city centre is the **Hatay Archaeological Museum**. This is most impressive, housing some extraordinarily fine floor mosaics, full of colour and life, which date from the first six centuries AD. We see a drunk Dionysus, an infant Hercules, some Bacchic dancers, a dark-skinned fisherman, as well as a vivid portrait of the four seasons. Here at least one can sense something of Antioch's wealth and vitality.

## Daphne and Seleucia

Other places nearby are worth a visit. Five miles (8 km) away was a beautiful cypress grove, the sanctuary of Apollo's oracle at **Daphne**. Despite the area's pagan associations (and its theatre and stadium), we know this was a popular suburb for Antioch's Jewish population – perhaps because a high priest (Onias III) had once fled here for escape (2 Maccabees 4:33). Quite possibly, the synagogues here were some of the first to hear the message about Jesus. Little now remains, but the general vicinity can be appreciated by going on the main road towards the suburb of Harbiye.

Acts 13:4 explicitly mentions Antioch's port, **Seleucia** (also known as Seleucia ad Pieria, after the nearby Pieria Mountains). Due to silting, however, both the inner and outer harbours are now up to a mile (1.5 km) from the shoreline; but in its heyday the lower and upper cities had a combined population of up to 30,000.

The Orontes was navigable for its first 25 miles (40 km), so it was possible to sail right into Antioch itself. In practice, however, many disembarked at Seleucia, located some 6 miles (10 km) to the north of the Orontes estuary, and then travelled overland. Quite probably this is what Paul did on the other occasions when travelling to Antioch (Acts 14:26; 15:30; 18:22); in which case Paul would have known this shoreline well – as the welcome prelude to his 'homecomings' in Antioch.

The key spectacle for modern visitors dates to just *after* Paul's time, however. Seleucia was subject to several damaging flash-floods (known locally as 'donkey-drowners'); the harbour's silting up was also a concern. To solve both these problems, Vespasian and Titus commissioned an ambitious project (enlisting some of those taken captive during the First Jewish Revolt): the creation of a bypass tunnel, which would take the stream's waters directly into the sea, bypassing the harbour. The overall length of this water-course was 1,530 yards (1,400 m), but the last 140 yards (130 m) had to be cut through solid rock. It was a staggering achievement, which took nearly 70 years to complete. The inscription (dated to c. AD 132) is still in place, crediting the emperors who first planned the operation; and, as you walk (carefully) through the tunnel, it is hard not to be mightily impressed with the ingenuity and determination of the project's managers. Despite their efforts, however, the harbour eventually silted up, and Seleucia came to an end.

4

CHAPTER

# Cyprus

*The two of them… went down to Seleucia and sailed from there to Cyprus. When they arrived at Salamis, they proclaimed the word of God in the Jewish synagogues. John was with them as their helper.*

*They travelled through the whole island until they came to Paphos. There they met a Jewish sorcerer and false prophet named Bar-Jesus, who was an attendant of the proconsul, Sergius Paulus. The proconsul, an intelligent man, sent for Barnabas and Saul because he wanted to hear the word of God. But Elymas the sorcerer… opposed them and tried to turn the proconsul from the faith. Then Saul, who was also called Paul, filled with the Holy Spirit… said, 'You are full of all kinds of deceit and trickery. Will you never stop perverting the right ways of the Lord? Now the hand of the Lord is against you. You are going to be blind for a time, not even able to see the light of the sun.'*

*Immediately mist and darkness came over him… When the proconsul saw what had happened, he believed…*

**Acts 13:4–12**

## First adventures

Paul's first 'missionary journey' out of Antioch was to the scenic island of Cyprus – probably in AD 46. We saw in Chapter 3 how this first expedition was launched with prayer and prophetic words (Acts 13:1–3). Now we see what happened as Paul and Barnabas, together with the young Mark, struck out south-westwards. Going down to Antioch's port on the Mediterranean (Seleucia, some 9 miles or 15 km away), they found a cargo ship travelling to Cyprus and went on board.

### Three men in a boat

We can imagine some of their feelings as they ventured out into the unknown and as the mountains of Cyprus, some 90 miles (145 km) from Seleucia, at last came into view on their starboard horizon.

For one of them, Barnabas, this journey was nothing new. He was a native of Cyprus (see p. 60) and was quite used to travelling in the triangle between Cyprus, Jerusalem and Antioch. So he was not making a total 'leap into the unknown' – indeed, starting the expedition with a visit to Cyprus may have been his idea. A few years later he would decide to come this way again (Acts 15:39). For him this was home.

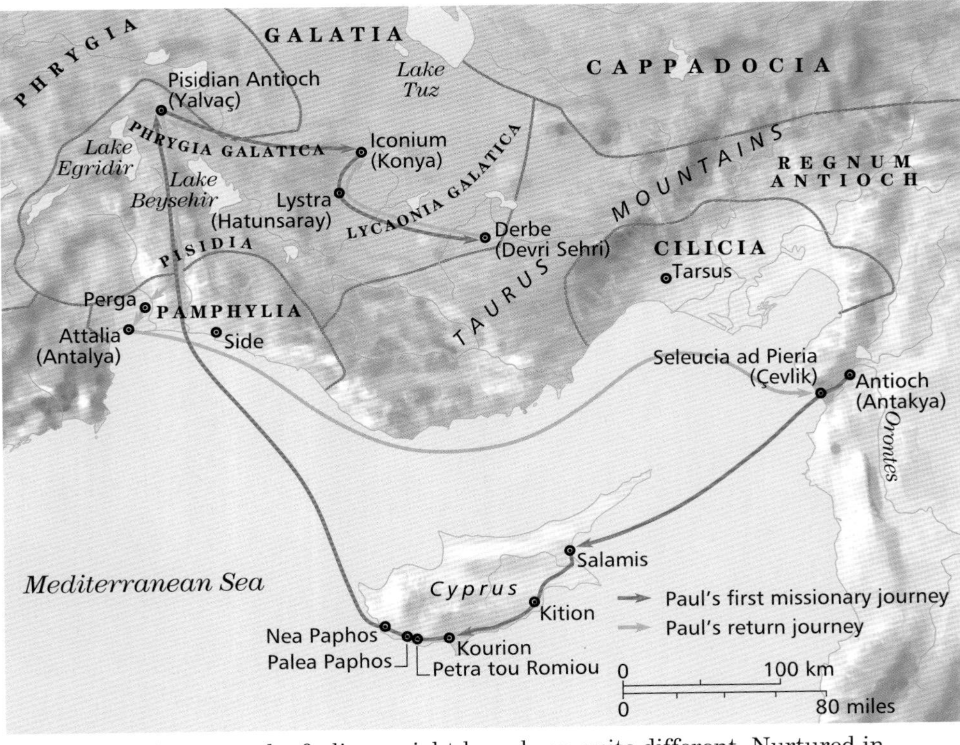


**Map of Paul's first 'missionary journey' (AD 46–47).**

For Mark, however, the feelings might have been quite different. Nurtured in Jerusalem and only recently having tasted the cosmopolitan atmosphere of Antioch, this was indeed a voyage of fresh discoveries. Yes, he was travelling with a trusted family member, Barnabas, to an area that *he* knew well (see p. 60); but he himself had little idea, for example, how synagogues functioned so far away from Jerusalem. And how would they respond to this message of a messiah? More worrying still, how would he cope with it all? Would he prove useful to his seniors, or somehow get in their way? Would he feel homesick?

Paul too had some questions. This was possibly his first night on the open sea (with his previous sailings being safely along the Mediterranean coast), so he was doing something new. So as they set sail, he might have sensed how his calling to be Jesus' 'apostle to the Gentiles' was coming to fruition – at long last. He had preached the gospel to Gentiles before, but Cyprus gave him opportunities to break new ground. Yet, even as the shoreline of Cyprus came more closely into view, Paul may have been thinking of further shores. For his own long-term sights were probably set on the large territory of *his* native area of Asia Minor and its shores on another sea – the Aegean to the west. For Paul, Cyprus was just the first step towards something much larger.

The three men in the boat, each with their slightly different hopes and fears, but joined by a single shared commitment, picked up their few belongings and, interspersed with the other passengers, made their way down the gangplank onto the busy harbour walls of Salamis. What would happen next?

The eastern colonnade of the Gymnasium at Salamis, with the walls of the bath complex beyond.

## Arrival in Salamis

Cyprus, a beautiful island clad with forests and with two distinctive mountain ranges, lay in the eastern Mediterranean at a strategic location. It was only 40 miles (65 km) south of Asia Minor, 90 miles (145 km) west of Syria, and some 250 miles (400 km) north of Alexandria. For this reason, and also because of its rich deposits of copper (in Greek *kupros*), it played a vital role in the trade routes of the ancient world. Settled originally by the Phoenicians and then the Greeks, its unique position meant inevitably it was rarely left alone by the 'superpowers' – the Persians, the Ptolemies and, since 58 BC, the Romans.

One of its chief settlements on its southern shore was called Kition. As a result, the Hebrews had referred to the island as 'Kittim'. From the various references to 'Kittim' in the Old Testament the biblical writers evidently saw it as an island with naval power, connected with the traders of Tyre and Assyria; but, above all, it was a land far away, across the treacherous sea.

Salamis, the main town on the east coast, had been settled around the eighth century BC by the Greeks, soon becoming the island's principal city. By the first century AD, like most Cypriot cities, it had a small but recognizable Jewish community – note how Luke refers to 'synagogues' in the plural (Acts 13:5). For the three travellers, landed on the quayside, the synagogue was the obvious first port of call.

In this we see the first clear example of what will become a common theme as we follow Paul in his travels: his first visit in any place was always to the local synagogue. There were some obvious, practical reasons for this: as Jews themselves, this was a natural point of connection. Each Saturday morning they would find a group of people committed to studying the Hebrew Scriptures. And, as a visiting rabbi, Paul would regularly be invited to address the worshippers as a matter of courtesy – just as happened to Jesus himself when he made *his* visit to Nazareth's synagogue (Luke 4:14–28).

Yet there was a deeper point, drawn from Paul's theology. Though an 'apostle to the Gentiles', he was convinced that Jesus was *Israel's* Messiah. This good news was all about, and for, Israel. Israel's long-held expectation that God would act to fulfil his promises *had at last come true*: he had sent a Messiah–King to rescue his people. So the good news about Jesus had to be proclaimed in the synagogue first – because it was ultimately *Israel's* good news for the world. The good news was therefore 'for the Jew first, then for the Gentile' (Romans 1:16). Paul was so convinced of this that he resolutely continued this policy – even though it invariably led to his being rejected from the synagogue (see pp. 80–81). In the Cypriot city of Salamis he started what he meant to continue.

So, perhaps on three or four Saturdays, 'they proclaimed the word of God in the Jewish synagogues' (Acts 13:5). On this occasion Luke makes no comment on how the synagogues responded to this preaching. Nor do we know how many of those attending these synagogues were already believers in Jesus. Presumably there was a handful, since it was *Jewish believers* from Cyprus who had first travelled to Antioch with the good news (Acts 11:20). In this sense, Salamis was not quite 'virgin territory'.



## Onwards to Paphos

In due course the three travellers decided to move on. Perhaps on foot, perhaps on mules or donkeys, they travelled about 100 miles (160 km) 'through the whole island'. Almost certainly they travelled along the road that skirted round the south of the island, not through the interior.

Their goal was the capital of the new Roman province of Cyprus – Nea Paphos. This 'New' Paphos lay on the far south-western corner of the island, some 7 miles (11 km) beyond 'Old Paphos' (or 'Palea' Paphos). Originally a Greek settlement, it had been taken over by the Ptolemies of Egypt (as a useful trading port and as a good source of timber for their shipbuilding) and now by the Romans.

Because Cyprus was a senatorial province, the governor (as Luke correctly points out) was known as the 'proconsul', and the occupant of this position in AD 46 was one Sergius Paulus (Acts 13:7). We know nothing about this man from other sources; clearly he had some acquaintance with Judaism, inasmuch as he had a Jewish magician within his court circle – something that the governor Festus

Plan of ancient Paphos.

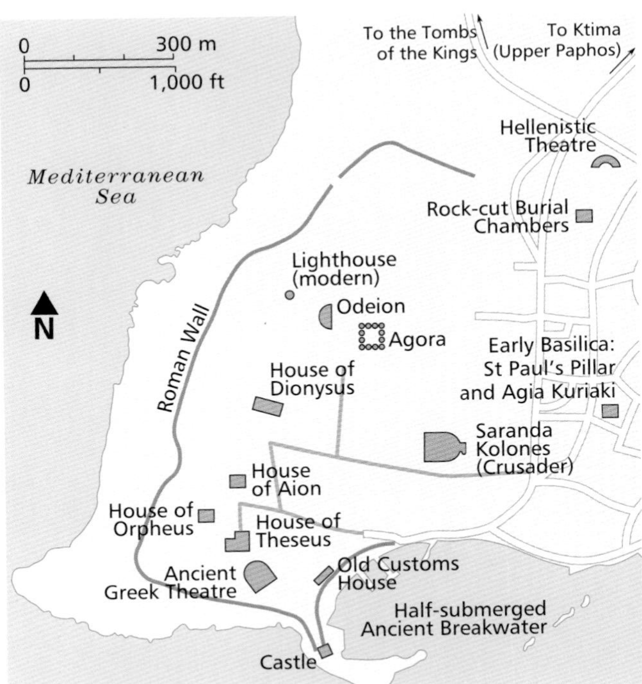

*'The things that mark an apostle – signs, wonders and miracles – were done among you with great perseverance.'*
**2 Corinthians 12:12**

also had in his court in Caesarea, according to Josephus (*Antiquities* 20.142).

Presumably, Paul and the others visited the local synagogue. At some point, the proconsul heard news of this (perhaps via Bar-Jesus, the magician) and invited them to his residence to speak. Opposed in his preaching by the magician, Paul effectively speaks out a curse upon him that leaves him temporarily blinded. This, the first of several such 'miraculous' events associated with Paul in Acts (see also Acts 16:18; 19:11–12), made a powerful impression upon the proconsul: when coupled with what he had already heard, it was sufficient, claims Luke, to bring him to a point of 'faith' (Acts 13:8–12).

## Jesus and the Roman authorities

A natural implication of Luke's wording would be that Sergius Paulus went on to be baptized, becoming a full 'believer'. Yet Luke does not expressly say this, so conceivably the matter was left more open-ended. For Luke, however, the governor's response marks a sufficient climax to his account of Paul's visit to Cyprus – with none other than the

### Key dates: Cyprus

|  |  |
|---|---|
| c. 6500 BC | First arrivals of people from mainland by raft. |
| 2400 BC | Ebla tablets refer to the island's copper exports, as do the later Mari tablets (1800 BC) and the Amarna letters (1400 BC). |
| 1300 BC | Founding of 'Palea Paphos' by Phoenicians (later the centre of a cult of Aphrodite). |
| 1000 BC | Phoenician settlements, such as those at Kition (modern Larnaca). |
| c. 800s BC | Founding of Salamis by the Greeks ('Salamis' was also an island near Athens, scene of the famous sea battle against the Persians in 480 BC). |
| 700–500 BC | Various references to 'Kittim' in the Old Testament (Numbers 24:24; Isaiah 23:12; Daniel 11:30). |
| 333 BC | Alexander the Great's navy brings his rule, then (later) Ptolemaic rule (from Egypt). |
| c. 320 BC | Founding of new city at Paphos ('Nea Paphos') by King Nicocles. |
| 200s BC | 'Tombs of the Kings' in use near Nea Paphos. |
| c. 100 BC | First reference to Jews on Cyprus (1 Maccabees 15:23). |
| 58 BC | Cyprus annexed by Rome (initially included in the province of Cilicia). |
| 22 BC | Cyprus becomes a senatorial province, governed by its own proconsul. Augustus confirms Salamis' Temple of Zeus as a sanctuary of asylum. |
| 15 BC | Salamis badly affected by an earthquake. |
| 12 BC | Augustus leases to Herod the Great all the island's copper mines for half their revenue. |
| AD 46 | Paul, Barnabas and Mark arrive on the island. Sergius Paulus might be related to Lucius Sergius Paulus (curator of the Tiber in Rome) or Quintus Sergius Paulus (whose name appears on an inscription from Kythraia in northern Cyprus). |
| AD 50 | Barnabas returns to Cyprus with Mark (Acts 15:39); according to much later tradition, Lazarus becomes the first 'bishop' of Kition. |
| AD 75? | Traditional date for the martyrdom of Barnabas (see *Acts of Barnabas*, dating from the fifth century AD). |
| AD 115–17 | Widespread Jewish revolt (originating from Egypt) is crushed by Trajan, who orders that 'no Jew is to appear on the island'. |
| AD 368–403 | Epiphanius serves as bishop of Salamis, famous for his *Panarion* (a treatise refuting numerous heresies). |
| c. AD 478 | Anthemius, bishop of Salamis, discovers the body of St Barnabas. The self-governing nature of Cyprus is recognized in relation to the patriarchate of Antioch. |
| AD 647 | Salamis invaded by Arabs, causing Christians to flee to Famagusta. |
| 1100s | Building of many monasteries in Troodos Mountains. |
| 1192–1489 | Island ruled by the descendants of Guy de Lusignan. |
| 1489–1571 | Venetian occupation of the island (building the walls of Nicosia and Famagusta). |
| 1878 | The British are allowed by the Sultan of Turkey to establish military outposts in Cyprus. |
| 1960 | Creation of Republic of Cyprus, led by Archbishop Makarios. |
| 1974 | Separation of Greek and Turkish Cyprus. |

island's Roman governor expressing some faith in the 'teaching about the Lord'. Here was Paul's message receiving recognition from the highest Gentile authorities.

For Luke this was very significant. Within just fifteen years of Jesus himself being sentenced to death under a Roman governor in Jerusalem, here was another Roman governor responding positively to the message about him through Paul. Here too was the Roman empire beginning to take note of a new, distinct teaching from within Judaism. The potential clash between Jesus and Caesar – which would become so acute in Rome within twenty years, and which would run as a painful sore for nearly three centuries – had come to its first expression here in Paphos. And the first signs were promising.



## Cyprus today

Cyprus is a beautiful island, tragically divided. Since 1974 the northern half has been administered from Ankara by the Turkish government; the southern half is an independent Greek-speaking state. For students of Paul, there are two sites to be seen, but on opposite sides of the 'green line': ancient Salamis on the east coast in the Turkish sector, Paphos on the south-west coast in Greek Cyprus. Tourists are now allowed through the checkpoint in Nicosia, so both sites can be seen in one visit.

**Bottom: Plan of ancient Salamis.** Top: Detail of the northern gymnasium area.
1 Cold rooms (*frigidaria*)
2 Latrines
3 Swimming pools
4 Stoking rooms (*praefurnia*)
5 Hot rooms (*sudatoria/caldaria*)

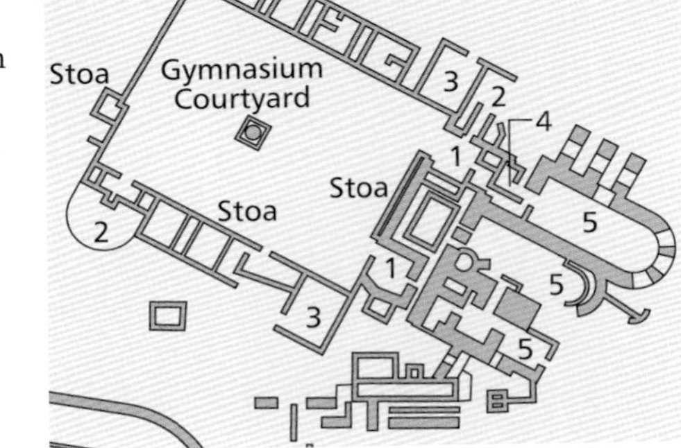


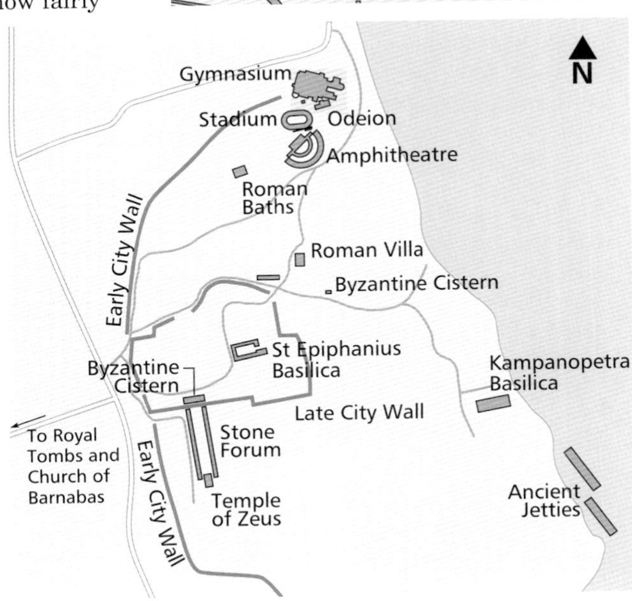


### Salamis

Visiting Salamis can be a great experience. Turkish Cyprus is marked by the strong contrast between the (now fairly barren) flat central plain and the sharp ridge of the Kyrenian Mountains running along the island's northern edge and eastwards along its so-called 'pan-handle'. Salamis itself is on the flat plain, but with great views northwards to the mountains.

There are few modern buildings in the area. Instead, much lies unexcavated under sand dunes. The whole site covers more than 5 square miles (13 sq km), so it is quite possible for visitors to feel they have the place to themselves. Moreover, although the entrance is at the north-east corner, the site is also accessible from the sandy beach. Along the beach there is now little evidence of the ancient harbour, but near a spur of land jutting out into the sea the foundations of some of the breakwaters can be seen just below the water level.

## Barnabas and the Byzantines

In Luke's account, Barnabas, Paul's chief companion on his early journeys, is expressly described as a native of Cyprus: 'Joseph, a Levite from Cyprus, whom the apostles called Barnabas (which means son of encouragement) sold a field he owned and brought the money and put it at the apostles' feet' (Acts 4:36–37).

### Barnabas in Jerusalem and Cyprus

We do not know why Barnabas had gone to Jerusalem: was he there to study (like young Paul from Tarsus)? Or was he there to gain some experience of Jerusalem's Temple worship (since he belonged to the priestly tribe of Levi)? He evidently had some (ancestral?) property in the Jerusalem area, some of which he sold for the apostles. Moreover, John Mark (as we learn much later from Colossians 4:10) was Barnabas' 'cousin', which means that Barnabas had family connections in Jerusalem. Quite probably, on first arriving in Jerusalem, he had stayed in John Mark's home with his mother Mary (Acts 12:25). And then, as Mark's whole family joined the new messianic movement, he did too. Indeed, were he, Mary and Mark among the 120 believers gathered in Jerusalem even before the day of Pentecost (Acts 1:15)? In any event, he and Mark had known each other for quite some time before they journeyed to Cyprus.

We also, of course, do not know how many times Barnabas had made a return visit to Cyprus in the intervening years. Intriguingly Luke records that after Stephen's martyrdom, believers had been scattered to 'Phoenicia, *Cyprus* and Antioch' (Acts 11:19); so Barnabas might well have come home at this time, no doubt spreading the message of Jesus among the Jewish population on the island. Luke then goes on to say that it was Jewish believers from '*Cyprus* and Cyrene' who then caused a stir by travelling over to Antioch and speaking to Greeks about Jesus (Acts 11:20). Barnabas was not in this particular group, for we know he was back in Jerusalem at this juncture. But his Cyprus connections may well have commended him to the Jerusalem apostles as the ideal person to be sent down to Antioch to investigate what was going on – which he promptly did (Acts 11:22–23).

Barnabas' link with Cyprus made it an obvious first choice for the first 'missionary journey'. It was also the place to which he later returned after he and Paul had decided to go their separate ways: 'Barnabas took Mark and sailed for Cyprus' (Acts 15:39). This is the last time Barnabas is mentioned in the text of Acts. We do not know for sure what happened on this, his second 'missionary journey', or precisely how he spent the rest of his life.

Early Christian tradition has it that Barnabas stayed on Cyprus (based at Salamis?) as the founding leader of the church on the island until his death around AD 75, when he was put to death by the local Jewish community. During this period Cyprus also played host, it is claimed, to Lazarus – the man raised from the grave by Jesus in Bethany just outside Jerusalem (John 11:38–43). He was reputedly the first 'bishop' of Kition (modern Larnaca).

### Barnabas and the later church

In later centuries the Cypriot church made much of this historic link with Barnabas. By the end of the fourth century AD, the Christian faith had spread quite deeply across the island. Epiphanius, one of the bishops of Salamis at this time, became famous for his unstinting work in the eastern Mediterranean, describing and hunting out various heresies from the church (writing the *Panarion* as a 'cure for all heresies').

A century later, there was some controversy between the bishops on Cyprus and the bishop (or archbishop) of Syrian Antioch, with the latter claiming that Cyprus must come under *his* jurisdiction (because his church was an 'apostolic' one, founded by the apostle Peter). The Cypriot church pleaded its case to be similarly 'apostolic' (because of Barnabas). Just when they looked like losing the argument, there was a mysterious occurrence.

The bishop of Salamis, Anthemius, had a dream in which Barnabas appeared to him and revealed where his corpse had been buried – under a carob tree a little inland (for its site, see pp. 62–63). Upon excavating the next day, a corpse was duly found (clutching a Hebrew version of Matthew's Gospel). The Cypriots immediately took these relics to Constantinople where the emperor Zeno (AD 474–91), suitably impressed, granted some special privileges to the island.

Chief among these was that the Cypriot church was recognized as an 'autocephalous' (or self-governing) church, able to appoint its own archbishop. The archbishop was also able to do certain things that were normally the preserve of the emperor himself (namely, wearing imperial purple, holding a sceptre rather than a pastoral staff, and signing his letters in red ink!). This blurring of the boundaries between the religious and political spheres made it natural (much later under the Ottomans and then into the twentieth century) for Cypriot archbishops to be recognized as being also the civic and political leaders of their people (hence Archbishop Makarios' use of the title 'ethnarch' in the 1960s).

Greek Cyprus (as opposed to the northern section of Turkish Cyprus) has remained a bastion for Greek Orthodoxy throughout the centuries. Up in the Troodos Mountains, for example, there are numerous churches and monasteries, many dating from before the Middle Ages, several of which contain fine frescoes.

TOP: the small church over the tomb of Saint Barnabas, 2 miles (3 km) to the south-west of Salamis.

BELOW: an example of the rich mosaics in Kykko Monastery, the largest of the many Orthodox monasteries located in Cyprus' Troodos Mountains.

The first site is the **gymnasium**. The large courtyard, with its fine columns, would have served as the *palaestra* (exercise yard). At its south-western corner there are some well-preserved latrines in a semi-circular format. The courtyard's eastern colonnade had two small swimming pools at each end, surrounded by marble statues set into niches in the walls. From this colonnade there were two entrances into the bath complex: first into some octagonal cold rooms, then into further sweat rooms and the hot water baths. In some of these rooms some fine mosaic fragments have been preserved.

Just a short distance to the south of the *palaestra* was an **amphitheatre**, but it is now scarcely recognizable due to the undergrowth. One's eye goes instead to the vast **theatre** just beyond. Originally built during the reign of the emperor Augustus, it had 50 rows of seats, accommodating up to 15,000 spectators. A major earthquake in the fourth century AD led to its demise. Its stones were quarried for other use, thus reducing the number of rows to fewer than twenty.

To the south-west of the theatre there has been some recent archaeological work, uncovering various dwellings and a colonnaded street that ran north–south. Following this street southwards you rejoin the dirt track at a small junction. Going eastwards brings you to the **'Kampanopetra' Church** and the beach; continuing southwards brings you eventually to the large ***agora***. Unlike many later *agorae*, this Hellenistic market place, lined with colonnaded shops on either side, is not a square but a very long rectangle dominated at its southern end by the **Temple of Zeus** (originally a large Hellenistic structure but rebuilt by the Romans shortly before Paul's visit). We can imagine Paul and his companions wandering through the *agora*, observing the traders about their daily business,

*'... we came to the synagogue near the place called Biblia; and Barnabas, having unrolled the Gospel which he had received from Matthew, began to teach the Jews...*

*'But they... took him by night and bound him with a rope by the neck... and having gone out of the city... they burned him with fire, so that even his bones became dust. And straightaway that night, having taken his dust, they cast it into a cloth...*

*'We came to a certain place, and having found a cave, put it down there; and having found a secret place in it, we put it away, with the documents which he had received from Mark.'*

***Acts of Barnabas* (fifth century AD)**

perhaps making discreet enquiries about the location of the Jewish synagogues, and all the time being watched over by the towering façade of Zeus' pagan temple.

Retracing one's steps northwards, on leaving the *agora* the visitor passes the city's large reservoir tanks, which collected the water brought by miles of aqueducts. Then after a hundred yards or so there are the impressive ruins of a **Byzantine church**. This was Salamis' largest church, associated with the city's famous bishop, Epiphanius, and probably built during his term of office (AD 368–403); his tomb still lies encased in marble in front of the southern apse.

This famous bishop gained a reputation as an ardent champion of orthodoxy, travelling to Jerusalem and elsewhere in the critical period around the Council of Constantinople (in AD 381). His major work is called *Panarion*, meaning a 'cure for all heresies'. Although disadvantaged by the political manoeuvres of others, Epiphanius certainly put the Cypriot church 'on the map'. Standing in the basilica's apse to the east of the communion table, it is easy to imagine Epiphanius standing in that same spot, looking out on his congregation in the aisles.

Similar thoughts may spring to mind at the other large Byzantine church quite close to the beach, the so-called **'Kampanopetra' Basilica** (also dating to the fourth century AD). Built with three apses and with a large courtyard to the west, its eastern walls backed onto another courtyard that included bathing facilities and a sweat room. One of these rooms has a fine circular mosaic, with triangular tiles in red, black, white and light brown.

Basilicas such as these can affect later Christian visitors quite powerfully. From an educational point of view, they show how church architecture first developed: the orientation to the east; the adoption of the basilica style (formerly used for public or 'royal' buildings); the gradual preference for a structure with three apses; and the semi-circular seats for the clergy. Of particular interest are their low chancel barriers (perhaps just above knee height) that surrounded the communion table. So, although the 'sanctuary' and nave were distinct, there was still a very open feel – in contrast to later churches, which put great distance between clergy and people.

From a spiritual point of view, their ruined state gives them a simplicity that breaks down the years that separate us from our forebears. To see the remains of a communion table is to be poignantly reminded of one common action that has not changed through the centuries; for Christians across the world still meet regularly to remember Jesus' death through taking bread and wine together.

What would Paul have made of this – to see large churches built near where he first landed on Cyprus and to see a building expressly designed for celebrating the Lord's Supper? Surely he would feel deeply moved and gratified? Through breaking bread, he later wrote, believers 'proclaim the Lord's death until he comes' (1 Corinthians 11:26). And now, three hundred years later, believers were doing precisely that – proclaiming the importance of Jesus' death in this unique way. Here in Salamis, the sands of time may have blown over the site, but somewhere, deeper down, there are sure signs of a solid rock.

Another poignant site, just two miles to the south-west of ancient Salamis, is the **traditional tomb of Barnabas**. Almost certainly Barnabas, as a native Cypriot, *did* die somewhere on the island. This particular site, however, inevitably raises some questions because it was only identified several hundred years later – and in slightly bizarre circumstances motivated by politics (see p. 60).

The small square church built over the tomb remains to this day, in a beautiful quiet location, surrounded by carob trees; nearby is the monastery dedicated to St Barnabas. The tomb itself is reached by descending a flight of steps; in the niche visitors have placed many candles and there is a lengthy inscription proclaiming the unique role Barnabas played in bringing Christianity to the island of Cyprus. Meanwhile, in the (now unused) monastery, there is a church filled with quite recent icons and a small museum with pottery and artefacts ranging from the Neolithic and Bronze ages through to the Roman period.





## Paphos

The other Pauline site on Cyprus is on the opposite end of the island. Until the early 1980s Paphos was a comparative backwater – a small, remote fishing harbour with few restaurants. The building of a new international airport and of numerous hotels, together with the influx of (mainly British) expatriates, has now changed the area out of all recognition. The main site of **ancient Paphos**, however, remains undeveloped. Now cordoned off as an archaeological site, this large area is on a promontory by the sea, marked by a modern lighthouse.

Within this area are found a small **theatre**, the so-called **House of Dionysus** (a dwelling from the second century AD with a feast of mosaics), and other houses built for the Roman nobility. There is also a building which, because of its size and elaborate mosaics, may well have been the **governor's residence** at some period. It may date to after Paul's time, but it may yet be on the same site that Paul himself would have known when he appeared before Sergius Paulus (Acts 13:7).

More tentative still is **St Paul's Pillar** – identified as the supposed site of Paul's

ABOVE: the small church of Agia Kuriaki near 'St Paul's Pillar', surrounded by the remains of a much larger church (dating back to the fifth century).

LEFT: the famous mosaic of Hippolytus and Phaedra, found in the House of Dionysus.

BELOW: St Paul's Pillar.

flogging. It lies in some archaeological remains to the east of the main archaeological site, close to the seventeenth-century Greek church of Agia Kuriaki (now used by Roman Catholics and Anglicans). Visitors, however, can now readily see that this pillar is part of a later complex of church buildings. The area is covered by a five-aisled basilica dating to the fifth century AD, complete with a large narthex (or courtyard) at its western end. One of the aisles has been covered by **Agia Kuriaki**, and some of the northern side was redeveloped by the Crusaders. The so-called 'St Paul's Pillar' clearly dates from one of these two church buildings and thus would not have been in this location in Paul's time (when, in any case, this area would have been well outside the city). Until 1985, however, this area had not been excavated – indeed there was a tarmac road going straight across the site – so this pillar was one of the few ancient remains that was visible. As such, a local tradition developed, quite understandably, which identified this solitary object from antiquity with Paul.

The beautiful bay of Petra tou Romaiou, the traditional 'birth-place' of Aphrodite in Greek mythology, on the south coast of Cyprus.

So visiting Paphos today only gives a small idea of what it was like in Paul's day. One key part of Cyprus' ancient reputation, however, has continued into the present. This is the island's mythological connection with the goddess Aphrodite. On the north coast just to the west of Polis is her supposed bathing place and on the south coast (at **Petra tou Romaiou**, 11 miles or 18 km east of Paphos) her supposed birth place as she rose up from the surf of the Mediterranean. Cyprus is still promoted as Aphrodite's island, the 'island of love'. If the same was true in Paul's day, he would have responded that his message was also about love – but a divine love of a quite different order.

5

CHAPTER

# Pamphylia

*From Paphos, Paul and his companions sailed to Perga in Pamphylia, where John left them to return to Jerusalem. From Perga they went on to Pisidian Antioch. On the Sabbath they entered the synagogue and sat down.*

**Acts 13:13–14**

*After going through Pisidia, they came into Pamphylia, and when they had preached the word in Perga, they went down to Attalia. From Attalia they sailed back to Antioch, where they had been committed to the grace of God for the work they had now completed.*

**Acts 14:24–26**

## Divergent paths

In the late summer of AD 46, Paul, Barnabas and Mark set sail from Paphos towards the coast of Asia Minor. With the sailing season due to close in the autumn, it was presumably all part of their original plan to leave the island at the end of the summer. Yet, by heading west across to Paphos, they had effectively committed themselves already to landing back on the mainland much further to the west of Paul's native Cilicia. Hence they came to Pamphylia.

Pamphylia was the Roman province on the south coast of Asia Minor, located on the fairly narrow coastal plain to the south of the Taurus Mountains. Further to its east was the province of Cilicia; to its south-west the mountainous and fairly inaccessible area of Lycia. In Rome's administration at this period Lycia and Pamphylia were currently joined together in a united Roman province, with Perga, a large harbour city on the Cestrus River, serving as the capital of the region.

**Map of ancient Pamphylia's southern coast.**

### Approaching from the sea

There were at least three potential ports that Paul and his companions could have used, depending on the weather conditions. Some 30 miles (50 km) further to the east of Perga was Side, a bustling city set on a small promontory, which was a natural port for ships travelling along the coast. Meanwhile, some 9 miles (15 km) to the south-west of Perga was the attractive harbour of Attalia. This was becoming the

The foreboding, snow-capped Taurus Mountains towering above the port and city of Antalya: when Paul chose to travel on through the mountains, John Mark decided it was time to turn back.

major port in this region, a natural enclosed harbour surrounded by quite steep cliffs, which lay at the eastern edge of a beautiful gulf overlooked by the high peaks of the Lycian Mountains. For those sailing northwards from Cyprus, this was perhaps the most obvious harbour to aim for, and it remains possible that they did land here. Luke, however, records that 'they sailed to Perga' (Acts 13:13), which (though it could mean they landed first at Attalia) probably indicates they went to Perga directly.

In any event we can picture again the journey's last moments as our three travellers saw the large Taurus Mountains coming closer on the horizon. The previous day they had been in Paphos, setting sail in a north-westerly direction to skirt round the rocky, deserted peninsula on Cyprus' north-west corner. Soon after those peaks had receded over the starboard horizon, the Taurus peaks would have taken their place. By now, it was probably late August, so these mountains, covered in snow until late spring, would instead have been stark and barren – but probably softened somewhat by the heat-haze that hovers here at the end of a long, hot summer.

Again the three men may have approached this new landscape with some divergent feelings. When first approaching Cyprus six months before, Barnabas was perhaps the most enthusiastic, with Paul having his sights ultimately set elsewhere. However, this time things may have felt quite different. It was Barnabas who was now leaving his homeland behind, arriving in an area he had probably never visited.

RIGHT: View of Perga looking north-eastwards from the theatre, across the stadium towards the city's gate complex and *agora*; the acropolis lies out of view to the left; the ancient harbour would have been in the middle distance.

ABOVE: The Byzantine *agora* looking westwards toward the city gate.

Meanwhile for Paul this was something of a return – if not to Tarsus, then at least to somewhere not so far away; he was coming back to the same landmass of Asia Minor. Moreover, this adventure into pastures new was precisely the cutting-edge, frontier-style missionary work that Paul had been waiting for for a long time. At last he was genuinely hitting 'virgin territory'. For, unlike in Cyprus, the good news about Jesus had probably not yet reached the synagogues here in Pamphylia.

But 'one man's meat is another man's poison'. Spare a thought, then, for young John Mark: for what was thrilling Paul's heart was probably inwardly killing Mark. Antioch, then Cyprus – these had been challenges enough for the young man from Jerusalem. Arriving now in Pamphylia he was two, if not three, stages removed from his home and family. At some point it all got to be too much, and he decided to quit.

## John Mark's desertion

From Luke's account we actually know very little about what missionary work went on in Pamphylia – either when they first landed or when they came back this way after visiting Galatia. Instead Pamphylia is chiefly remembered in Acts as the place of John

Mark's desertion (Acts 13:13; 15:37–38). This was when there was a painful 'parting of the ways', with Mark going back to Jerusalem.

At this distance in time we cannot know for certain why Mark made this decision. There is a sliding scale of possible reasons – from those that Paul and Barnabas might have begrudgingly seen as fairly 'legitimate', down to those that spoke to them almost of betrayal. Was he physically ill? Was sea travel not agreeing with his constitution? Or perhaps he had never imagined being away from home for more than a year and was just feeling plain homesick?

All of these might have surfaced while Mark was at sea. Perhaps he plucked up the courage to raise the issue with his seniors even before they disembarked. Yet it is possible that the trigger to Mark's finally abandoning his colleagues came a fraction later – when Paul made it clear he was not staying long in Pamphylia but heading inland up to Galatia. For we get the impression from Acts 13 that almost immediately Paul decided that Pamphylia was no more than a stepping-stone – a place from which to launch into the big unknown of the 'interior'. *This* may have been what for Mark was the 'last straw'. Was there no stopping Paul?



## Paul's motivations

Again we cannot reconstruct Paul's reasons for making this big decision. Some have suggested (not unreasonably) that here too there were some practical factors at work. In late August the Pamphylian plain is unbearably hot; so going inland to Galatia would have taken them up more than 3,000 feet (900 m) to a region far less hot and humid. Not inconceivably, one of them (without knowing the medical reasons) may have been suffering from malaria – a common problem in these low-lying parts. In fact some such medical problem is exceedingly likely. For there is a hint in Paul's later letter to the Galatians that he arrived there with an illness badly affecting his eyes (Galatians 4:13–15).

*'It was because of an illness that I first preached to you. Even though my illness was a trial to you, you did not treat me with contempt… if you could have done so, you would have torn out your eyes and given them to me.'*

**Galatians 4:13–15**

If so, Mark's advice at this critical juncture may have been that they should all travel back home before winter. Paul's decision, however, characteristically, was instead to travel 'onwards and upwards'. Despite infirmities, this was not the time for beating a retreat. Having got this far, one can almost hear him saying, it would be shameful to turn back.

And behind all this there may have lurked some other, more strategic, motivations in Paul's mind. Although there is no evidence that he had visited the inland region of South Galatia while resident in Tarsus, it was not all that far away 'as the crow flies' from his home town. So, if things turned out badly, they could always return home by taking the inland route south-eastwards. All this made it a natural next step for Paul in his expanding vision – indeed, perhaps one that he had dreamed about and plotted for a long time. Here was his chance.

Moreover, there was one other potential attraction about going through the Taurus mountain range towards Galatia. Although Paul had been given the 'green light' for his Gentile mission by Jerusalem's church leaders (see pp. 45–46), he probably knew that there were aspects of it that remained controversial. There would still be (what are now known as) 'Judaizing' believers, who might try to 'rein in' this missionary work that they viewed with such alarm. Perhaps even on Cyprus his work among Gentiles had caused some eyebrows to be raised.

In such circumstances what Paul needed, then, was a *non-retractable surge forward* – something that provided undeniable evidence of God's power to reach 'all nations', something that would also act as a clear endorsement of his apostolic ministry. Or, in more political terms, what he needed was to change the facts on the ground – to present any Jerusalem critics with a *fait accompli*. Seen in this light, we realize that for *John Mark* a period of extended mission during the winter season in a cold, remote region tucked out of sight beyond the Taurus Mountains held no attractions whatsoever; but for *Paul* it was just what he needed! For it would take months for anyone back in Jerusalem to hear about it, and by that time, it would be too late.

## The painful split, later healed

Some such reasoning, we suggest, was running through Paul's mind. If so, we have no idea when the thought first occurred to him, nor when he first broached it with Barnabas. Whenever it was, Barnabas clearly came down on Paul's side, rather than siding with his cousin Mark. Nor, of course, do we know how much Paul shared his

### Key dates: Pamphylia

|  |  |
|---|---|
| c. 1000 BC | Traditional date for founding of Perga after the Trojan War (by Calchas and Mopsus), though its acropolis probably was inhabited from much earlier (in the Bronze Age?). |
| 466 BC | Famous battle at the Eurymedon River (close to Aspendos) between the Persians and the Athenians. |
| 333/334 BC | Alexander the Great takes control of Pamphylia; in Aspendos he buys 4,000 horses described as the 'best in the world'. |
| 200s BC | In Callimachus' poem, Artemis is depicted as praising Perga above all other cities (*Hymn* 3). |
| c. 210 BC | Apollonius, a mathematician from Perga, makes significant contributions to astronomy and geometry (the first to set out the properties of conic sections). |
| 189 BC | The Romans' defeat of the Seleucids (at Battle of Magnesia) results in Perga becoming part of a Pergamene kingdom. |
| 140 BC | King Attalus II of Pergamum founds Attalia, naming it after himself. |
| 133 BC | King Attalus III of Pergamum bequeaths Perga to the Romans, but Attalia becomes a free city for a while. |
| 77 BC | Attalia comes under Roman rule. |
| c. AD 42 | Pamphylia begins to be administered as a regular Roman 'province' under the emperor Claudius. |
| AD 46 | Paul and Barnabas arrive in Pamphylia, but John Mark returns from here to Jerusalem. The following summer Paul and Barnabas return through Perga and Attalia en route for Antioch (Acts 13:13–14; 14:24–25). |
| AD 130 | Emperor Hadrian visits Attalia, making it a Roman colony; the triple-arched gate is built in commemoration. |
| c. AD 160–70 | Building of the Roman theatre at Aspendos – the gift of two wealthy brothers. |
| c. AD 120s? | Building expansion in Perga, partly due to the benefaction of a priestess and magistrate known as Plancia Magna (daughter of a previous proconsul of Bithynia). |
| AD 250s? | Perga shares title of 'metropolis' with nearby Side (itself in its most prosperous period); Nestor and Tribimius, two Christians from Perga, are martyred in the Decian Persecution (AD 251). |
| AD 325 | Bishops from Perga at Council of Nicaea. |
| AD 431 | Bishops from Perga at Council of Ephesus. |
| AD 600s | Arab invasion of area leads to gradual abandonment of Perga over subsequent centuries. |
| 1207 | Seljuk Turks conquer Adalia (formerly Attalia), which had been used by the Crusaders as a port. |
| c. 1390s | Ottoman Turks take control of Adalia (now Antalya). |
| 1919 | Antalya is given to Italy after the First World War, but it is soon liberated by the Turkish army (1921). |

heart and ambitions with Mark. Yet there is evidence of a kind that suggests Paul *did* entrust some of these private plans to Mark. The evidence for this comes from what happened a few years later.

In Acts 15 we read Luke's honest account of how the partnership between Barnabas and Paul ended after the Jerusalem Council. Paul point-blankly refused to take Mark with them again on another journey because of what had happened in Pamphylia: 'they had such a sharp disagreement that they parted company. Barnabas took Mark and sailed for Cyprus, but Paul chose Silas' (Acts 15:39–40). Barnabas wanted to give Mark a second chance, but Paul would have none of it. Perhaps this was because Paul saw anyone who could not keep up with his pace (however legitimate their reasons) as an inherently unreliable team-member. Yet possibly the reason ran deeper: he felt he had trusted Mark, and his trust had been abused.



For, when we note that in the intervening years some 'agitators' had troubled the Galatians, insisting that they should be circumcised, we have to ask: how did these Judaizing agitators (almost certainly from Jerusalem) learn so quickly what Paul was doing in remote Galatia? The most obvious answer is that they *learnt it through none other than John Mark*. Whether Mark was an eager or a reluctant informant we do not know; but almost certainly, when Mark got home to Jerusalem, the news got out of Paul's expansive bid into central Anatolia. The Judaizers soon responded, despatching emissaries to Galatia and to Antioch. The storm that led to the Jerusalem Council was brewing. And young John Mark, the 'deserter' in Paul's small team, was – even if unwittingly – the culprit or, at least, the 'weak leak in the chain'.

*'Some time later… Barnabas wanted to take John Mark with them, but Paul did not think it wise to take him, because he had deserted them in Pamphylia.'*
**Acts 15:37–38**

Seen like this, we can now see why Paul would not even consider taking Mark back onto his staff. He had shown he had the capacity to 'stab Paul in the back'. Paul's trust had been savagely repaid, giving Paul months of anguish. He would not risk that happening again.

Happily, there is a brighter ending to this episode. Over a decade later Paul expressly asks that Mark be sent to him 'because he is useful to me in my ministry' (2 Timothy 4:11). Imprisoned in Rome, Paul knows he will not be going soon on any new 'missionary journey'; so Mark, with his Jewish background and his knowledge of Jesus' teaching, might prove very useful in the complex issues facing Christians in Rome in the early 60s AD. In this different context, Paul charitably acknowledges Mark's good points, and Mark, after years of working alongside Barnabas and then the apostle Peter (1 Peter 5:13), is himself in a much better place to respond. So we learn a little later that 'Mark, the cousin of Barnabas', is there with Paul in Rome (Colossians 4:10). Paul and Mark are reunited, working together. The deep rift that opened in Pamphylia was evidently healed some fifteen years later in Rome.

## Back to Perga

So Mark found a ship going back along the coast (via Antioch and Caesarea?) heading homeward for his family in Jerusalem. Hopefully he completed the necessary sea travel before the sailing season became problematic in late September. Meanwhile Paul and Barnabas headed up one of the two roads that cut through the Taurus mountain range, reaching (perhaps up to ten days later) the Roman colony of Pisidian Antioch in Galatia (see p. 78).

Then, probably in the late summer of the following year (AD 47), they made their way back down into the Pamphylian plain. They too needed to board a ship going eastbound before the sailing season closed. Eventually they would sail out of the scenic harbour of Attalia; but first there was time, they reckoned, for some ministry in Perga.

Perga was an ancient city that, like other cities along this coastline, had been under Greek rule for many centuries until the recent arrival of the Romans. During the first century it would have been a city of some significance – a busy port replete with other civic amenities such as bath complexes, colonnaded streets and courtyards.

So, not for the last time in his life, Paul would find himself in a thriving Greek city where, quite conceivably, he and his travelling companions were the only ones in the region to believe what they did – namely, that God had recently done something in far away Jerusalem that would challenge the very foundations on which such Greek cities were established. A time-bomb was waiting to go off, and Paul was there gently lighting the fuse – perhaps in a synagogue (if there was one) or perhaps on a street corner (wherever he could gain a hearing). Luke simply recounts that 'they preached the word in Perga', giving no hint of any repercussions (Acts 14:25). Yet that 'word' was potential dynamite, and preaching it in such solitary circumstances was always an act of daunting courage.

## Pamphylia today

Pamphylia corresponds roughly to what in modern Turkey is known as the region of 'Antalya' – the quite narrow coastal plain on the southern coast bounded by the mountains to the north and to the west. On a clear spring day there can be brilliant views of snow-peaked mountains going down towards the blue-green waters of the aptly called 'turquoise sea'. Later in the summer (the likely time of Paul's first visit in AD 46), however, the coastal plain can be obscured by a shimmering heat-haze.

The Roman theatre at Side.

The sites of interest for students of Paul lie on or near the coast: going westwards, Side, Perga and Antalya itself (ancient Attalia). By Paul's day **Side** (pronounced 'See-day', an ancient word for 'pomegranate') had been a significant port for many centuries. We are not sure where Paul landed on his first missionary journey (see p. 66); but, if he did not visit Side then, he may have done so later (see, for example, Acts 18:21). With its fertile hinterland and the wealth brought by piracy and the slave trade, it had flourished since Hellenistic times. Unlike Attalia it never came under Pergamene rule but was always friendly towards Rome. Its days of greatest prosperity would be in the second and third centuries AD and the extent of its walls would then contract considerably in the Byzantine period.

The ancient city lies on a promontory, bounded by the sea on three sides. Visitors are encouraged to walk southwards from the car park through the Hellenistic walls, following the line of a colonnaded street. Just beyond the *agora* is the city's vast

**theatre** (built in the second century AD for an audience of around 13,000). With no natural hill-side, the entire edifice was built up on sub-vaults from the ground. Walking past some modern shops (over the site of the silted harbour) and then turning left, one reaches the spectacular ruins of the two **Temples of Athena and Apollo** – their few re-erected columns making for an impressive sight when set against the sea. The Byzantines later used these temple foundations to build a huge church (and, later, a much smaller one, still quite well preserved). Back in Paul's day, however, these pagan temples, perched on the water's edge, might well have caught his eye as he sailed past en route to Jerusalem (see Acts 27:5).

**Perga** lies a further 10 miles (16 km) to the west, located on a river (the Cestrus) that was navigable in its day, but which has long since silted up. It began to flourish in the second century BC and would continue as a major port for a further five or six centuries. Although the site entrance is on the south side, the city is perhaps best appreciated today by making one's way first to the **acropolis** (on its northern side) and then retracing one's steps carefully through the site.

Although no remains have yet been found, this acropolis would have been the location for Perga's temple in honour of Artemis (worshipped as the 'princess of the city'). From here there is a great panorama over the whole site, making it easy to imagine the city in Paul's day as he walked through its streets: to the east the outline of the harbour area; to the south the main colonnaded street towards the city-gate complex; and to the west the clear line, interrupted by towers, of the impressive Hellenistic walls. In the foreground, running east–west, there is another, shorter colonnaded street that divided Perga into four quarters.

A water channel runs the entire length of the main colonnaded street (itself roughly 65 feet or 20 m wide), sourced by a **Nymphaeum Fountain** (built later by Hadrian) at the foot of the acropolis. At the main intersection of the colonnaded streets, an arch has been reconstructed (built by two brothers, Demetrius and Apollonius, in honour of Domitian around AD 95). Continuing southwards you then pass (some distance to the

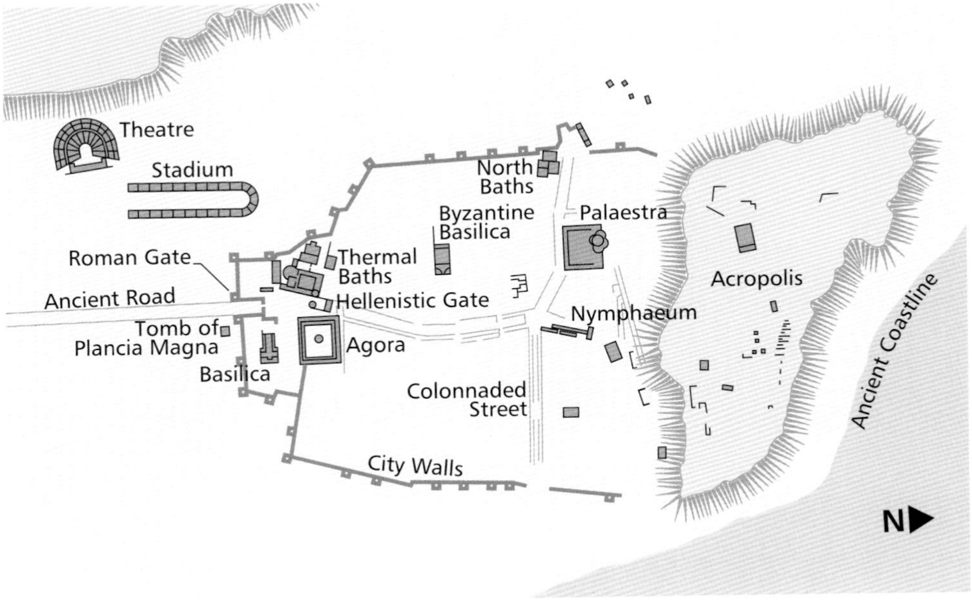

Plan of ancient Perga.

## Visiting modern Turkey

Modern Turkey is a fascinating place to visit. Surrounded by a beautiful coastline, its southern shores overlooked by the steep Taurus Mountains, it is land of beautiful colours and widely diverging scenery: from the harsh barren landscape in the far east near Lake Van, to the unique and bizarre rock formations of Cappadocia (modern Goreme) nearer to its central capital, Ankara.

It is a country evidently indebted to the pioneering work of Kefal Ataturk in the 1920s, who introduced some radical reforms (including the adoption of the Western script to write down the nation's distinctive language). Turkey has been a Muslim country since the arrival of the Seljuk Turks in the eleventh century. Yet among the Turkish people can be found the ruins of sites that are famous throughout the world because of their role in the history of later Western civilization, such as Hector's Troy, or Croesus' Sardis.

Students of the classical world keep finding familiar treasures – not least two of the seven wonders of the ancient world (the Temple of Artemis in Ephesus and the Mausoleum of Halicarnassus) or the stunning ruins of Aphrodisias. This was the home of fierce Hittite warriors, ancient Lycians and the creative Ionians (with their philosophers and astronomers such as Thales, or medics such as Hippocrates). From Pergamum we derive our word for 'parchment'; from the winding River Meander, the English verb 'to meander'. And modern Istanbul stands on the site of ancient Byzantium or Constantinople, which enjoyed a hegemony for over 1,000 years, as the guardian of a Christian culture.

With the exception of Antioch (Antakya) and Tarsus, the New Testament sites all lie on the western side of the country, focused in a quadrant that arks round from Alanya to Kusadasi. This includes the so-called 'turquoise coast' ('turquoise' took its name from the beautiful blue-green colour of the shallow sea waters here): brown-soiled hills meet the waters of the Mediterranean and the Aegean, giving some stunning views.

Key sites near the southern coast include Alanya (with its impressive acropolis rising up sheer from the sea), ancient Side, the theatre at Aspendos, and the mountaintop ruined city of Termessos. Further round to the south-west one finds the sunken underwater city of Kekova, the beautiful harbour of Kas, the stunning lagoon of Olu Deniz, the turtle bays of Dalyan (by ancient Caunos), the Crusader castle in Bodrum (ancient Halicarnassus) and the vast ruins of the oracular temple at Didyma. Even more remote sites (such as ancient Cnidos) can best be reached through travelling on one of the popular *gulet* boats, which in summertime cruise in and out of beautiful remote inlets.

Until recently several of these places on the shore-line were inaccessible by road. Modern airports (in Antalya, Dalaman and Izmir) have done much to open up the area to travel. Those following in Paul's steps may alternatively take advantage of Konya airport and so access the inland sites of ancient Galatia, as well as the upper regions of the Lycus

Valley (with the biblical sites of Colossae and Laodicea). Nearby Hierapolis is also mentioned in the Bible (Colossians 4:13) and is now known as Pamukkale (or 'cotton castle') because of its famous hot springs spilling over to form limestone 'travertines'.

So visitors are often amazed by the wealth of beautiful or historic sites on offer (on one recent visit I clocked up over twenty ancient theatres in ten days!) and are touched by the warm welcome of local people. *'Çok güzel!'* (Turkish for 'very good!') becomes an oft-repeated catchphrase.

Turkish highlights (anti-clockwise from top left): the scenic lagoon of Olu Deniz (near Fethiye); the harbour of Bodrum (ancient Halicarnassus) with the castle of St Peter; the theatre at Aspendos (built around AD 170), which could host 7,500 spectators and still has superb acoustics; the quiet harbour of Kas; the high-level aqueduct, that brought water from the Taurus Mountains down to Aspendos.

right and in an overgrown area) a fifth-century Byzantine church (the seat of Perga's bishop?) and then eventually (on the left) the large fourth-century **Byzantine *agora***. With its Corinthian columns and some mosaics from its shops still visible, it is impressive. At its centre stands a round building – possibly a temple dedicated to Hermes or Tyche.

Nearby is the well-preserved **city-gate complex**, perhaps Perga's most significant ruin. The two large round towers, together with their oval courtyard, date back to the Hellenistic period, but much of it was decorated and developed around AD 120. To this period can be attributed the two-tiered gateway with its triple arch on the north side, as well as the extended courtyard to the south. With the city's expansion to the south during this period, a new city gate was eventually built in the fourth century AD. The intervening area (developed around AD 200) includes the *propylon* (or entrance) to the large **Roman bath complex**. Walking westwards the visitor moves successively through a colonnaded *palaestra*, then the *frigidarium*, *tepidarium* and eventually the *caldarium* (the cold, warm and hot baths respectively); their pools and hypocaust (underfloor heating) systems are particularly noteworthy.

There are two further sites to note (outside the main kiosk entrance to the city): the vast **theatre**, set against the neighbouring hill-side, with an estimated capacity of

Antalya's distinctive harbour on the turquoise coast: from here, beneath these same cliff-faces, Paul and Barnabas set sail on their way home to Antioch.

15,000 (though currently closed for restoration); and the large **stadium**, built in the second century AD, which is one of the best preserved in Asia Minor. Underneath the raised seats on its eastern side are no fewer than thirty large chambers; twenty of these would have been shops, the other ten serving as corridors for the 12,000 spectators as they entered and left the stadium.

Finally, there is the large, sprawling city of **Antalya**. The well-resourced **Museum of Archaeology** houses the many artefacts found in the regions of ancient Lycia, Phrygia and Pamphylia (as well as some retrieved from the sea-bed of the Mediterranean), including a small reliquary supposedly containing the bones of St Nicholas, the bishop of Myra. The numerous statues and sarcophagi from Perga (mainly dating to the second century AD) are very impressive, reflecting the city's wealth and the skill of its craftsmen at this period.

Antalya's **ancient harbour** is still preserved – as a yacht marina in a natural hollow surrounded by shallow cliffs. This harbour area is surrounded by ancient walls and towers, dating back originally to the Hellenistic period. The Romans reused these walls and then in AD 130 built a **triple-arched gate**, finely worked in marble and granite, in honour of the emperor Hadrian. Looking out over the harbour, we know with some certainty that this was precisely where Paul and Barnabas embarked on their return journey to Syrian Antioch (Acts 14:25–26). Surrounded by these same harbour walls, looking out on the same beautiful Gulf of Antalya, and gazing over to the massive Lycian Mountains to the west, they set sail 'homeward bound' – presumably with many positive memories of their time in the region of Pamphylia.

6

CHAPTER

# Galatia

*From Perga they went on to Pisidian Antioch. On the Sabbath they entered the synagogue... Standing up, Paul motioned with his hand and began to speak...*

*On the next Sabbath almost the whole city gathered to hear the word of the Lord... The word of the Lord spread through the whole region. But the Jews... stirred up persecution against Paul and Barnabas, and expelled them from their region. So they shook the dust from their feet in protest against them and went to Iconium.*

*[The apostles] fled to the Lycaonian cities of Lystra and Derbe and to the surrounding country, where they continued to preach the good news.*

**Acts 13:14–16, 44, 49–51; 14:6–7**

## Into the interior

In early September AD 46 Paul and Barnabas travelled up through the Taurus Mountains. The mountain passes would soon be blocked with snow and the journey could take at least a week – whether they used the recently constructed *Via Sebaste* or the slightly shorter (but more hazardous) trail directly to the north of Perga. Eventually they reached the southern segment of the large Roman province known as Galatia and entered the city of Pisidian Antioch, a city set on seven small hills and famous for its health spas.

Whatever their original reasons for coming to this remote area, Paul and Barnabas would be in Galatia until the following autumn for what proved to be a very significant year of ministry. Luke describes at some length their exploits in four Galatian cities (Acts 13:13 – 14:21), giving us for the first time thus far in Acts some real detail and insight into what Paul actually said and did when on his missionary travels.

### Pisidian Antioch: in and around the synagogue

This Antioch was known as 'Antioch *near* Pisidia' (Strabo, *Geography* 12.8.14). Strictly speaking, it was just within the borders of Phrygia, not Pisidia; but for the Romans this colony became known as 'Pisidian Antioch' because of its role in keeping a watchful eye over the former region of Pisidia (further to the east). It was over 3,600 feet (1,100 m) above sea level, set against the backdrop of some further hills, with a good vantage point overlooking the plains to the south and east, and a commanding position over the main east–west 'trunk' road that crossed the plateau at this point.

A Jewish community of considerable size had been settled here for some time. Paul and Barnabas visited the synagogue on their first Saturday, and Paul was invited to give a 'message of encouragement'. In Acts this is the first time we hear Paul preach;

Storm clouds above Pisidian Antioch: being 3,000 feet (900 m) above sea level, the region can be bleak and cold with a comparatively short summer season. Paul and Barnabas had certainly chosen a remote area.

and, although Luke has clearly only given a very short synopsis (Acts 13:16–41), we gain a good idea of the kind of things Paul would have said when explaining to synagogue congregations the news about Jesus:

- He rehearses Israel's history and then presents Jesus as the culmination of this story, in fulfilment of 'what God promised our fathers';
- He refers to John the Baptist's ministry (with its challenge to repent in preparation for the Messiah);
- He introduces Jesus as the 'Saviour' and describes how, despite his innocence, he was executed under 'Pilate' at the request of Jerusalem's 'people and rulers' – though this paradoxically was in fulfilment of the 'words of the prophets that are read every Sabbath';
- He announces the news of Jesus' resurrection (again in fulfilment of Scripture), which, unlike the Law of Moses, now makes possible the 'forgiveness of sins'.

*'I want you to know that the gospel I preached is not something of human origin… I received it by revelation from Jesus Christ.'*

**Galatians 1:11–12**

The sermon evidently caused a stir (Acts 13:44–52): after the service, members of the synagogue invited Paul and Barnabas to come back the following Sabbath. And the news got around, for the next Saturday 'almost the whole city gathered to hear the word of the Lord' – presumably congregating in the open air. This provoked the synagogue members to 'jealousy', but Paul retorted that this message about Jesus was for *all* people – God intended it to be 'a light for the Gentiles' (quoting Isaiah 49:6). Though some Gentiles then believed in Paul's message about Jesus, the Jewish listeners were not pleased; and, in due course, through the agency of some of their contacts among the city's leadership, they got Paul and Barnabas 'expelled from their

region'. So the apostles moved on, 'shaking the dust from their feet' as they went – precisely what Jesus himself had advised his first disciples to do when encountering rejection (Luke 9:5).

## Jews and 'God-fearers'

This experience of being rejected by the synagogue would recur frequently in Acts. Paul's message, although he presented it as the fulfilment of Israel's Scriptures and as the 'good news' that Israel had been longing for, was not often received as such. Instead – being focused on a crucified Messiah, himself rejected by Israel's rulers – it was seen as almost scandalous. It also challenged the status of Israel's Law. Yet there was another reason for this strong negative reaction.

Wherever there were synagogues throughout the empire, there were always many people who saw themselves on the 'fringes' of Judaism. Attracted by its monotheism, and perhaps especially by its ethical teaching, these so-called 'God-fearers' might have attended synagogue meetings quite regularly, but few actually became 'proselytes' (full converts to Judaism) – a process which, for men, would require circumcision.

ABOVE: One of many Latin inscriptions found at Pisidian Antioch, a Roman colony.

BELOW: View of Pisidian Antioch, looking westwards down the *decumanus*.

Twice in his speech here in Pisidian Antioch, Paul expressly addresses these 'God-fearing Gentiles' (Acts 13:16, 26); and we can easily imagine some of their reactions. For Paul was announcing that they could now join God's people on an equal footing with Jews – and to do this, they no longer had to be circumcised! No wonder the Gentiles, in Luke's understatement, were 'glad' (Acts 13:48) – they were delighted! For the Jewish members of the synagogue, however, things looked quite different: this was an attack on their previous status and privilege, so they were 'filled with jealousy' (Acts 13:45).

Moreover, it was galling to see Paul effectively 'stealing' the synagogue's fringe members with his too-easy talk about 'faith'. As the Bible commentator F. F. Bruce put it: 'It was as natural for God-fearing Gentiles to embrace the blessings of the gospel on these terms as it was for Jews to decline them on these terms.' And this had a paradoxical result for Paul's ministry: 'only by visiting the synagogue could Paul establish contact with these God-fearers, but the almost inevitable result of his policy was a breach with the synagogue'.

This difficult situation clearly bothered Paul throughout his life. He longed that Israel would come to see the coming of Messiah Jesus as her moment of glory (Romans 9:1–5) and fervently hoped that the 'jealousy' which his ministry aroused might yet provoke some of his fellow Jews to faith (Romans 11:14). Yet his own task was to be an 'apostle to the Gentiles', and this would not be thwarted by the hostility he received from those in the synagogues. Just as Jesus was truly the 'light for the Gentiles' (Luke 2:32), so Paul understood this phrase from Isaiah to be also a neat description of what *he and Barnabas* were seeking to do as apostles (Acts 13:47). This prophecy gave them a special mandate to bring the light of Jesus to the Gentiles. It was a task they would not shirk.





## Similar events in Iconium

Paul and Barnabas went along the *Via Sebaste*. Turning left at Misthia they came to Iconium, some 90 miles (150 km) to the east of Antioch – a journey of three or four days. Around this time the emperor Claudius had allowed the city to adopt his own name, so for a while it also took the name 'Claudiconium'. It lay at an important road junction set in a wide plain, from where major roads led off in all four directions.

Undeterred, they went to the synagogue (Acts 14:1–6). This time they were able to stay in the area for a 'considerable time', resulting in a 'great number of Jews and Gentiles' coming to faith. Yet eventually things took a similar turn for the worse. When Paul and Barnabas learnt of a plot to stone them, they fled the city.

## Lystra: the encounter with paganism

They fled to a Roman colony called Lystra, some 18 miles (30 km) to the south-west. As a Roman colony (like Pisidian Antioch), there would once again have been Roman army veterans here, together with some Jewish residents. There would also have been many 'native' people (known to the Romans as *incolae*) from the surrounding area – in this case from Lycaonia. Their mother tongue would not have been Greek but Lycaonian, which explains the confusions the apostles soon encountered (Acts 14:6–20).

For at some point Paul pronounced a word of healing on a man lame from birth. When the man promptly stood up, the crowds were amazed. But the result was not quite as the apostles had hoped: the Lycaonians presumed they were gods in human form (identifying Paul with Hermes and Barnabas with Zeus); and soon a pagan priest was bringing a bull, preparing to sacrifice it to them. Paul and Barnabas were horrified at this blasphemous sacrifice in their honour and rushed into the crowd, trying to reason with them: 'we are only human beings like you!' Despite the language barrier (with presumably the apostles speaking in Greek and the crowd shouting in Lycaonian), the message got through and the sacrifice was aborted.

*'In the hills of Phrygia, an oak and a lime tree stand side by side, surrounded by a low wall. Zeus went there, disguised as a mortal.'*

**Ovid, *Metamorphoses* 8.611–724, in which Zeus visits a poor elderly couple whom he transforms into trees**

This fascinating account is the first one in Acts to show what happened when Paul moved completely outside the orbit of the Jewish synagogue and began to engage with raw paganism. At such times he reveals himself to be an authentic Jewish proponent of Israel's creational monotheism, vehemently opposed to idolatry in all its forms. In later letters he would reflect on how Jesus, as the true Lord of the world, calls people to 'turn to God from idols to serve the living and true God' (1 Thessalonians 1:9).

The other intriguing point is the way Paul was compared to Hermes 'because he was the chief speaker'. Local inscriptions confirm that both Zeus and Hermes were highly regarded in this region. Hermes was seen as the special messengers of the gods, Zeus as the leading god of the Greek pantheon. So, conceivably, Barnabas gave signs of being





## Paul and Thecla

*A man named Onesiphorus, hearing that Paul was coming to Iconium, went out speedily… to meet him and invite him to their house… They went in the king's highway to Lystra and stood there waiting for him, comparing all who passed by with that description which Titus had given them.*

*At length they saw a man coming, of a small stature with meeting eyebrows, bald head, bow-legged, strongly built, hollow-eyed, with a large crooked nose; he was full of grace, for sometimes he appeared as a man, sometimes he had the countenance of an angel. And Paul saw Onesiphorus and was glad…*

So begins a document from the second century AD, known as the *Acts of Paul and Thecla*. It is one of several apocryphal works dating to this period, which look back to the apostolic age with some nostalgia. It tells the tale of an aristocratic young woman, aged eighteen, called Thecla, who, when she hears the preaching of Paul in Iconium, renounces her family to follow him.

Perhaps its most intriguing feature is this description of Paul's physical appearance – the only such description that has survived. There is nothing in the canonical New Testament that would help us here. The fact that in Lystra Barnabas is likened to Zeus (see above) might suggest Paul was of shorter stature than his colleague (but it might have been due to his being slightly younger?). We know too that some Corinthians found Paul's overall presentation slightly less appealing than that of the refined Apollos. Yet this hardly gives us a clue as to his facial features.

This second-century account, however, might well be drawing on a true recollection. Certainly, later iconic depictions of Paul match this description quite closely – though, of course, they may themselves have been influenced by this description! It is fascinating to see some of these early icons and to note their common features. At the least, Paul is invariably bald and bearded. The result is that, although biblical scholars suggest we have no real clue about Paul's appearance, the Orthodox Church comes to quite the opposite conclusion.

The plot line of the *Acts of Paul and Thecla* is simply told: Thecla, though pledged in marriage, overhears Paul's preaching by sitting at a neighbouring window. Her fiancé is enraged and ensures Paul is brought before the governor, accused of teaching against marriage. Thecla visits Paul in prison and then is herself condemned to be burnt; but miraculously the fire is extinguished. Thecla, meeting up with Paul again (who is praying in a cave), pledges that she will follow him, so he takes her to Pisidian Antioch.

As soon as they arrive there, a leading citizen falls in love with her, but, when rebuffed by her, his love turns to hatred and she again is brought before the local governor, who promptly condemns her to the lions. A local woman, Trifina, adopts her for a while and then faces the lions herself with Thecla, but the animals do not touch them. Fiercer animals are used and more savage torture, but to no avail. Eventually the panicked governor listens to her testimony and releases her, pronouncing her as a 'servant of God'.

During all this Thecla had been baptized. She now goes to find Paul (who is preaching in Myra); he sends her back to her home in Iconium, but she soon moves on to Seleucia and establishes a small convent on a hill overlooking the city, which attracts many visitors. Many years later (aged 90) some men attempt to rape her but she miraculously disappears into a rock and is seen no more.

The account is shot through with unlikely happenings, sometimes seeming to be a Christianized version of pagan myths such as those concerning Adonis and Astarte. Paul himself spoke out expressly against those who forbade marriage (1 Timothy 4:1–3), so its presentation of the sexual challenges of Paul's preaching are clearly overplayed. Nevertheless it shows something of the effect Paul's ministry in south Galatia was remembered to have had; and there are fascinating historical touches about life in these remote cities such as Antioch.

the more 'senior' of the two, while Paul was clearly developing as the chief speaker. One gains the impression that Barnabas was happy, when necessary, to play a more supportive role compared to Paul – that great crafter of words and master of argument.

But any popularity the apostles had in Lystra – even if of the wrong kind – was soon dispelled when 'some Jews came from Antioch and Iconium and won the crowd over. They stoned Paul, and dragged him outside the city, thinking he was dead.' In fact Paul must only have been knocked unconscious, for 'he got up and went back into the city' (Acts 14:19–20). Yet this experience would mark him for life. Later he would cite this occasion in his list of his sufferings as an apostle ('once I was stoned': 2 Corinthians 11:25). And, in a more literal sense, his body may well have shown the scars for years to come – hence perhaps his asking at the end of his letter to the Galatians that 'no one cause me trouble, for I bear on my body the marks of Jesus' (Galatians 6:17). For the believers in Galatia would have known very well precisely what Paul had gone through in trying to bring them the gospel of Jesus.



## Heading back from Derbe

Knocked down, but not knocked out, Paul with Barnabas sets off to another city, called Derbe, some 60 miles (100 km) to the south-east. This city too had recently been honoured by the emperor Claudius and was known as Claudio-Derbe for quite some time. Some suggest that its name was associated with the Lycaonian word for 'juniper'. Once again the apostles 'preached the good news' and again 'won a large number of disciples' (Acts 14:21).

But time was running on. Instead of pressing on by the land-route back south-eastwards towards Tarsus, they decided to retrace their steps through Galatia. While risky (because of their recent unpopularity), they wanted to encourage the new believers. Yet they would also need to keep an eye on the time, since sailing along the Mediterranean would become hazardous in the autumn. They would need to be back down on the Pamphylian coast by early October at the latest if ever they were to reach Syrian Antioch by winter.

So they travelled back through the cities in reverse order, through 'Lystra, Iconium, and Antioch', appointing 'elders in each church' (Acts 14:21–23). Paul was a realist and knew that congregations work best when there is recognized leadership. These small churches would have been very vulnerable in the coming months, so it was vital to appoint appropriate leaders and also to lay down some agreed foundations on which the communities could prosper. They had left in haste, so they needed to return to finish what they had started – not least because they had no idea when they themselves would be returning that way, if at all.

A fishing boat on Lake Aksehir, one of three large inland lakes, each of which is within 35 miles (55 km) of Pisidian Antioch.

## Paul's return visit to Galatia: Timothy and news from Jerusalem

In fact, for Paul, the gap in time was about three years. 'Absence makes the heart grow fonder', and you can hear Paul's deep longing for the Galatians in what he wrote to them in the intervening period. He had learnt that some visitors from Jerusalem had unsettled them, requiring Gentile believers to be circumcised, and his letter is passionate and adamant:

*'You foolish Galatians! Who has bewitched you? Before your very eyes Jesus Christ was clearly portrayed as crucified! ... Have you suffered so much for nothing? ... You are all sons of God through faith in Christ Jesus. ...There is neither Jew nor Greek, slave nor free, male nor female, but all are one in Christ Jesus. If you belong to Christ... you are no longer a slave, but... an heir.'*

*'My dear children, for whom I am again in the pains of childbirth until Christ is formed in you, how I wish I could be with you now and change my tone, because I am perplexed about you! ... It is for freedom that Christ has set us free. Stand firm then and do not let yourselves be burdened again by a yoke of slavery.'*

**Galatians 3:1, 4, 26–29; 4:7, 19–20; 5:1–2**

Map of Asia Minor's road systems.

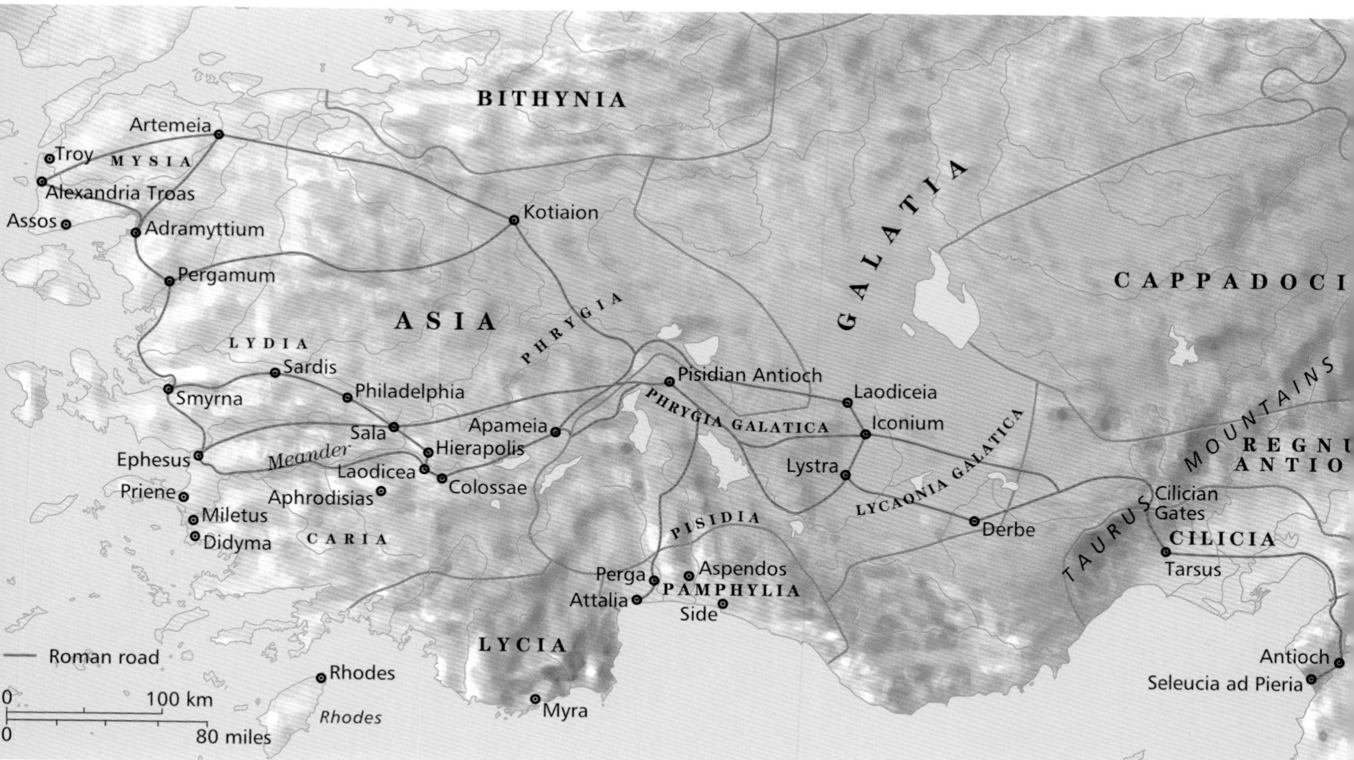

## Key dates: Galatia

| | |
|---|---|
| 300–250 BC | Founding of Antioch 'near Pisidia' by Seleucid rulers. |
| c. 195 BC | Antiochus III orders the transfer of 2,000 Jewish families from Babylonia to the 'fortresses and most important places of Phrygia' (Josephus, *Antiquities* 12.149). |
| 188 BC | Antioch is declared a 'free city' by the Romans. |
| 100s BC | Building of the temple to a local male god (known as 'Men Askaenos') 3 miles (5 km) to the south-east of Antioch. |
| 36 BC | The Romans put Antioch and Lystra under the rule of Amyntas, a client-king in the Galatian region. |
| 25 BC | A new province of Galatia is created by Augustus, bringing former territories such as Phrygia, Lycaonia and Galatia together under direct Roman rule. Eight colonies for army veterans are established in the area, but only Antioch is given the '*ius Italicum*' (a Roman legal status); it is known as 'Colonia Caesarea Antiochia'. |
| 6 BC | Augustus builds the *Via Sebaste*, with Antioch at the junction of roads going east, south and west. He also places some veterans in Lystra, to provide some protection from bandits located in the Taurus Mountains (to the south). |
| AD 46 | Paul and Barnabas arrive in Antioch (late summer) and then move on to Iconium, Lystra and Derbe. |
| AD 47 | Paul and Barnabas leave Galatia, going south into Pamphylia en route to Syrian Antioch. |
| AD 129 | Interior of Asia Minor visited by Emperor Hadrian. |
| AD 157 | Emperor Antoninus Pius is mentioned in an inscription made in Claudio-Derbe. |
| c. AD 160 | Montanus and two female prophets claim new authoritative revelation, teaching that the New Jerusalem (see Revelation 3:12; 21:2) would descend on the small Phrygian village of Pepuza, leading to fierce reaction from Tertullian and others. |
| AD 295 | Emperor Diocletian establishes a new province of Pisidia, with Antioch as its capital. |
| AD 325 | Galatian bishops (from Antioch, Iconium and Lystra) attend the Council of Nicaea, and then subsequent ecumenical councils (in AD 381 and 451). |
| AD 375–81 | Optimus, bishop of Antioch, builds its new basilica and then attends the Council of Constantinople (as does Bishop Daphnus of Derbe). |
| AD 718 | Antioch invaded by Arabs, under Abbas (son of Caliph Velid). |
| 1176 | Somewhere near Antioch the Byzantine emperor Manuel Comnenos loses the Battle of Myriakephalon to the Turkish sultan Kiliçarslan. In due course a new town emerges, named Yalvaç, which means 'prophet' (a reference to Paul?). |
| 1228–73 | Celaleddin Rumi (better known as Mevlana) lives in Konya and establishes Mevlevi dervish monasteries. |
| 1828 | First published identification of Antioch, by Francis Arundell (the British chaplain in Izmir). |
| 1907 | Sir William Mitchell Ramsay publishes *The Cities of Saint Paul* (based on his research since 1880). |
| 1912–14 | Excavations at Temple of Men Askaenos and in Antioch under Ramsay and others (including discovery of Augustus' *Res Gestae* in 1914). |
| 1924 | Excavations in Antioch with team from Michigan University (USA) cease because of disagreements with Ramsay. |



You can hear it too when Paul says to Barnabas after the Jerusalem Council (which endorsed his ministry amongst the Galatians): 'let us go back and visit the brothers in all the towns where we preached... and see how they are doing' (Acts 15:36). Paul was deeply anxious to know how they were. Had they been knocked out of the race (Galatians 5:7)? Had they buckled under the weight of persecution? So, when Barnabas decided instead to go to Cyprus with Mark, Paul teamed up with Silas and made his way 'through Syria and Cilicia'; then travelling overland, up through the Cilician Gates, he first reached Derbe and then Lystra (Acts 16:1–5).

*'I have been reminded of your sincere faith, which first lived in your grandmother Lois and your mother Eunice.'*
**2 Timothy 1:5**

At this point he was introduced to a young man (in his early twenties?) who would prove to be Paul's 'right hand man' for the rest of his life: Timothy, a native of Lystra, the son of a Greek father and a Jewish mother, who was recommended to Paul by the believers in both Lystra and Iconium. He had probably already begun a teaching ministry in these two towns, and Paul was quick to spot his potential.

For some reason (due to local sensitivities or perhaps with an eye to the future?) he decided that Timothy should be circumcised. Now that the Jerusalem Council had clarified that circumcision was not *required* for Gentile believers on theological grounds, Paul was relaxed if there were some more pragmatic reasons why it might be helpful. In fact, one of the chief reasons why Paul had come back to Galatia so promptly was precisely that he and Silas were carrying the 'apostolic decree' from Jerusalem in their hands. He was bringing them the good news that his gospel had been vindicated at the highest human level. The Gentile believers in Galatia, who had rejoiced so much that they could enter God's people without being circumcised, could now breathe a collective sigh of relief and rejoice again.





## Looking back on Galatia: suffering but resurrection

Paul would travel this way for a third and final time en route from Antioch to Ephesus in AD 55 when he passed through at the start of his third missionary journey, 'strengthening all the disciples' (Acts 18:23). Our final reference to Galatia, however, comes from one of Paul's letters to Timothy. Writing over a decade later to encourage his youthful assistant, Paul writes:

*'... we must go through many hardships to enter the kingdom of God'.*
**Acts 14:22**

*You, however, know all about my teaching, my way of life, my purpose, faith, patience, love, endurance, persecutions, sufferings – what kind of things happened to me in Antioch, Iconium and Lystra, the persecutions I endured. Yet the Lord rescued me from all of them. In fact, everyone who wants to live a godly life in Christ Jesus will be persecuted...*

**2 Timothy 3:10–12**

RIGHT: The temple of Augustus in Pisidian Antioch (viewed from the south-east), looking down from the surrounding cliff-face; there was a large open space in front of the temple, making this the obvious centre of the city's life.

The threat of such persecution had evidently not deterred Timothy. He had gladly left his family in the small town of Lystra and set out with Paul into the unknown, possibly never to return. Something had struck Timothy about the essential truth both of Paul and of his message. One can only speculate how Timothy gained this determination to follow Jesus regardless of the cost. Was it on that day when he and some of the other new disciples 'gathered around' this man, seemingly dead, lying in the rough ground outside Lystra's walls (Acts 14:20)? Why had this strange man come from Jerusalem? What was so important about this Christian message that this Jewish rabbi was prepared to give his life for people so far away in the remote plains of Lycaonia?

But then the man, seemingly miraculously, revived consciousness and got up onto his feet. This was no resurrection, but it spoke powerfully of the God who *did* have resurrection power. Timothy resolved to follow this God wherever it took him. And so, when Paul came back through Galatia three years later, Timothy was ready to follow him.

*'Caesar Augustus, son of a god, pontifex maximus... father of the fatherland.'*
**Dedicatory inscription on Augustus' temple, including reference to the 'Pater Patriae' title awarded to him in 2 BC**

# Galatia today

What Paul knew as south Galatia is a large inland area, separated from the Mediterranean by the Taurus Mountains. Much of it is over 3,000 feet (900 m) above sea level, so the winters are long. The two major cities in the area are now Konya and Isparta, the latter in the region known as the Turkish Lake District (because of the three substantial inland lakes here: Lakes Egridir, Beysehir and Aksehir).

# Pisidian Antioch

Paul and Barnabas visited four cities in Galatia (Antioch, Iconium, Lystra and Derbe); of these, the major site of archaeological interest today is **Pisidian Antioch**. Located close to the small modern town of **Yalvaç**, these deserted ancient ruins, situated 3,280 feet (1,000 m) above sea level and lying many miles from either the coast or major centres of population, strike the modern visitor with their remoteness. However, because it oversaw the important junction on the *Via Sebaste*, Antioch was in Paul's day a Roman colony with real significance.

Roman colonies were patterned on a Roman camp – with the *decumanus* road intersecting with the main street running north-south known as the *cardo maximus*. This can be clearly seen here. After passing through the large **triple-arched gate** (built after Paul's time), the visitor soon joins the *decumanus*, which makes its way up a slight gradient, complete with chariot ruts, towards the junction with the main street. To the left of the *decumanus* is the **ancient theatre**. Though originally dating from well before Paul's time, its chief renovation came much later (c. AD 310), when some of the seating was built up over an archway covering the *decumanus*.

Plan of ancient Pisidian Antioch.

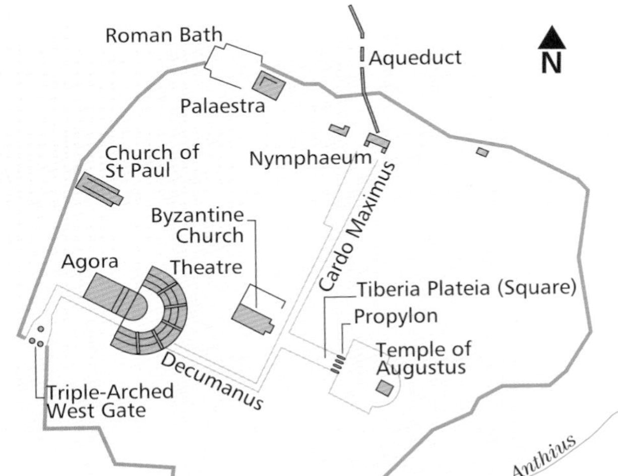


On the far side of the *cardo maximus* is the **Temple of Augustus**. This temple, begun during Augustus' reign but finally dedicated after his death, was built on the highest point of the city some 30 years before Paul's visit; it witnesses to the vast expansion of the imperial cult in Paul's day. Approaching through the broad colonnaded **Tiberius Square**, Paul would have seen people walking up twelve steps and then passing through the impressive triple-arched entrance gate (or *propylon*) on their way into the temple's courtyard. Commemorating Augustus' victories, the whole thing would have spoken volumes about the emperor's authority – not least because on the *propylon* was inscribed a copy (in Latin) of the *Res Gestae* (Augustus' own account of the achievements of his reign).

Beyond the *propylon* was a large, semi-circular courtyard, surrounded by colonnades, the eastern part of which was cut out from the hill-side's rock. And standing in the centre, towards the back, was the **sanctuary** of Augustus' temple.

Though quite small – some 15 by 30 feet (4.5 x 9 m) – it was set on a high foundation of natural rock and approached by a further twelve steps. Antioch's residents were expressing in impressive fashion their gratitude to the emperor for their city's increased prestige under his rule. However, for Paul it demonstrated the daunting challenge ahead. What room would there be for his own message, focused on a rival world-ruler, in a city where this imperial cult was evidently growing at such a pace?

Returning through the Tiberius Square, there is a ruined **Byzantine church** (sometimes known as St Bassus). Archaeologist Sir William Mitchell Ramsay claimed to have found some evidence for an earlier apse underneath this church (containing the names of some Christian martyrs from the Diocletian persecution, including that of Bassus); perhaps, then, this earlier church had been built over the ancient synagogue? If so, did Paul deliver his sermon here? Was this where his audience, while located so close to the Temple of Augustus, first heard the message about a Jewish messiah whom God had raised from the dead?

Ramsay's evidence is now disputed, so the precise location of the synagogue remains uncertain. Nevertheless, it cannot have been far away; and the fact that 'almost the whole city' turned out to hear Paul speaking again strongly suggests this all took place in some central location. Moreover, the fact that the Christian community later built a church here reveals the deeper historical reality – namely that Paul's seemingly bizarre message, which challenged the imperial ideology at its root, had ultimately conquered. So this church's ruined apse makes an ideal setting for visitors to listen to a rendition of Paul's sermon, and to ponder the eventual effect of what was begun here in the late summer of AD 46.

At the northern end of the *cardo* are the remains of a **monumental fountain** (or *nymphaeum*), a water tower 30 feet (9 m) high, which supplied the city's water, brought by aqueduct from the mountains to the north. Good views of the **aqueduct** can be seen from here. Built in the first century AD it was an impressive feat of engineering, bringing water down some 7 miles (11 km), with an average gradient of 2.6 per cent. This, however, was skilfully reduced to just 0.02 per cent on arrival at the *nymphaeum*, thus safely supplying the city's inhabitants with up to 660,000 gallons (3,000 cubic metres) of water each day.

Some 75 yards (69 m) further to the west is the city's **gymnasium complex**, with the floor stones of the *palaestra* still visible and several rooms from the bath complex still intact with their roofs. From here, further to the west, one can see the clear outlines of the city's **stadium**. However, the key site in this area (heading back in the direction of the site's entrance) is another Christian basilica, known sometimes as the **Church of St Paul**.

Expanded and renovated sometime around AD 500, this is one of the largest basilicas found in Asia Minor and gives a good idea of Byzantine architecture: the basilica is complete with three aisles, a central apse, and (at the western end) an inner and outer *narthex*. From an inscription in some of the surviving floor mosaics – now deliberately preserved under 12 inches (30 cm) of earth – an original, smaller basilica seems to have been built on this site during the era of Bishop Optimus.

In all probability the Byzantines dedicated this, their main church, to the memory of Paul. A large font, inscribed with Paul's name (*hagios Paulos*) and found in neighbouring **Yalvaç**, may well have come from this church. Even if the church's precise site had no known connection with Paul, clearly Antioch as a whole could lay claim, unlike many other cities, to a visit, clearly evidenced from Scripture, by this leading apostle.

LEFT: The scenic remains of Antioch's carefully-constructed aqueduct (with the blossoms and receding snow of late April).

The whole site gives plenty of opportunity to wander off for further exploration, but time would also be well spent in making a brief visit to the **Yalvaç Museum**. Several key artefacts from ancient Antioch and the surrounding area have been preserved – statues, coins, sarcophagi, and funeral *stelae*, not forgetting the font from St Paul's Church and the fragments of Augustus' *Res Gestae*.

## Iconium (Konya)

Of the other three places that Paul and Barnabas visited, the most easily accessed is **Iconium**, now identified with Konya (population 1.3 million). Located at the western edge of a large plain, one can well imagine the two travellers spending some cold months here in the winter of AD 46/47. However, Konya is now a large modern city and all traces of this small ancient town have effectively been removed. At its very centre, surrounded by a busy circular road, stands the mound of the **ancient acropolis**; but this is now covered with a city park and the Ala-et-tin Mosque.

Visitors find their attention taken instead to the various buildings from the time when the city became a key centre for the Islamic sultanate. There is the Monastery (or *Tekke*) of the Whirling Dervishes (together with the tomb of its thirteenth-century founder, Mevlana), which was a centre for mystic Sufi culture for many centuries until it was banned by Ataturk in 1925. Other places to visit, in addition to this **Mevlana Mausoleum**, include the **Ince Minaret** and the **Karatay Museum**. For those following in the steps of Paul, however, the most fruitful visit may be to Konya's small **Museum of Archaeology** (fifteen minutes' walk from the mausoleum). In addition to several splendid sarcophagi, there are some inscriptions of real interest within New Testament studies. One of these, more than 3 feet (1 m) high, was brought here from nearby Lystra and expressly refers to the colony of *Julia Felix Gemina Lustra*.

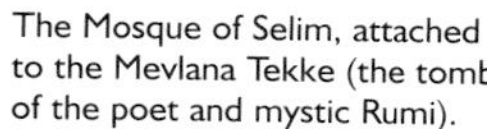

The Mosque of Selim, attached to the Mevlana Tekke (the tomb of the poet and mystic Rumi).

# Lystra and Derbe

The stone identifying the *tel* of ancient Lystra ('LVSTRA'), which has since been relocated to Konya's museum.

**Lystra** was the Roman colony to which Paul and Barnabas fled from Iconium. There is virtually nothing to be seen at the site today (some 21 miles or 34 km south-west of Konya, about a mile north of a village called Hatunsaray). However, the inscription (now transferred to Konya's museum), when discovered in the mid-1880s, confirmed the city's identity. The site is a natural military vantage-point, set on a sizeable hill, but it has never been properly excavated. However, its many Latin-filled inscriptions (also in the Konya Museum) confirm that this was a Roman colony. Intriguingly, some of the later ones make references to the 'priests of Zeus' and to the 'hearer of prayer and Hermes' – striking corroboration of Luke's account in which Paul and Barnabas are likened to Zeus and Hermes.

Looking at this mound, one is left asking why anyone would have come from Jerusalem to spread the news of a man crucified by the Romans just seventeen years before. No wonder Mark had turned back home for Jerusalem at the thought of being in these remote places. Yet Lystra would prove to be the place from where Paul, on his next visit, would select Mark's replacement, Timothy, his life-long companion. Lystra may now be little more than a mound, but here was born one of the 'unsung heroes' of the New Testament church.

There is perhaps even less to see on the site of ancient **Derbe**. Indeed the precise site is a matter of dispute – though a hill known as Keri Hüyük is increasingly favoured. This is located some 80 miles (130 km) south-east of Konya, 15 miles (24 km) north-east of Karaman (ancient Laranda) and 3 miles (5 km) across the fields from a village called Ekinozu. In Karaman's museum is a tombstone that refers to 'God-loving Michael, bishop of Derbe', which may have come from Keri Hüyük. And the discovery here in the 1950s of an inscription (referring to 'Claudio…') strongly confirms this is Derbe (since Derbe was also known in Paul's day as *Claudio*-Derbe; see p. 83).

Again this key evidence is found not on the site, but back in the **Konya Museum**. So a visit to the site, still totally unexcavated, yields little insight. Derbe was the remote home town of another of Paul's travelling companions, Gaius (Acts 19:29; 20:4). It was also not so far from Paul's own home town of Tarsus. Was Paul initially planning to return via the Cilician Gates: see p. 34)? Yet, though it would mean many extra days' travelling, they decided to return the way they had come in order to encourage the believers. It was a courageous decision – born of concern for those who lived in this remote area of south Galatia.

7

CHAPTER

# Macedonia

*During the night Paul had a vision of a man of Macedonia standing and begging him, 'Come over to Macedonia and help us.' After Paul had seen the vision, we got ready to leave for Macedonia... From Troas... we sailed straight for Samothrace, and the next day on to Neapolis. From there we travelled to Philippi, a Roman colony and the leading city of that district of Macedonia.*

*When they had passed through Amphipolis and Apollonia, they came to Thessalonica...*

*As soon as it was night, the brothers sent Paul and Silas away to Berea.*

**Acts 16:9–12; 17:1, 10**

## First steps into Europe

Refreshed from his time in Antioch and fired up by the Jerusalem Council, Paul decided now to venture even further westwards in the cause of Christ, passing through south Galatia (p. 84) and coming eventually to the west coast of Asia Minor, where he experienced this compelling vision to sail across the Aegean to Macedonia.

We see this now as the historic first arrival of the Christian message on the shores of Europe. Paul himself, however, would not have seen it in quite these terms, but in leaving the landmass of Asia Minor, he was indeed going beyond his natural 'comfort zone'. Macedonia was one of Rome's largest and oldest provinces (established back in 167 BC), so Paul could not but have felt this heavy Latin influence and experienced some culture shock.

Paul arrived here, so he would claim, as a result of God's clear guidance. He himself wanted to enter the province of Asia (and its capital, Ephesus), but 'he was kept by the Holy Spirit' from going there (Acts 16:6). Was this a prophetic message received by the believers in Galatia (perhaps at Lystra) when they commissioned Paul on their journey and 'laid hands' on him and his companions (2 Timothy 1:6)? We do not know; but in obedience, they avoided entering Asia and then also Bithynia – being prevented by 'the spirit of Jesus'. Eventually they reached the coast at Troas and it was here that they at last received some clear guidance: Paul saw a man in his dreams saying, 'Come over to Macedonia and help us.'

Travelling with Paul was evidently a matter of constant prayer, trying to discern God's will at each moment. Much of the time this small group simply *did not know* what they were doing from one day to the next. They had to be ready for the unexpected. We then see this necessary flexibility of approach when Paul comes to Philippi.

## Paul's developing strategy

At this stage in his travels Paul is developing quite a clear strategy, evidently heading for important centres of population. He is not opposed to more 'rural' ministry, but he sees his pioneering role as requiring him to target the large urban centres around the Mediterranean. He had come from Syrian Antioch, the largest city in the East, and he was looking for similar places to preach his message.

In this second 'missionary journey', the size of his chosen cities is gradually expanding. Some of the towns in Cyprus, and especially in Galatia, may have been quite small. Now something larger is at work: Philippi, then Thessalonica, then Athens, and eventually Corinth. With hindsight these large cities can be seen as a preparation for the biggest city in this Aegean region, namely Ephesus. Paul had wanted to head straight there, but the 'Spirit of Jesus' had prevented him (Acts 16:6). Maybe this was precisely so that he might develop his skills in slightly smaller cities before tackling somewhere so vast as Ephesus.

Paul appears to have been thinking in terms of ever-expanding circles or arcs: first, Cyprus and southern Anatolia (AD 46–47); next, the arc of the Aegean seaboard going down the east coast of Greece, with Ephesus as the acknowledged hub (AD 50–55); then a slightly wider arc, which went 'all the way round to Illyricum' (Romans 15:19) and came down the *west* coast of Greece (AD 55–57); and then...? Rome was clearly the next objective on this line of westward expansion. But the gospel had already reached Rome by other means (see p. 124), and Paul preferred to cut fresh ground (Romans 15:20). So Paul probably began to think of his own arc, which would use Rome simply as a springboard for work *even further to the west* – hence his references to the possibility of heading off to Spain (Romans 15:24). One has to admire the man's vision and sheer determination.

### Teamwork

We can also sense something of his strategy in terms of personnel. Travelling with a minimum of two others seems to have been the ideal – whether Barnabas and Mark (Acts 13), or Silas and Timothy (as here in Acts 16), or, when in Illyricum, two from among Sopater, Secundus and Aristarchus (Acts 20:4). Likewise, once stranded in Caesarea for two years, six of the original eight, who travelled up to Jerusalem, seem to have returned home; but *two* (namely Luke and Aristarchus) are asked to stay, and end up travelling with Paul all the way to Rome. Thus once in Rome, when 'only Luke' is with him, he strongly feels the need for a *second* companion – hence his urgent call to Timothy (2 Timothy 4:11).

Evidently, then, Paul liked to work in threes – a preference perhaps only reinforced by the difficulties experienced after Mark deserted him in Pamphylia. That would not happen again. No doubt, this was partly driven by the obvious need for mutual encouragement. After all, if left on his own for a while (as he was in Athens), Paul seemingly could become slightly depressed (see p. 116). Yet it also gave an ideal opportunity for a less experienced person to be trained in the company of two more senior colleagues. In addition it meant the task of catechizing or baptizing new converts could be delegated more easily by Paul to his colleagues (see pp. 126, 138).

Paul took this 'mentoring' side to his role very seriously – as seen in his letters to both Timothy and Titus, his closest colleagues. Yet these two men seem to have been quite different from each other. Titus, who was with Paul from the mid-40s AD (Galatians 2:1), was seemingly the most effective trouble-shooter, the person who was most successful in bringing the Corinthians 'into line' (2 Corinthians 2:13–14; 8:17). Timothy, however, was younger and more timid (1 Timothy 4:12; 2 Timothy 1:7), and for him the Ephesus job would be a major challenge. He was also someone with whom Paul perhaps felt some emotional rapport: 'I have no one else like him... he has served with me like a son with a father' (Philippians 2:20, 22); he was a 'dear son' in Christ (2 Timothy 1:2). If so, no wonder Paul summonsed him immediately to Rome; and no wonder his arrival did much to revive Paul's flagging spirit (see p. 192).

It is tempting to analyze Paul's inner 'cabinet' in terms of modern management psychology. What were the personal dynamics, for example, between the eight Gentiles who accompanied Paul by boat from Troas to Caesarea (Acts 20:6–21:8)? We cannot tell. Yet it is interesting to note how Luke himself may have been a kind of 'sheet-anchor' within the team. As a medic and then a historian, he was perhaps instinctively or by training someone who was good at administration, taking notes and keeping archives up to date. One does not get the impression he was especially exuberant or extrovert, but more the solid, dependable type. In this he may have been quite a contrast to Paul! Yet Paul had the management insight and the self-knowledge to value this rather different member of his team, his 'dear friend, doctor Luke' (Colossians 4:14).

## By the river in Philippi

Philippi was 'a Roman colony' and 'the leading city of that district of Macedonia' (Acts 16:12). Founded by Philip II of Macedon, it had only become a Roman colony, settled by army veterans, after the horrific Battle of Philippi in 42 BC; but it had established itself as the major city in the region. Its coins were overwhelmingly Roman; it was fiercely proud of its Roman status, a veritable outpost of Rome itself but on a foreign shore. Close communication with Rome was kept up through frequent use of the *Via Egnatia* that linked Philippi to Dyrrachium on the Adriatic coast, from where boats sailed for Italy. From Philippi, in a real and particular sense, it was true that 'all roads led to Rome'.

Paul and his companions arrived mid-week and began asking where, the next Saturday, they might find the 'synagogue' (technically just a gathering of ten Jewish men). Instead they were directed to a gathering of a few Jewish women, known to have a place where they prayed – somewhere outside the city, down by a nearby stream. Imagine, then, the women's surprise when these travelling Jewish men joined them!

They were invited to speak, and a woman named Lydia responded positively, asking immediately to be baptized in the river. Almost certainly she had some financial means, being described as a 'dealer in purple cloth from the city of Thyatira', a city to the south of Pergamum. Her home was ample enough to house Paul's team and she also managed a small 'household' (some of whom asked to be baptized). Luke also describes her as a 'worshipper of God' – in other words, she was not Jewish by birth but a 'God-fearer' on the fringe of Judaism. Paul's message, as we have seen, had particular appeal for such people (see pp. 80–82).

So far so good. Paul's team continued to visit the small 'place of prayer' each

The central remains of ancient Philippi, looking across the Roman forum; the Battle of Philippi was fought in the plains beyond the city (to the west) beneath the distant mountains.

Saturday, but they may have wondered how, if at all, things were going to develop after that. Evidently they were winning a few more people into the faith by various means (Acts 16:40), but how would they get an entrée into this Roman colony? The answer came from a surprising quarter.





## A change of fortune

A slave-girl with an aptitude for fortune-telling (and who thereby earned her owners 'a great deal of money') began stalking Paul's team. She kept shouting loudly to all and sundry that they were 'servants of the Most High God, telling you how to be saved' (Acts 16:16–17). Paul would not have disagreed with the description – in fact it was a very insightful, concise way of describing precisely what they were about! Yet after this had gone on for several days, it got irksome, perhaps embarrassing. Although on some occasions 'bad publicity is better than no publicity', Paul did not want his message being first heard about in this way. So 'in the name of Jesus Christ', he exorcized her (Acts 16:18).

This did not go down too well with the slave-girl's owners when they sensed they could no longer hope for a fortune through fortune-telling. Paul and Silas (perhaps because they looked the most obviously Jewish of the team) were dragged off to the city forum, there to be denounced before the Roman praetors as troublesome Jews 'advocating customs that are unlawful for us Romans to practise' (Acts 16:19–20). Officially Jews were not to proselytize Roman citizens and the apostles' activity could probably be described under that heading. So, with the crowd clamouring against them, they did not receive any proper hearing but were promptly flogged.

Almost certainly this was one of the three times when, as Paul later records, he was 'beaten with rods' (2 Corinthians 11:25). This was the Romans' preferred mode of flogging, so the other two occasions were probably when Paul was in a Roman colony, possibly Pisidian Antioch and Corinth. Of a piece with this is the fact that in Philippi as a Roman colony the praetors (magistrates) had supporting officers (or *lictors*) whose badges of office were bundles (or *fasces*) of rods and axes. Luke's word for them (in Acts 16:35) means literally 'rod-bearers'.

So Paul and Silas were beaten with rods and then put in prison. With hindsight, it now appears that the praetors were probably only putting them there for the night (Acts 16:35). Before that welcome (and unexpected?) news reached the prisoners, however, something else happened: an earthquake around midnight caused the prison doors to open and the prisoners' chains to come loose. The jailer, panicking that the prisoners had escaped and therefore ready to commit suicide, discovered to his delight that Paul and Silas were still there. Mightily relieved, and now overcome with awe at these strange happenings, he 'fell trembling' before them, asking 'What must I do to be saved?' (Acts 16:26–30).

We do not know if he meant this in a more practical sense (in other words, how was he to face the praetors' wrath the next morning?), but Paul and Silas did not miss their opportunity to speak about a more important 'safety' – that found in Jesus. The result was a new believer – and not only him but 'all his family', who at that unlikely 'hour of the night', after listening to Paul's speaking the 'word of the Lord', were all 'baptized'. It is unlikely anyone slept much that night; instead they all had a meal together – and the jailer was 'filled with joy because he had come to believe in God' (Acts 16:32–34).

## Faith and baptism

We note here how, as with Lydia, a response of faith in Jesus led on immediately to the necessity of baptism. Passing over the vexed (and ultimately unanswerable) issue of whether the jailer's family included tiny children who could not have understood Paul's teaching (and who therefore provide the precedent for the practice of 'infant baptism'), we note the more important point: that Paul's preaching always had the goal of faith followed by baptism. Elsewhere Luke takes this somewhat for granted, but from his narrative about Philippi we see a window into Paul's regular practice: what Jesus had commanded (Matthew 28:19), this he would do.

Baptism for Paul was the sign of the 'new covenant' established by Jesus, the sign of truly becoming part of God's new people. As such, as he had already argued in Galatians, it became one of the prime reasons why Paul saw circumcision (the previous sign for entering God's people) as no longer necessary: 'because all of you who were *baptized* into Christ have clothed yourselves with Christ', 'you are *all* sons of God through *faith* in Jesus Christ' (Galatians 3:26–27). Clearly one of the great advantages of baptism over circumcision was precisely that women could now be included on an equal footing with men – indeed everyone, of whatever background, found themselves equal at the waters of baptism. Thus Paul continued: 'there is neither Jew nor Greek, slave nor free, *male nor female*, for you are *all one* in Christ Jesus' (Galatians 3:28). No wonder Paul's message found a special resonance with those who until then had felt themselves to be on the margins. Now, through faith in Jesus, they were brought right onto 'centre stage', to the very centre of God's purposes for his world.

*'For we were all baptized by one Spirit into one body – whether Jews or Greeks, slave or free – and we were all given the one Spirit to drink.'*
**1 Corinthians 12:13**

## Taking leave of the Philippians

The next morning, when news reached them that they were being released, Paul decided to kick up a little fuss. In the mob violence the day before an important fact had been overlooked (perhaps drowned out by the crowd's shouting): Paul and Silas were Roman citizens and, as such, they should never have been put in prison without some kind of hearing. If they were now to be dismissed, they would first demand an apology in person!

We do not know how Silas had received his Roman citizenship (though it may have been another factor in his favour when Paul chose him as his chief travelling companion). The reasons for Paul's citizenship are also unclear (see pp. 34–35). But presumably it was statistically unusual for Jews to have this privilege – at least the Philippian praetors had not given it a moment's thought when Paul and Silas were arrested. So they were duly surprised and 'alarmed' when the lictors brought them word of this. They came to apologize (knowing they themselves could be in trouble if the prisoners pressed the matter) and requested them to leave the city – which Paul and Silas were now willing to do. They had made their point. Conceivably Paul may have hoped that 'playing the card' of their Roman citizenship at this point would lead on to his being able to give a more public account of what he was doing in Philippi; but the praetors' demeanour probably indicated that was not wise. So they made a brief visit to Lydia's house to say farewell to the believers gathered there (perhaps no more than 30 maximum?) and then went on their way. And if we are correct that Luke himself was a resident of Philippi (see p. 16), then those left behind included Luke – no doubt entrusted by the apostles with building up the small congregation. It would be another four or five years before Paul came that way again.

## Onwards to Thessalonica

The three of them set out westwards along the *Via Egnatia*. This was a busy, paved road – one of the major arteries of the Roman empire – and many travelling with them would have been people headed for Rome. The journey time from Philippi to Rome has been estimated at about 40 days (assuming roughly 20 miles or 30 km per day and one day's voyage from Dyrrachium to Brundisium); however, imperial couriers may have halved this. Meanwhile those coming the other way would have been bringing the latest news from the imperial city. Thoughts of one day going to Rome himself may well have begun to percolate through Paul's mind at this point.



They decided to pass through Amphipolis without stopping (though it was the capital of one of Macedonia's four districts). They also kept going through the smaller port of Apollonia. Their sights were set on the provincial capital some 90 miles (145 km) away to the west, Thessalonica (Acts 17:1–9).

*'The Thessalonians are populous and easy-going, open to everything new – good and bad.'*

**Strabo, *Geography* (c. 30 BC)**

Unlike Philippi this was a decidedly Greek city – as the coinage found there indicates. As the largest city in Macedonia, they could hope that here at least (unlike in Philippi) there was a sizeable Jewish synagogue – which there was (Acts 17:1). Once again ('as his custom was') Paul made his way there and spent at least three Saturdays arguing from the Old Testament that the Messiah 'had to suffer and rise from the dead' (Acts 17:2). This sounds very similar to what Jesus himself had done on the Emmaus road (back in Luke 24:26) and indeed even before his death (Mark 8:31). We see here the centrality that Paul gave to both the cross and the resurrection, and his need in the synagogue context to argue for this as a fulfilment of the messianic passages in the Hebrew Scriptures.

The Roman forum of ancient Thessalonica, where Jason and others were brought before the 'politarchs'.

This time there was a reasonable response from the Jewish members of the synagogue. Again, the new believers also included a significant number of 'God-fearing Greeks', including several 'prominent women' (Acts 17:4). Paul would comment later on how the Thessalonians had 'turned to God from idols' (1 Thessalonians 1:9) – an indication that a fair proportion of the first believers had come from a Gentile background. And once again (as in Pisidian Antioch and Iconium) it was this that triggered a violent response from the other Jews who had not been persuaded by Paul. 'Renting a crowd' from the forum and rushing to the house of Jason (presumably a recent convert), they hunted for Paul and Silas, but unsuccessfully. Instead they dragged Jason and some other believers before the city officials (known here, uniquely, as 'politarchs': Acts 17:6). They then accused them of harbouring some visiting Jews who had 'caused trouble all over the world' by 'defying

Caesar's decrees' and 'saying there is another king, one called Jesus' (Acts 17:6–7).

Not surprisingly, this caused quite a turmoil. In recent years the emperor Claudius had sent out edicts (for example, to Alexandria) warning officials against the increase and spread of Jewish nationalists, who were fostering rebellion against Rome in their longing for messianic freedom (see p. 47). Likewise in Rome he had expelled all its Jewish residents because of their rioting (see p. 192). Now, so it appeared, Thessalonica was going to be taken over by rioting caused by some dispute about Israel's 'Messiah'.

Moreover the city council (or *demos*) of Thessalonica had probably taken an oath in which they had sworn full allegiance to the emperor. A charge of this kind could therefore not be ignored or brushed aside. We know too that both Augustus and Tiberius had issued decrees against prophets who claimed to make predictions about the future (Dio Cassius, *History* 56.25.5; 57.15.8). Since Paul's teaching to the Thessalonians clearly included some strong teaching about the future return of Jesus – his *parousia* or 'royal appearing' (see 1 Thessalonians 4:13–5:3) – this too could have been used against him in some shape or form.

However, this accusation made before the politarchs is more revealing than it looks for another reason. Paul had been proclaiming Jesus as the Messiah of Israel (Acts 17:3), but his accusers were interpreting this as a challenge to Caesar's authority –

**Map of Paul's second 'missionary journey'.**

Jesus is '*another* king'. This manoeuvre sounds remarkably similar to that which was tried on Jesus himself, when his messianic claim before Caiaphas was converted into the more political charge before Pilate that he was claiming to be a king (Luke 23:1–2; John 18:33–37). Yet, despite the malicious 'spin' intended, there was in both cases more than a hint of truth. For in Hebrew thought (based on passages such as Psalms 2 and 72), the true Messiah of Israel automatically *was* the true Lord of the world as well.

This means that when claiming that Jesus was Israel's Messiah, Paul would also have been (either implicitly or sometimes explicitly) claiming that he was the true Lord over the world – including the Roman empire. In a culture where the imperial cult was growing apace (with previous emperors being divinized after their deaths), and in an era when the reigning emperor could claim to be 'lord' of pretty much the whole world, Paul was advancing a radically rival concept: the world's true ruler was not Caesar, but someone called Jesus. Given that Jesus had been crucified on a Roman cross twenty years earlier, this was a bizarre thing to claim and certainly risky. Yet the evidence from Thessalonica suggests this is precisely what Paul did claim. He was heard, rightly, to be claiming that there was 'another king' or 'emperor' – Jesus of Nazareth.

In such circumstances it was probably a good thing that Paul himself was not brought before the politarchs. Would he have tried to speak? Would this meddling visitor from the East have been lynched? The time would come when he would be hauled before Roman officials with even higher standing (in Corinth and in Caesarea: see p. 126, 168), but that time had not yet come. In his absence, Jason and the others, as fellow Thessalonians, were given a reprieve and simply released on bail. But when they got back home the decision was quickly made that Paul and his team had better slip away as soon as possible. They fled that night.



*'The Macedonians' broad-rimmed hat – their shelter in snow-storm and helmet in war'.*

**Antipater of Thessalonica (early first century BC)**

## Paul looks back to Thessalonica

It was a very sudden departure, with no time for proper farewells or extended instructions. We can sense this in the letter Paul writes a few months later (1 Thessalonians). He says he had been 'intensely longing' to see them again and was being gnawed away by sheer worry lest they had succumbed to further persecution and had given up on their faith (1 Thessalonians 2:17–3:5). But now, after hearing of them through Timothy, he is overjoyed to know that they are standing firm (1 Thessalonians 3:6–13). He senses that the friends and families of the young believers will have been trying to poison their minds against him – Paul's visit was a 'failure', they might have been told, and his teaching just a form of clever trickery. So Paul reminds them that this simply was not true:

*We had previously been insulted in Philippi, but we dared to tell you his gospel in spite of strong opposition. For the appeal we make does not spring from error or impure motives, nor are we trying to trick you… We were gentle among you, like a mother caring for her little children… We loved you so much… We worked night and day not to be a burden to you… We dealt with you as a father deals with his own children…*

**1 Thessalonians 2:1–12**

And, referring to the hard reality of persecution in Thessalonica, he reminds them that they are not alone but are like 'God's churches in Judea', who similarly have experienced hostility from their 'own countrymen' – from those Jewish people who 'want to keep us from speaking to the Gentiles' (1 Thessalonians 2:14–16).

It is a very frank, yet tender, letter in which we see something of the inside story that Luke has described only from the outside. We see something of Paul's strategy of sharing his life with believers, something of his personal vulnerability, and something of the emotional 'roller-coaster' he was on as he waited anxiously for news of whether his 'efforts' had proved 'useless' (1 Thessalonians 3:5). In this case, it appeared, his labours had not been in vain; but after any such visit Paul could never be sure.

## A better response in Berea

So Paul, Silas and Timothy moved on discreetly to Berea, a town 12 miles (19 km) south of the *Via Egnatia* at Pella. The Thessalonian believers may have suggested this as a suitably quiet place off the main road, where they might be unnoticed for a while. Cicero himself had described it as an 'out of the way town' (*In Pisonem* 89).

In such circumstances one might have thought Paul and his team would 'lie low' for a while; but, once again, they went to the synagogue. This time they received one of their most positive responses: the Jewish residents 'received the message with great eagerness and examined the Scriptures every day to see if what Paul said was true' (Acts 17:11). Many Jews believed, but so too (again) some 'prominent Greek women and many Greek men' (Acts 17:12). Luke does not mention any of their names, but later one of Paul's companions is named as 'Sopater, son of Pyrrhus, from Berea' (Acts 20:4).

Modern mosaic of Saint Paul in a niche of the monument built in his memory in Veria (see p. 107).

For a while there was calm. However, as perhaps they could have expected by now, the calm was soon broken. Sure enough, some members of Thessalonica's synagogue arrived to stir things up (Acts 17:13). At this it was decided that Paul had better leave Macedonia straightaway. So some of the new believers acted as his bodyguards and personally took him down (by land or sea?) to Athens, returning with Paul's instructions to send Timothy and Silas to Athens as soon as possible (Acts 17:11–12).

The fact that Silas and Timothy stayed in Berea, if only for a few weeks, is a clear sign that Paul was the one who was provoking the most violent opposition. He was probably the chief speaker and the one who argued in most detail from his knowledge of the Hebrew Scriptures. For all we know, his style may have been a little more combative. Certainly, during the team's time in Macedonia, we hear little of young Timothy. He was probably encouraged by the others to learn as much as possible by observing them in action. His time for heroics would come. For now he was valued for his steady companionship and loyalty. And, unlike Mark (who had occupied this 'number three' position before), this young man showed no signs of shirking.

## Paul's return visits to Macedonia

Despite the risks to himself Paul clearly wanted to come back into the province of Macedonia fairly soon – at least initially (see 1 Thessalonians 2:17–18). In fact it would be four or five years before he could return. Luke describes this return visit in Acts 20:1–2:

*When the uproar had ended [in the Ephesus theatre], Paul... said good-bye and set out for Macedonia. He travelled through that area, speaking many words of encouragement to the people, and finally arrived in Greece, where he stayed three months [in Corinth].*

## Key dates: Macedonia

|  |  |
|---|---|
| c. 480 BC | Xerxes the Persian passes through Macedonia (as recounted in Herodotus, *History*, Book 7). |
| c. 360 BC | Neapolis ('new city') founded by Thasians, motivated by gold deposits in Mount Pangaion (a few miles to the south). |
| 358 BC | Philip II of Macedon captures Amphipolis. |
| 356 BC | Philip founds 'Philippi', building walls around the acropolis of a mining town previously known as Crenides (meaning 'spring'). |
| 330 BC | Alexander the Great (Philip's son) sets off from Macedonia for the East (Arrian, *Anabasis* 1.11.4). |
| 315 BC | King Cassander founds Thessalonica in honour of his wife, Thessalonike, the half-sister of Alexander the Great. |
| 168 BC | After the Third Macedonian War, the area is subdued by the Romans and divided into four districts. |
| 148 BC | 'Macedonia' becomes a full Roman province, with Thessalonica as the provincial capital and seat of the proconsul; Illyria (on the Adriatic) is included, with the *Via Egnatia* (named after proconsul Cnaeus Egnatius) being built from there – first as far as Thessalonica, then on to Neapolis. |
| 49 BC | Pompey and his army take refuge in both Berea and Thessalonica during his campaign against Julius Caesar. |
| 42 BC | Battle of Philippi, in which Octavian (later Augustus) and Mark Antony defeat the republican forces led by Julius Caesar's assassins – Cassius (who is killed) and Brutus (who commits suicide); recounted in Appian, *Civil Wars* 4.105–38. |
| 31 BC | Mark Antony uses Amphipolis as his naval base, preparing for the Battle of Actium. After his victory, Augustus renames Philippi as 'Colonia Augusta Julia Philippensis', giving it the privilege of the '*ius Italicum*' (see Dio Cassius, *History* 51.4.6). Thessalonica is given the status of a free Greek city, ruled by five 'politarchs'. |
| AD 44 | The emperor Claudius restores Macedonia to senatorial control. |
| AD 50 (July) | Paul, Silas and Timothy arrive in Macedonia, landing at Neapolis (Acts 16:11). |
| AD 55 (Sept?)– AD 56 (Dec?) | Paul travels through Macedonia towards Illyricum and eventually Nicopolis (Acts 20:1–2; Titus 3:12; Romans 15:19). |
| AD 57 (April) | Paul, en route to Jerusalem, stops in Philippi with Luke for the week of Passover (Acts 20:6). |
| AD 292 | Galerius is proclaimed ruler of the east while in Thessalonica, but instigates major persecution of Christians there (including a martyr known as Demetrius). |
| AD 380 | After his conversion in the city, Theodosius the Great issues the 'Edict of Thessalonica', prohibiting pagan worship; the city is his base of operations against Gothic invaders. |
| c. AD 400 | Construction of octagonal basilica in Philippi as the city's cathedral. |
| c. AD 475 | Construction of Basilica 'A' in Philippi. |
| c. AD 550 | Unsuccessful construction of Basilica 'B' in Philippi (after earlier one destroyed by earthquake), with some features similar to those in 'Hagia Sophia' (in modern Istanbul). |
| AD 600s | Philippi falls gradually into decline (with presence of Slavs in the area). |
| AD 900s | Small church built at west end of Basilica 'B'; Byzantine fortress built on Philippi's acropolis. |
| 1204 | Thessalonica occupied for some years by the knights of the Fourth Crusade. |
| 1387 | Turkish rule in Thessalonica (until 1912); in time there were up to 48 mosques, but also 36 Sephardic Jewish synagogues. |
| 1453 | Fall of Constantinople to the Turks; Macedonia brought under Turkish rule. |
| 1876 | Discovery in Philippi of a cave with murals (from seventh century?) depicting Paul's imprisonment, leading to its identification as 'St Paul's Prison'. |
| 1917 | Major fire in Thessalonica causes widespread damage. |
| 1962 | Discovery of Thessalonica's Roman forum. |
| 1978 | Earthquakes cause further damage in Thessalonica. |
| 2000 | Discovery of a gold wreath and then fortifications near Nea Appolonia suggest the finding of ancient Appolonia. |

The length of this visit through Macedonia is unclear but it may well have been up to fifteen months – from late summer AD 55 to late winter in AD 56 (see p. 12). Paul would have been returning to established churches but also breaking new ground. This time he would not be lured south towards Berea but would resolutely stay on the *Via Egnatia*, heading towards the west of Macedonia (see map on p. 143). This area on the Adriatic was also known as 'Illyricum' – an area that Paul, writing Romans in early AD 57, claims to have visited (Romans 15:19).

Quite possibly he was joined in this venture by two men from Thessalonica, Aristarchus and Secundus, who later are in Paul's team setting out from Corinth to Jerusalem (Acts 20:4); perhaps also by Sopater from Berea (also named in Acts 20:4). Paul would be training them in frontier mission and doing again that which he did best – pioneering evangelism in 'virgin territories'. 'It has always been my ambition', he wrote the following year, 'to preach the gospel where Christ was not known' (Romans 15:20). At last, now that the (quite different, but very draining) troubles of Corinth and Ephesus could be left behind him, Paul could re-energize himself by using his primary skills – those of 'cutting edge' mission.

So this should be our lasting memory of Paul in Macedonia. Yes, he would pass through this province in great haste in April AD 57 when racing to get to Jerusalem (on that occasion he would spend Passover in Philippi: Acts 20:6); but his longest time in Macedonia may well be this 'hidden' time back in AD 55 and 56.

As he travelled westwards, the Roman influence would have become stronger and stronger, the Greek influence waning all the time. Jewish synagogues too would be becoming increasingly rare to find, and some of the cities bitterly remote. Yet still this 'apostle to the Gentiles' pressed on with his few young companions, determined to preach the good news about Israel's Messiah. And then, when the opportunity to sail across to Rome itself disappeared from view, he chose to come south, heading via Nicopolis for Corinth (Titus 3:12).

It had been a risky time, perhaps a lonely time, but he was doing what he loved best. And, when he arrived in Corinth, his batteries were so thoroughly recharged that he was able to pen the single most influential piece of theological writing the world has ever seen – his life's masterpiece, his letter to the Romans. So Macedonia, for all its earlier stresses and near-death experiences, may also have been the seed-bed from which new life sprung. It was all part of what it meant to be following someone who had suffered but who had then been raised from the dead.

## Macedonia today

Most of what was Paul's 'Macedonia' now lies within modern Greece. However, parts of the Roman province would take one into Albania or the 'Macedonian republic', once part of the former Yugoslavia. So the region today is the meeting-point of quite different peoples and has witnessed some significant border conflicts; the Greek area, for example, has had periods of being under Turkish and then Bulgarian rule.

## Kavalla

If travelling today, Paul would have landed at **Kavalla**, the large, modern port on the ancient site of **Neapolis** (meaning 'new town'). It is a natural place for a harbour: the coastline further eastwards is unsuitable for constructing harbours, and the town is built on two hills that surround the harbour in a neat semi-circle. A stone in the grounds of **St Nicholas' Church** (originally dedicated to St Paul before it became a mosque) marks the traditional site of Paul's landing; and, given the way the shoreline has receded, this may not be too far from the mark. The **Museum** contains some good artefacts from Macedonia's troubled history, but what reminds us most of Paul are the remains of the ***Via Egnatia*** (some surviving in quite long stretches), as this ancient road makes its way over the hill through Kavalla's suburbs towards Philippi.

## Philippi

**Philippi** is about 9 miles (14 km) north-west of Kavalla. The *Via Egnatia*, itself normally about 10 feet (3 m) in width, cuts through the middle of the ancient site. The city lies at the foot of a steep hill, overlooking a large plain. This area (which in Paul's day would have been quite marshy) had been the scene of the dramatic **Battle of Philippi** almost exactly 100 years before, which effectively brought to an end the Roman 'republic'. (The precise site is marked by two low hills about 2 miles or 3 km to the south-west of Philippi). After a 'stand-off' lasting twenty days, the hungry army of Octavian and Mark Antony finally overcame Brutus' men. Then, when Octavian later defeated Mark Antony at Actium, he sent yet more veterans to Philippi, which he was establishing as a Roman colony. It was soon known as a 'little Rome', covering a vast amount of the local area, and was, as Luke rightly terms it, the 'leading city of that district of Macedonia' (Acts 16:12).

The site of ancient Philippi is truly impressive. After entering the site, visitors walk along some of the *Via Egnatia* before reaching the **ancient forum**, a large rectangular court surrounded by long *stoas* and with significant city buildings nearby (such as the library to the east). Much here dates to the second century AD, when the emperor Marcus Aurelius (AD 161–87) rebuilt the forum (over the site of the

The fishing harbour of modern Kavalla (ancient Neapolis), where Paul and his companions first set foot in 'Europe'.

previous one), dedicating a temple here to his predecessor, Antoninus Pius.

Along its northern colonnade there is a line of four steps, which probably led up to the tribunal (or *bema*) – quite possibly the very place where Paul and Silas were brought under arrest. To the south is a smaller **'commercial' forum** and (on the west side of this second forum) a ***palaestra*** and its latrines. On its south side the Byzantines began building a **large basilica ('B')** with three apses and a square nave, but its dome collapsed during construction; centuries later a small church was built in its *narthex*.

To the east of the main forum, the visitor comes across the so-called **'Octagon' Church**, identified recently as Philippi's 'cathedral'. It was built around AD 400 over the site of a previous chapel dedicated to St Paul, and its mosaic flooring was commissioned (according to its inscription) by a 'Bishop Porphyrius'. Nearby is the **bishop's residence** (*episcopeion*), together with various offices, storerooms and two large wine presses.

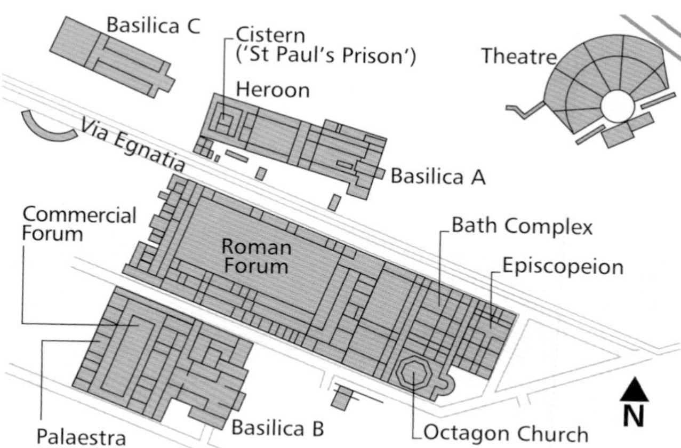


**RIGHT: Plan of Philippi ruins.**

BOTTOM: Remains of 'Basilica B' in Philippi with the slopes of the acropolis in the distance. The building of several such large Christian churches, so close to the centre of the ancient city, indicates how the Christian faith had come to be firmly established in Philippi four centuries after Paul's brief visits.

One of the main buildings on the other (north) side of the *Via Egnatia* is a **three-aisled church** (known as **Basilica 'A'**), built around AD 480 with marble flooring, and also a second storey. Nearby is the so-called **St Paul's Prison**, but this is most unlikely to be authentic. More probably, when Basilica 'A' was destroyed by an earthquake, this former cistern started being used for discreet Christian worship and then became associated with Paul. During this period it was decorated with Christian frescoes and later a small chapel was built above it.

Other sites worth visiting include: the Roman **bath complex** to the south-west of the commercial forum; the **Hellenistic theatre** (to the north-east of Basilica 'A'), which was renovated in the second century AD for gladiatorial fighting and may have held up to 50,000 people; some of the **small sanctuaries**, dedicated to pagan gods, and rock-cut **grave-reliefs** that are dotted around the northern half of the site; and the **acropolis** itself (chiefly for its fine views back over the entire site).

**MIDDLE: Plan of wider Philippi area.**

BOTTOM: The *Via Egnatia* runs through the centre of Philippi.

## Baptismal site

There remains the question as to where Paul first encountered the Jewish women who were praying 'outside the gate by the river' (Acts 16:13). Three sites have been suggested: somewhere on the River Gangites (1.5 miles or 2.5 km to the west of Philippi); in the modern village of Krenides (half a mile to the east of the ancient city), where there are the remains of two churches (from the fourth and fifth centuries) located in a previous cemetery area; or (most likely) somewhere along the Krenides stream in the area now known as **'Lydia'** (named after the woman from Thyatira converted by Paul's preaching). This last area, marked by a line of trees, is suitably close (about a quarter of a mile outside the city's western gate) and was approached by a Roman road. Some of the area may have been a cemetery at that time. During the twentieth century the octagonal **baptistery of St Lydia** was built, together with some seating by the stream, which Christian visitors may use for worship or, not unnaturally, for baptisms.

(camp of Brutus)
Traditional (more likely?) site known now as 'Lydia'
Via Egnatia
Acropolis
(camp of Antony and Octavian)
Colonial Arch
to Neapolis (modern Kavalla)
Less likely site of Jewish 'place of prayer' (Acts 16:13)
PHILIPPI
(camp of Cassius)

## The *Via Egnatia*

Paul left Philippi, going westwards along the ***Via Egnatia***. The Romans had paved this in the second century BC – 450 miles (725 km) in length and, in places, up to 20 feet (6 m) in width – to establish the main communication corridor from Rome to its eastern provinces. It could be incredibly busy. Cicero had once delayed departing from Thessalonica, waiting for when there was less traffic (*Letters* 69); his letters also indicate that it could be

The Lion of Amphipolis (reassembled and erected in the 1930s, but dating back to the fourth century BC) may have been commissioned by Alexander the Great for his loyal admiral Laomedon.

dangerous, due to occasional attacks by barbarians. At various points along the road there were places to exchange animals (*mutatia*) and places to stay (*mansiones*).

Paul and his companions, being determined to reach Thessalonica, passed through some of these staging-posts without stopping for long: Luke mentions Amphipolis and Appolonia (Acts 17:1). **Appolonia** is little known in Greek history but may recently have been discovered (just outside Nea Appolonia, 30 miles or 50 km east of Thessalonica). **Amphipolis**, which is 65 miles (105 km) east of Thessalonica, has a natural acropolis located on a sharp bend in the Strymon River. The Byzantines would later build no fewer than five churches on its acropolis, some with elaborate mosaics. Below the acropolis one can still see Hellenistic and Roman houses, a large gymnasium complex and various small sanctuaries to local deities. Perhaps most fascinating are the fossilized timbers of the **ancient bridge** over the river (some dating back to the fifth century BC) and the famous **Lion of Amphipolis**.

## Thessalonica

Eventually, after a journey of 95 miles (150 km), Paul reached **Thessalonica**. Thessaloniki is now the second largest city in Greece (after Athens). Despite this, some significant archaeological remains have survived – all within walking distance of the city centre. And one of the city's main streets, **Egnatia Odhos**, takes its name and route from the ancient *Via Egnatia* that ran through the city in Paul's day.

Those interested in Macedonia's history before the New Testament (and especially the era of Philip II and Alexander) should visit Thessalonica's **Archaeological Museum**, as well as the museum located at **Vergina**, 75 miles (120 km) west of the city, which displays the splendid **Royal Tombs of Macedonia**. For those interested in the Roman period, however, there are the **Roman baths and street** (visible in the crypt under Agios Demetrius Church) and the **Roman forum** (on the site of the Hellenistic *agora*). This large area, surrounded by two-storeyed *stoas* and civic buildings (for example, the **Odeion theatre**) almost certainly contained the judgment tribunal in which Jason was brought before the city's rulers (Acts 17:6). The rest of Roman Thessalonica would have been nearer the acropolis. From the acropolis there are fine views, giving a good idea of the ancient city – for example, from the wall ramparts near the Chain Tower. In this area diligent visitors can also discover a **stone** traditionally associated with Paul's preaching (in the southern transept in the chapel of Vlataddon Monastery) and a **'well of St Paul'** (in a garden near the Chain Tower).

Those interested in later periods cannot avoid the impact left by the emperor Galerius during his reign (AD 293–311). The **Arch of Galerius** was built along the *Via Egnatia* to commemorate his Persian victory. Nearby is the **Rotunda**, which was originally part of Galerius' mausoleum (but was later used as a Christian church, then a mosque, and is now known as **Agios Georgios**). Also not far away, but in the opposite direction, is the **Palace of Galerius**, where the octagonal-shaped ruins probably mark the site of his throne room.

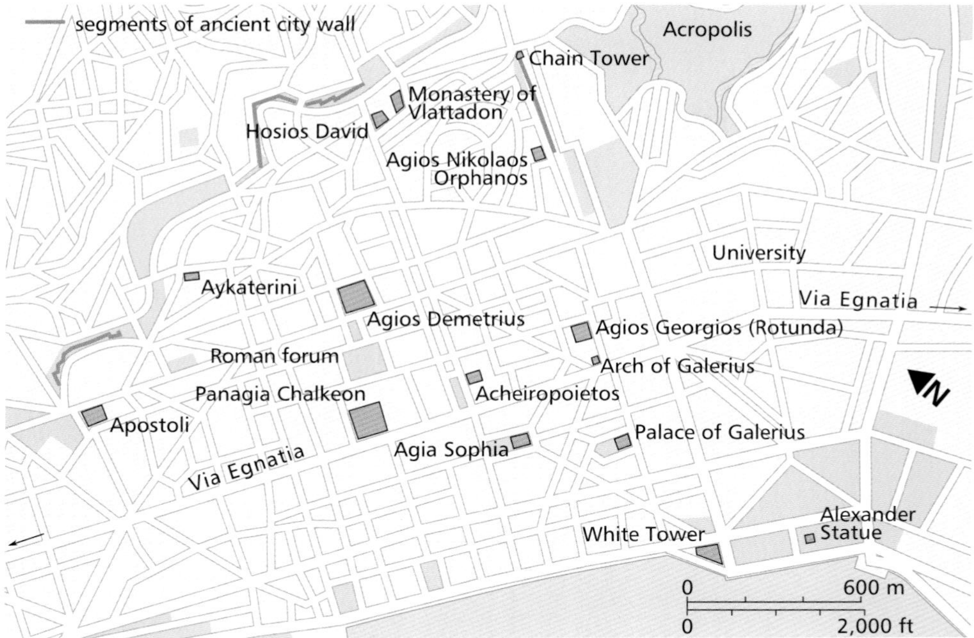


**Plan of ancient sites in Thessaloniki.**

Galerius' persecution of Christians led to the death of one Demetrius, who is now heralded as Thessalonica's patron saint. In the fifth century AD a major church was built in his honour, but this was destroyed by a city fire in 1917. The present church of **Agios Demetrius** was rebuilt (partially from original materials) in the 1940s; its vast crypt area may well be the Roman baths in which Demetrius (according to tradition) was kept prisoner. There are at least six other Byzantine churches in the city (ranging from the fifth to the fourteenth centuries), several of them with fine mosaics; one of the earliest, **Hosios David**, for example, depicts a young, beardless Christ, seated in glory.

## Ancient Berea

Paul's final stop before leaving Macedonia was one of the largest cities in Macedonia, but there is little of ancient Berea that is visible today. In its place is the small town of **Veria**. As you approach from the north some of the ancient wall can be seen, and there are also scattered remains of some ancient streets and shops along Elia Street and Parodos Edessis Street. The chief point of interest from a Pauline perspective is the large **modern monument**, built in 1961 in honour of the apostle Paul. Understandably, within local tradition it is suggested that this might have been on the site of the synagogue Paul visited, but there is now no means of confirming this.

8

CHAPTER

# Athens

*While Paul was waiting in Athens, he was greatly distressed to see that the city was full of idols. So he reasoned in the synagogue with the Jews and the God-fearing Greeks, as well as in the market place day by day with those who happened to be there. A group of Epicurean and Stoic philosophers began to dispute with him. 'What is this babbler trying to say?... He seems to be advocating foreign gods.' They said this because Paul was preaching the good news about Jesus and the resurrection.*

*Then they brought him to a meeting of the Areopagus, where they said to him, 'May we know what this new teaching is that you are presenting? ... You are bringing some strange ideas to our ears, and we want to know what they mean.' (All the Athenians... spent their time doing nothing but talking about and listening to the latest ideas.)*

**Acts 17:16–21**

## At the centre of culture

Saul the Pharisee, now Paul the 'apostle to the Gentiles', wandering around the streets of ancient Athens on his own. It is a powerful picture. In Paul's time Athens was acknowledged as having been the historic centre of the ancient classical world. Over 500 years before it had led the way in architecture, sculpture, philosophy and all kinds of literature (whether tragic and comic drama, or poetry and history); it had enjoyed a brilliant 'golden age', never equalled again, which had left the ancient world forever in its debt. Now this man from the (not so insignificant) university city of Tarsus, a protégé of the great Gamaliel of Jerusalem, finds himself at the very epicentre of that whole classical tradition – a tradition that he could not but admire, but which as a Jew he had been trained to dismiss as ignorant and idolatrous. What would he make of it all?

### One man in an alien world

This clash of worldviews would have confronted a Jew in almost any city in the empire. Every street had altars and statues depicting the pagan gods, and the civic community found its coherence through a long-established way of life that was enmeshed in various religious rituals associated with local temples. For a Jew there was only one city that afforded any escape from this relentless barrage of paganism – Jerusalem (which may explain in part why Paul had been sent there to finish his training).

So Paul had had to work out a response to paganism long before and in other cities. Yet there was something about Athens – with its unique history, its beautiful temples and its continued love of engaging with new philosophical ideas – that inevitably brought the issue to its finest point. And Paul, remember, was there on his own.

But as he looked out on the Parthenon, set resplendent atop Athens' Acropolis, he did so not simply as a Jew. He came as one believing that Israel's God had recently done a decisive new thing in the history not only of Israel but also of the world. What did it mean, then, for Paul to walk around Athens' streets as an *apostle* believing that *he* – just one man among the many others going about their daily business – was the *only person* in the city that day who had the key to the universe? No one else around him knew God's 'secret' or 'mystery' (Mark 4:11; Ephesians 3:4); but who was he among so many?

So, as Luke says, Paul was 'greatly distressed to see that the city was full of idols'. This provoked him to 'reason in the synagogue' and then to branch out into the 'market place'. Paul's Jewish abhorrence of idolatry came bursting forth from his inner being; and Paul's convictions about the true Messiah, the Lord of the world, meant he could not contain himself in solitary silence – he simply *had* to speak out and to reason with those in the city, both Jews and Gentiles.





## Paul among the philosophers

The 'market place' was almost certainly the large *agora* to the north-west of Athens' distinctive rocky outcrop known as the Acropolis (or 'high city'). Meanwhile to the west there was another, much lower, hill, but with its own claim to fame – the 'Areopagus' (or 'Mars Hill'). This was where Athens' citizens had first gathered for their parliamentary assemblies (giving birth to 'democracy'); and then, long after these had moved elsewhere, it became the meeting place for the senior 'Areopagus council'.

Paul's regular speaking in the *agora* eventually sparked a response from some 'Epicurean and Stoic philosophers' who dubbed him a *spermologos* – a local word of abuse for a 'babbler' or, perhaps better, a 'charlatan'. They thought he was prattling on to no effect, or else was up to some kind of (as yet undetected) trickery. Meanwhile, others imagined he was introducing some 'foreign gods' to the already well-stocked array of gods available in the Greek pantheon. This was because Paul kept speaking about 'Jesus and the resurrection', which Paul's hearers might easily imagine was a reference to one new male god ('Jesus') and a new female goddess (the Greek for 'resurrection' is a feminine noun: *hee anastasis*): perhaps 'Anastasis' was Jesus' female 'consort'? Their pagan mythology led to a total mis-hearing.

The small outcrop of rock on which the Areopagus council often met; a possible location for Paul's speech to the Athenian philosophers.

Even so, they were intrigued. They invited Paul to the next meeting of the Areopagus council (meeting either on Mars Hill or perhaps, if very hot, down in the shade of the Royal Portico within the *agora*). So Paul was handed a golden opportunity to put forward his case:

*'People of Athens! I see that in every way you are very religious. For as I walked around and looked carefully at your objects of worship, I even found an altar with this inscription: TO AN UNKNOWN GOD. So you are ignorant of the*

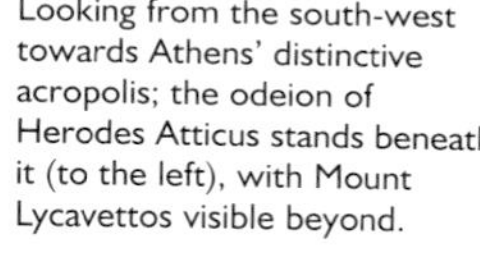

Looking from the south-west towards Athens' distinctive acropolis; the odeion of Herodes Atticus stands beneath it (to the left), with Mount Lycavettos visible beyond.

*very thing you worship – and this is what I am going to proclaim to you.*

*'The God who made the world… is the Lord of heaven and earth and does not live in temples built by hands. And he is not served by human hands… because he himself gives everyone life and breath and everything else. From one man he made all the nations, that they should inhabit the whole earth; and he marked out their appointed times in history and the boundaries of their lands. God did this so that they would seek him and perhaps reach out for him and find him, though he is not far from any one of us. "For in him we live and move and have our being." As some of your own poets have said, "We are his offspring."*

*'Therefore since we are God's offspring, we should not think that the divine being is like gold or silver or stone – an image made by human design and skill. In the past God overlooked such ignorance, but now he commands all people everywhere to repent. For he has set a day when he will judge the world with justice by the man he has appointed. He has given proof of this to everyone by raising him from the dead.'*

**Acts 17:22–31**





## Paul addressing a pagan audience

Even though Paul engaged with pagan crowds most days of his life, this Areopagus speech is all that has come down to us in the New Testament that can give us any insight into his preferred topics when speaking to pagan crowds.

We note first how he tried to find a local point of connection with his audience – hence his reference to an altar he had seen in the city dedicated 'to an unknown god'. Drawing on this part of their local culture, he could build on the religious longing that this altar's inscription evoked. Even if some in his audience might have had an outlook on life that was more 'philosophical' than 'religious', Paul wanted to anchor his message by appealing to this innate religious instinct within humankind.

*'For in him we live and move and have our being.'*

**Poem attributed to Epimenides the Cretan (only preserved now in a Syriac version)**

It was a useful strategy, because it allowed him to open up the theme of how God had made himself 'known'. In other words, the message about Jesus was rooted in an understanding of 'revelation' – that is, God's ability to reveal himself to humankind. This was the deep presumption of his biblical faith – that Israel had not invented her God in her own image, but rather had been the (often unwilling and always undeserved) recipient of God's own revealing actions and words.

*'We are his offspring.'*

***Natural Phenomena*, by Paul's fellow-Cilician, Aratus**

## The hidden biblical story

What he then unpacked was the major framework of that biblical faith in its three main stages (relating to the past, present and future): namely, God as *Creator*, *Sustainer* and *Judge*. First, God *created* 'the world and everything in it'. This included human beings whom God created 'from one man' (Adam) – that is, as equals (the Athenians were no better than others simply because they lived in the centre of the classical world). In speaking of this Creator God Paul was also implicitly ruling out the idea (quite common in Hellenistic thought) that there was perhaps a 'second god' (or *Demiurge*), who was responsible for creation (because the 'primary god' was too holy to be involved with physical matter).

Next, God was the *sustainer* of this world, giving all people 'life and breath', determining where the different nations should live. And, as such, this God, though he accepted human worship, did not lack anything in himself; no, he was utterly transcendent and above humankind. Even so, he was not remote. Subtly quoting from two authors from his own acquaintance with classical literature, Paul argued that the true God was 'not far from each one of us'. Building on these quotations he then launched his critique of pagan idolatry. For, if God can live *within* human beings (and they are in some sense God's 'offspring'), then it follows that God himself cannot be *less* then human. Pagan idols, however, made from materials such as 'silver or stone', are the objects of human craftsmanship – they *are* so much less than human. Such idol worship reflects a profound 'ignorance' of the true God.

Then Paul moves in for the jugular: 'But now God commands all people everywhere to repent.' Idolatry, though born of ignorance, requires repentance. *Judgment* (the third key building-block in biblical thought) will therefore be a reality in the future. And the sure sign of this is *hee anastasis* (Jesus' resurrection). Paul saw Jesus' resurrection as the clear sign that the living God was powerfully at work in the world and that he was putting that world 'on notice' concerning the reality of future judgment. The one thus raised from the dead by God was thereby appointed by God to 'judge the world with justice'.

## Noting Paul's strategy

*'My purpose was... simply "to give the general sense of what was said"'*

**Thucydides, *History* 1.22.1**

The original speech presumably went on for around fifteen minutes or so. (In giving us what is only a skeleton outline, Luke here is following in the footsteps of Athens' own great historian, Thucydides.) Yet it is amazing how much this densely packed summary reflects the deep contours of Paul's thought.

The deeply biblical nature of Paul's speech is particularly intriguing – even though with this pagan audience he does not use the Hebrew Scriptures as an agreed authoritative source. Thus, behind Paul's presentation of God we see the clear influence of passages such as Genesis 1–2 (God as universal Creator); Deuteronomy 32:8 (God's allocation of nations to their lands); Psalm 98 (God's righteous judgment of the world) and Daniel 7:13–14 (the 'son of man' appointed by God to have authority over the nations). The Athenians are being introduced to the God revealed in the Hebrew Scriptures – yet without those Scriptures being quoted even once!

*'Paul upstages the claims and systems of paganism in the name, and for the glory, of the one God of Israel, the God now revealed through Jesus and the Spirit.'*

**N.T. Wright**

Evidently then, Paul, though now a Christian, had not departed from the basic Jewish substructures of his thought. If he had been making this speech in his pre-Christian days, he would have started with all the same points: Israel's creational monotheism stood radically opposed to pagan idolatry. What was new, however, was that Israel's God had now brought further definitive revelation into the world (in Jesus), which meant that previous ignorance was now inexcusable. The idea, for example, that God actually *lived* in human-made temples (Acts 17:24) could now be seen as doubly ludicrous – because he had just entered the world *in human form*. Paul is countering paganism with the truth of the God of Israel – but now as revealed *through* and *in* Jesus.

Seen like this, there is little doubt that Luke has accurately given the gist of what Paul would have said in such a situation. Indeed there are some striking parallels with what Paul himself will say in the opening chapters of Romans, as he prepares people to understand the good news: human idolatry is inexcusable in the face of God the Creator;

## Key dates: Athens

|  |  |
|---|---|
| 1100s BC | Athens emerges unscathed from the Dorian invasions in the north. |
| c. 594 BC | Solon appointed as ruler (*archon*) of the city-state of Athens. |
| 493 BC | Themistocles builds a fleet of 200 ships and fortifies the Piraeus harbour. |
| 490 BC | Athenians under Themistocles defeat Darius the Persian at Marathon (recounted by Herodotus in *History* Book 6). |
| 480 BC | Athenians defeat Darius' son, Xerxes, at the sea battle of Salamis (recounted by Herodotus in *History* Book 8); the start of Athens' 'Golden Age'. |
| 461–429 BC | Rule of Pericles, who commissions the building of the Parthenon on the Acropolis, the rebuilding of Athens' harbour, Piraeus, and the construction of the Long Walls (linking Athens to Piraeus). |
| 449–440 BC | Building of Temple to Hephaestus. |
| 431–404 BC | Athens eventually defeated by Sparta (recounted by Thucydides in his *History of the Peloponnesian War*). |
| 399 BC | Death of Socrates. His pupil, Plato (427–347 BC), writes philosophical works, followed later by Aristotle (384–322 BC). |
| 338 BC | Philip II of Macedon defeats Athenians at Chaeronea. |
| 168 BC | Athens backs Rome against Macedonia. |
| c. 150 BC | Attalus II of Pergamum, grateful for his earlier Athenian education, commissions the *stoa* in the *agora*. |
| 88 BC | Athens joins Mithridates VI of Pontus in an unsuccessful revolt against Rome. |
| 86 BC | The Roman general, Sulla, quashes the revolt, destroying Athens' Long Walls. |
| 15 BC | Marcus Agrippa (Augustus' son-in-law) commissions the Odeion in the centre of the *agora*. |
| AD 50 | Paul stays in Athens for several months (Acts 17:16–34). |
| AD 131-32 | Hadrian commissions the Temple of Olympian Zeus, placing his own statue beside that of Zeus. |
| AD 159 | Pausanias describes Athens in his *Description of Greece* (Book 1). |
| AD 161 | Herodes Atticus commissions the Odeion to the south-west of the Acropolis. |
| c. AD 170 | Marcus Aurelius endows four chairs of philosophy within the university of Athens. |
| AD 267 | Athens sacked by a Gothic invasion. |
| AD 500s | Justinian closes Athens' philosophical school and converts the Parthenon into a church (dedicated to Mary). |
| AD 584 | Athens ransacked by Slavs. |
| 1687 | During a siege, a Venetian cannonball hits the Parthenon (being used as a gunpowder store by the Turks). |
| 1821 | Athens becomes the capital of the independent Greek nation. |



God will judge human secrets, but now this God, who has passed over former sins in his forbearance, has done a new thing in Jesus to which all people everywhere can and must respond (Romans 1:19–21; 2:16; 3:21–24). What we see in Acts 17 is essentially the same – but cast for an entirely Gentile audience and without any explicit use of the Scriptures.

## The challenge of the resurrection

There is one thing, however, that Paul does not expressly mention: the cross. Probably this was because *both* the cross and the resurrection were potentially awkward ideas to convey to a cynical audience and he therefore had to focus on one, not both. In this light, the resurrection was the obvious choice – since the cross without the resurrection made little sense. If so, Paul was not intending to minimize the cross, but was simply making a strategic choice about how much his hearers could absorb in one sitting.

This may be confirmed by noting how Paul's speech comes to an end at precisely the moment when he mentions the resurrection. For, evidently, this concept of 'Anastasis' caused some confusion or even hilarity – such that Paul may well have been interrupted: 'When they heard about the resurrection of the dead, some of them sneered' (Acts 17:32). Were they still thinking of 'Anastasis' as a female goddess? Or did they simply judge this

## Visiting modern Greece

The modern nation of Greece contains a whole range of sites that testify to the vibrancy of its classical civilization (in addition to the sites discussed in Chapters 7 to 9).

Corinth is the gateway into the **Peloponnese**. From here it is not far to **Argos**, **Mycenae** and **Tiryns**, each dating back to the era of the Trojan War (c. 1200 BC). This was the world inhabited by characters such as Agamemnon, Electra and Orestes, known to us through the writings of Homer and tragedy writers such as Aeschylus and Euripides. Nearby too is the Venetian-influenced harbour of **Nauplion** and then **Epidaurus**, with its large theatre, still used regularly for summer performances and concerts.

**Sparta** was Athens' fierce enemy in the Peloponnesian War, famous for its military discipline. Moving westwards, as you begin to cross over the forbidding Mount Taigetus range, there is the deserted Byzantine hill-side town of **Mistras**. The western side of the Peloponnese hosts the site of ancient **Pylos** and, of course, the original 'Olympic stadium' at **Olympia**.

Returning towards Athens and crossing over the Corinthian Gulf by ferry you come to Greece's premier ancient site: **Delphi**, the location of the famous oracle. Perched in a beautiful niche among the mountains, the site still has an enthralling charm. Going up past various shrines and temples, you eventually reach the stadium, where there are stunning views across the valley.

Those interested in Byzantine culture will find other sites compelling: the beautiful **monastery of Hosios Loukas** (on the road returning from Delphi to Athens); the phenomenal rock formations of the **Meteora** (in central Greece) with their remote monasteries perched tantalizingly on the top; and the monastic beauty of **Mount Athos** (on the easternmost 'finger' of the Halkidiki peninsula in the northern Aegean), with its numerous **monasteries**. Its famous policy of only allowing men onto the peninsula is, of course, not popular with all, but those who do have the opportunity to spend a few nights there can find a unique experience, surrounded by beautiful countryside and the powerful history and faith of Greek Orthodoxy.

The sanctuary of Athena Pronaia (or '*tholos*') in the valley beneath Delphi's main sanctuary buildings.

LEFT: One of the Byzantine monasteries perched precariously on the distinctive rock-formations (the 'Meteora') above Kalambaka in central Greece.

BELOW: The monastery of Hosios Loukas.

*'When the dust has soaked up a man's blood, once he is dead, there is no resurrection'*

**Aeschylus, *Eumenides*, 647–48**

whole concept of anyone experiencing a physical resurrection after death to be ludicrous? Ever since the days of Aeschylus (writing a play, ironically, which was concerned with the establishment of this same Areopagus court), it had been a common place in Greek thought that there was 'no resurrection', no returning after death to physical life. Only some far away Jews (and indeed only those belonging to one of their strange sects, the Pharisees) entertained this absurd idea as a possibility. 'Immortality of the soul' would have been acceptable, but 'resurrection' was simply ridiculous and out of the question.





## Paul takes his leave

So Paul's brief opening into the heart of classical culture comes to a close. Some of his hearers want to hear more, and there are one or two listeners who show signs of positive faith (Acts 17:32–34); but the door for effective ministry, he judges, has shut.

Paul now decides to move on. This decision to relocate may have been influenced too by some other, quite practical, considerations. Paul had arrived on his own, but had immediately sent word back that Silas and Timothy should join him from Berea as soon as possible (Acts 17:15). They would have arrived perhaps six weeks later. Even then, however, Paul was still exceedingly anxious about the believers in Thessalonica whom they had left so suddenly (see p. 99). So he decided to send Timothy all the way back up to Thessalonica. This meant Paul continued to be in Athens but in a state of high anxiety. Writing later from Corinth, Paul describes this inner turmoil which had beset him in Athens in these words:

*Brothers and sisters, when we were torn away from you for a short time, out of our intense longing we made every effort to see you. For we wanted to come to you – certainly I, Paul, did, again and again... So when we could stand it no longer, we thought it best to be left by ourselves in Athens. We sent Timothy... to encourage you in your faith... When I could stand it no longer, I sent Timothy to find out about your faith. I was afraid that in some way the tempter might have tempted you and our efforts might have been useless...*

**1 Thessalonians 2:17–18; 3:1–5**

From this we realize that much of Paul's time in Athens was marked by this acute anguish over the situation back in Thessalonica. Thus his spirit was distressed not just by the idolatrous nature of Athens and the enormity of the task facing an 'apostle' like him. He was also 'cut up' inside by sheer worry about whether his earlier labours in Thessalonica had all been in vain.

We should not underestimate the power of this kind of mental pressure. When listing the many physical dangers he had endured, he capped the entire list by saying: 'Besides everything else, I face *daily* the *pressure* of my concern for all the churches' (2 Corinthians 11:28). An itinerant preacher like Paul would find, in the days before telecommunication, that many months went by anxiously waiting for news. And it took its toll.

So before Timothy left for Thessalonica, Paul and Silas had to make a decision about a future rendezvous point: when should the three of them meet again? It was decided they should leave Athens and aim for Corinth. And in due course Paul and Silas would head out on the road leading south-westwards, with Athens' proud Acropolis gradually fading into the distance behind them. Perhaps instinctively they knew they might never be visiting this famous city again.

# Athens today

Athens, the capital of modern Greece, is a vast city (population around 5 million). Its harbour, the Piraeus, is a major international port. Until recently, the best time to see Athens was on a spring day just after some rain, when the normally polluted air was clear. However, with tighter traffic controls (and the transport investment in hosting the Olympic Games in 2004), this is beginning to be a thing of the past.

## Buildings on the Acropolis

Athens' **Acropolis** is a very striking natural phenomenon – a massive rock rising up with sheer cliffs from the surrounding plains. It dominates any skyline. As an impregnable fortress, located just 7 miles (11 km) inland from the Aegean Sea, it was a natural place for an ancient city to be formed. Visitors like Paul (and the geographer Pausanias who describes his visit a hundred years later), having docked at Piraeus, would set their sights on the Acropolis, following a road surrounded by the rubble of the ancient Long Walls that once had securely linked the city to its harbour.

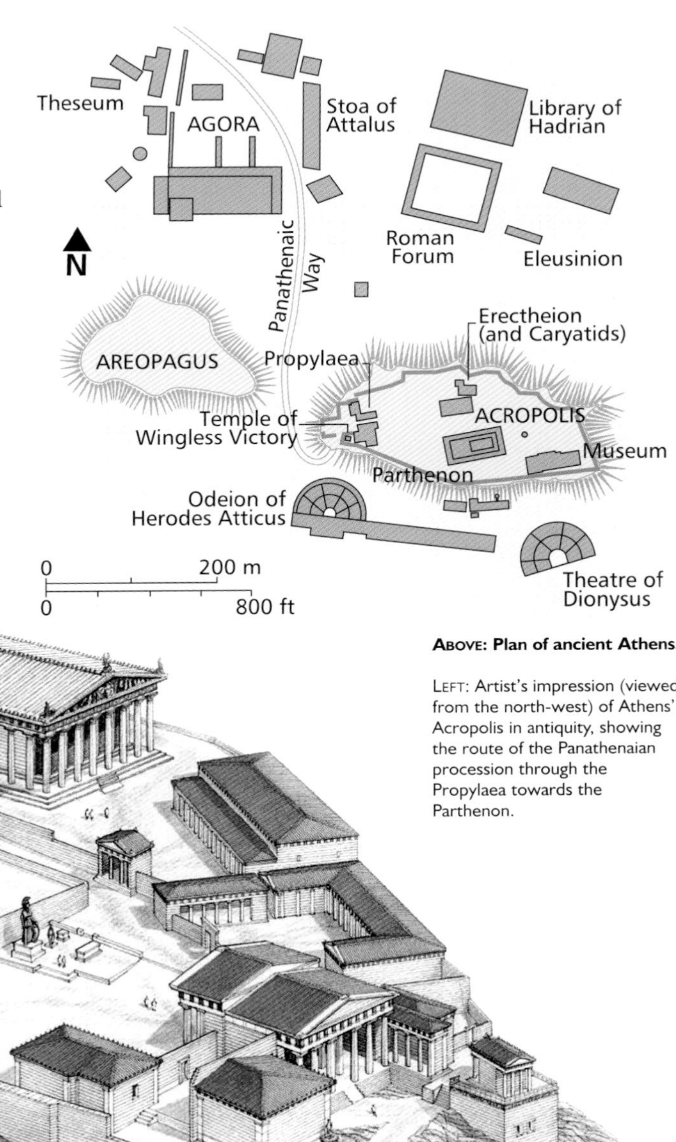


**Above: Plan of ancient Athens.**

Left: Artist's impression (viewed from the north-west) of Athens' Acropolis in antiquity, showing the route of the Panathenaian procession through the Propylaea towards the Parthenon.

We are not told expressly whether Paul went up onto the **Acropolis** – conceivably he chose not to, given its focus on pagan worship – but it is a 'must' for any modern-day visitor with the energy to climb the steps leading up to its western entrance. As you approach, there is on your right the small (reconstructed) **temple of 'wingless victory'** (or Nike); a little further, on your left, is a monument in honour of Agrippa. Then, after a final zigzag incline, you pass at last through the central aisle of the main entrance way (or **Propylaea**). You are walking along the route followed by every ancient visitor to the Acropolis, as well as the route of the famous four-yearly Athenian festival known as the 'Panathenaia'. And in front of you is Athens' gem, which dominates its skyline from every angle – the Parthenon.

The **Parthenon** (which in Greek is a title for the virgin goddess, Athena) is widely heralded as the epitome of ancient classical architecture. Surrounded by Doric columns (eight at the ends, seventeen along the sides), it exhibits incredible scientific skill – both in the solidity of its construction and in its awareness of the need to make various optical adjustments. So the vertical columns appear straight but actually bulge in the middle by a few inches and then taper towards the top, where the diameter is 17 inches (43 cm) less than at the bottom. And the figures on the frieze are similarly distorted to make them appear life-like to the viewer on the ground.

It takes an effort to imagine how it would have looked in Paul's day. For, although most of it was constructed from white marble (brought from the nearby Pentelic hills to the east), much of this would have been painted in a variety of strong colours.

The Parthenon, built in honour of Athena in the mid-fifth-century BC, which stood intact for over 2,000 years (until the Venetian siege of 1687).

Meanwhile there would have been statues in its pediment and carvings in all its 'metopes' (the square gaps between the so-called 'triglyphs'). There would also have been a continuous, 525-foot- (160-m) long frieze, going round all four sides and depicting the Panathenaic procession. Many of these are the so-called **'Elgin Marbles'** (taken in the 1820s by Lord Elgin and now preserved in London's British Museum), but some are to be seen in the **Acropolis Museum** (just beyond the Parthenon). Finally, within the shrine itself there would have been a vast, 40-foot- (12-m) high, statue of Athena, with ivory features and clad with nearly 250 lbs (115 kg) of gold plate. The Parthenon, the glory of Athens' 'golden era' in classical antiquity, would have been a truly impressive sight.

To the north of the Parthenon is the **Erectheion** (named after a legendary 'god-king' in Athens' past, Erectheus). This small temple with its Ionic columns and graceful figures plays quite a contrast to the Doric strength of the Parthenon. Some see this contrast in expressly masculine/feminine terms – helped by the fact that the temple's southern columns have been replaced by the famous 'Caryatids' (six sculptured female figures). The temple preserved the memory of earlier Athenian cults – an old wooden idol of Athena, a rock struck by Zeus' thunderbolt, and the olive tree which Athena had supposedly produced in her contest with Poseidon to gain possession of Athens' surrounding territory, Attica.

Before descending carefully it is worth pausing to enjoy the many views: to the north-east lies another strange hill, the almost triangular **Mount Lycavettos**, where the Greek Orthodox hold an Easter midnight vigil – the candles on Lycavettos are lit from the 'holy fire' flown in from the Holy Sepulchre in Jerusalem. To the south-east lie the immense **Temple of Olympian Zeus** with its Corinthian columns (rebuilt by Hadrian in AD 131–32) and the **stadium** of the 1896 Olympic Games.

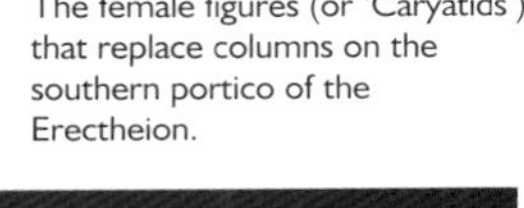

The female figures (or 'Caryatids') that replace columns on the southern portico of the Erectheion.

## Below the Acropolis: in the *agora*

Round to the south, immediately below the Acropolis, are Athens' ancient theatres. The later one, to the right, is the **Odeion of Herodes Atticus**. The original Greek one, some 250 yards (230 m) further to the left, is the **Theatre of Dionysus**, and is more difficult to see from on the Acropolis. It is well worth a separate visit, however – to see the very place where the plays of Aeschylus, Sophocles, Euripides and Aristophanes were first performed 500 years before Christ. The semi-circular 'orchestra' would originally have had no 'backdrop' stage (the *proscenium* here dates from the third century AD), but we can still

imagine the first rendition of these classical works, performed before crowds of over 15,000 and presided over by the priest of Dionysus (whose marble chair can still be identified).

Meanwhile, towards the north-west of the Acropolis there are good views over Athens' **ancient *agora***. This large area (some 25 acres or 10 hectares) was the central heart of the ancient city. Luke says that Paul was here 'in the market-place day by day' (Acts 17:17). The **Stoa of Attalus** (nicely reconstructed in 1953 and which also houses the **Agora Museum**) indicates how the many surrounding porticoes would have looked. The museum contains a fine selection of ancient finds – including the small *ostraka* (or potsherds) on which people scratched the names of any citizen to be 'ostracized' from the assembly for ten years. Democracy, clearly, had its limits.

On the opposite (west) side of the *agora* lies the distinctive **Theseum** (or temple to Hephaestus). Converted later into a Christian church (in the fifth century AD), it has been preserved in a remarkable condition. So, although it is eclipsed by the Parthenon in terms of finesse, it remains one of the finest extant examples of a *complete* classical temple. Built to honour Hephaestus and Athena (the gods respectively associated with metal-working and the arts), it would originally have had a wooden roof.

View from the Acropolis towards Mount Lycavettos.

From its entrance there are good views looking back over the *agora*: to the left the remains of various *stoas* (the **Painted Stoa**, associated with Zeno the 'Stoic', the **Royal Stoa**, where Socrates may have been tried and sentenced to death, and the **Stoa of Zeus**); to the right, the **Metroon** (where the state archives were kept), the **Bouleuterion** (a council chamber, shaped like a small theatre, to house the city's 500-strong 'parliament') and the circular **Tholos** (where leaders of Athens' ten tribes were housed on duty for a month in order to deal with civic affairs).

Through the middle of the *agora* (from the north-west corner in the direction of the Acropolis) ran the Panathenaic Way, associated with the four-yearly procession to the Acropolis. The centre of the *agora* had been a wide-open space, but two buildings went up in the hundred years before Paul's arrival: the **Temple of Ares** and the large **Odeion**, built by Marcus Agrippa. Paul would have passed these buildings, as well as presumably going on to the **Roman forum** (to the east of the ancient *agora*), which was famous for its markets, especially in oil products. Other buildings of interest in this area include the later **library of Hadrian** and the still-standing **Temple of the Winds** (a fascinating water-clock dating back to the first century BC).

There is so much else to see in Athens: the remains of the **gates and walls** (about 400 yards or 365 m north-west of the Theseum); the **potters' quarter** (hence known as the *Kerameikos*), which also contained a cemetery area with many fine funeral monuments visible in the so-called Street of the Tombs; and the **Byzantine Museum** and the **National Archaeology Museum**.

View westwards across the ancient *agora* towards the Theseum.

## The Areopagus

For those in the steps of Paul, however, the enduring memory of Athens must be the **Areopagus Hill**, which lies below the Acropolis to the west and itself overlooks the *agora* from the south. A very rough outcrop of limestone rock, this was the traditional location for the meeting of the Areopagite council. This senior body, however, had lost many of its powers in the democratic reforms of the fifth century BC. Though slightly re-established in Roman times, its functions remained somewhat limited – though it was able to hold murder trials (the two stones on which the judge and accused were seated can still be seen). We cannot be sure whether Paul addressed an actual session of this council meeting (which sometimes, confusingly, now met in the Royal Stoa) or instead was simply invited to come onto this hill as a convenient place for people to discuss his ideas. Quite possible it was the latter.

At the foot of the pathway leading up to the Areopagus is a bronze plaque that commemorates Paul's speech. Given the unevenness of the steps, many choose this more convenient location to remember Luke's story. Looking up at the glories of the Acropolis, one is made aware how solitary, and even stupid, Paul might have felt: one man announcing, in the centre of classical civilization, the news of something remarkable done by Israel's God in far-off Jerusalem. Paul's few words would play their part, as the centuries unfolded, in establishing the Christian message in the very heart of Athens. The classical world and the Christian church were being engaged in an age-long tussle, one fruit of which would include the great era of Greek Byzantium.

9

CHAPTER

# Corinth

*After this, Paul left Athens and went to Corinth… When Silas and Timothy came from Macedonia, Paul devoted himself exclusively to preaching… but when the Jews opposed Paul and became abusive, he left the synagogue and went next door to the house of Titius Justus, a worshipper of God… and many of the Corinthians believed and were baptized. Paul stayed for a year and a half, teaching them the word of God.*

*While Gallio was proconsul of Achaia, the Jews made a united attack on Paul and brought him into court… [But Gallio] had them ejected from the court…*

*Paul stayed on in Corinth for some time. Then he left the brothers and sailed for Syria… He had his hair cut off at Cenchrea because of a vow he had taken.*

**Acts 18:1, 5–8, 11–12, 16, 18**

## A cosmopolitan city

It had been an arduous few months for Paul. 'Hounded out' from three successive towns in Macedonia, then left isolated for some time in Athens, it comes as no surprise that Paul arrived in Corinth at a low ebb: 'I came to you in weakness and fear, and with much trembling' (1 Corinthians 2:3). As he travelled southwards towards this large city, the capital of the Roman province of Achaia, would he be treated in the same harsh way as in Thessalonica, the capital of Macedonia?

### A surprising scene of ministry

Corinth's reputation was certainly enough to cause this Jewish apostle of Jesus some hesitation. Since classical times people had coined the verb 'to Corinthianize' as a way of referring to fornication – such was the city's reputation for sexual immorality. So, as Paul approached the city, he would have seen the massive form of 'Acro-Corinth', rising up over 1,800 feet (550 m) above the surrounding plain, and would probably have known that this was the location for the temple dedicated to Aphrodite, famous for its cult prostitution. Although there were a good number of Jews already in the city, Corinth's lifestyle would have epitomized for the average Jew the sheer decadence of classical culture. Now here came Paul, a former strict Pharisaic rabbi, making his way into the city. It says much for the man and his message that he was even here at all.

Yet Paul's visit to Corinth would prove to be one of his most fruitful. He would stay for around eighteen months – far longer than he had stayed in any one place since leaving Antioch. And some four years later he would spend a further three months here. In the intervening period he would be in frequent correspondence with the young church, sorting out some of its many problems; yet when he left Corinth for the last time, he probably left behind a growing church made up of several hundred believers.

Behind all this, Paul would have asserted, was the hand of God. As he told the Corinthians, it was God alone who 'makes things grow' (1 Corinthians 3:7); and, back near the beginning of his stay, he had received in a vision a promise from God: 'Do not be afraid… because I have many people in this city' (Acts 18:9–10). Paul discovered that, though Corinth had not been part of his own original plans, it was clearly part of God's. And though Paul's involvement in Corinth was often difficult, this would only serve to develop his pastoral sympathy and theological acumen. As Professor of Divinity C. K. Barrett puts it: 'Paul, who learnt at Corinth what it is to be weak in Christ, shows there perhaps more clearly than elsewhere his full stature of Christian intelligence, firmness and magnanimity.'

The seven Doric columns of Corinth's ancient Greek temple of Apollo, set against the backdrop of the Acro-Corinth massif.

## City of mobility

Corinth occupied a unique geographical location by the narrow isthmus that formed the only connection between mainland Greece and the Peloponnese to the south. It thus sat astride both this key land-route (north-south) as well as the sea-route (east–west) – for those who wished to use its harbours rather than sail round the (often treacherous) shores of the Peloponnese. Corinth had one harbour (Cenchrea) facing eastwards onto the Aegean and the Saronic Gulf, and another (Lechaion) to the west of the isthmus facing onto the Corinthian Gulf. There was also a narrow road, which crossed the isthmus itself at its narrowest point (about 3½ miles or 6 km): constructed from wooden logs, this unusual road (known as the *diolkos*) could be used for dragging smaller boats across from one sea to the other.

Given this position, Corinth was a centre of thriving commerce. It also played host to the Isthmian Games, held every two years in honour of the god Poseidon. Back in 146 BC, however, the city had been destroyed by the Romans for its part in a revolt, leaving little standing apart from the Doric Temple of Apollo. Then in 44 BC Julius Caesar refounded it as a Roman colony for his army veterans, who automatically became Roman citizens. Its expansion was so swift that within twenty years it had overtaken Athens as the provincial capital.

So, when Paul arrived nearly one hundred years later, it was a multicultural city. With only a recent history (unlike Athens), it was not looking back nostalgically to the past, but pressing on to the future. This was a place for the *nouveau riche*, a place scarcely restrained by tradition – a city full of energy, vigour and life. Into this volatile mix, like a swirling sea, was placed Paul's message about new resurrection-life in Christ and freedom through experiencing God's Spirit. Would this novel 'experiment' work in such an environment? Or would it soon get dashed against the rocks, buffeted endlessly by the waves of Corinthian restlessness and ambition?

## Paul sets to work

Paul's letters, focusing on the 'inside story', reveal that launching the Corinthian church was indeed far from 'plain sailing'. Luke's account in Acts 18, however, naturally focuses more on the external aspects, describing how the church was started and its relationships with the synagogue and the local authorities.

First Luke refers to a married couple, called Aquila and Priscilla, with whom Paul stayed. Aquila himself was a Jew from Pontus (on the Black Sea); presumably his wife too was Jewish, though she may have been connected with the *gens Prisca*, one of the ancient families within Rome. They had been living in Rome (Acts 18:2), and were probably already believers – a sign of how quickly the Christian message was spreading across the empire. They were clearly very mobile – probably because of their trade as 'tent-makers' (though Luke's term may also include those who worked in leather). Since this was Paul's own profession, he 'stayed and worked with them'.

We see here how Paul always tried to earn his own keep, rather than becoming dependent on his converts for financial support (1 Corinthians 9:18; Acts 20:34). His chief speaking opportunities only came on Saturdays when he visited the synagogue

ABOVE: The modern canal (built in 1882–93) joins the Aegean Sea to the Corinthian Gulf. Though only 3.5 miles (5.5 km) long, it saves a sea journey round the Peloponnese of over 200 miles (320 km). Several ancient rulers thought seriously about building such a canal, but it proved impossible before the invention of dynamite. So the ancient alternative was the *diolkos*, a paved road (BELOW) along which small boats could be hauled on a wheeled platform.

**LEFT: Map of Corinth's ports and the isthmus.**

## Key dates: Corinth

|  |  |
|---|---|
| 600s BC | Building of *diolkos* across isthmus by Periander. |
| 550 BC | Building of Temple of Apollo. |
| 480–350 BC | Corinth becomes famous for its pottery and 'Corinthian' capitals (with their floral motifs). |
| c. 400 BC | 'Corinthianize' is coined as a word, referring to the city's immorality. |
| 338 BC | Philip of Macedon establishes the city as the centre of the 'League of Corinth'. |
| 146 BC | The Romans, under Lucius Mummius, raze the city to the ground. |
| 44 BC | Arrival of new colonists in Corinth, sent by Julius Caesar; Caesar's plans to dig a canal are aborted. |
| 27 BC | Corinth becomes the capital of the Roman province of Achaia, the seat of its proconsul. |
| c. 30 BC | Probably misunderstanding a passage in Herodotus, Strabo refers to the Temple of Aphrodite (on Acro-Corinth) having 1,000 priestess-prostitutes (*Geography* 8.6.20). |
| c. AD 40 | Emperor Caligula considers building a canal, but is deterred by Egyptian site-engineers who fear flooding due to the difference in the two sea levels. |
| c. AD 50–52 | Paul spends eighteen months in Corinth. Lucius Junius Gallio (younger brother of Seneca, the Stoic philosopher, tutoring Nero in Rome) is proconsul of Achaia for twelve months from 1 July, AD 51. |
| AD 57 (early) | After one or two brief return visits, Paul returns to Corinth for three months (January through March?), during which he writes Romans. |
| AD 67 | Emperor Nero himself breaks ground for a canal; Vespasian sends over 6,000 Jewish captives from Galilee to help, but the project is abandoned on Nero's death (AD 68). |
| AD 96 | Clement of Rome writes a long letter (1 Clement) to the Corinthian church, appealing for unity after the expulsion of some of the church's leaders. |
| c. AD 170 | Bishop Dionysus of Corinth says that Paul's letters to the Corinthians are still read in the local church each Sunday (Eusebius, *Ecclesiastical History* 2.25.8). |
| AD 521 | City destroyed by Goths, with some subsequent restoration by Emperor Justinian. |
| 1882–93 | Digging of modern isthmus canal. |
| 1896 | Archaeological excavations in ancient Corinth. |
| 1961–63 | Excavations of *diolkos*. |

(though presumably he was not silent when talking to customers at the front of his shop!). This weekly pattern changed, however, when Silas and Timothy finally arrived; Paul could now devote himself 'exclusively to preaching' (Acts 18:5) – quite probably because the Thessalonians had sent Paul a financial gift (2 Corinthians 11:9).

Once again Paul's preaching led to some divisive results. On the one hand there were some converts: the synagogue's ruler, Crispus, and a 'worshipper of God' (or 'God-fearer') called Gaius Titius Justus (whom Paul simply calls 'Gaius': Romans 16:23). These two, together with Stephanas, were the only people whom Paul himself baptized (1 Corinthians 1:14–16); perhaps this task was delegated to Silas and Timothy. On the other hand, the synagogue gradually became a hostile environment; so Paul set up a rival meeting-place in the home of Titius Justus (provocatively, right next door!). In due course, the synagogue members brought Paul before Gallio the proconsul, accusing him of encouraging people to 'worship God in ways contrary to the law' (Acts 18:12–13).

## Before the Roman tribunal

The phrasing seems deliberately ambiguous, immediately raising the key question: *which* law – Roman law or Jewish Torah? Presumably they wanted the proconsul to declare this new Christian message to be contrary to *Roman* law; and also to note that it was recognizably distinct from Judaism, which had been granted the status of a 'permitted religion' (*religio licita*). This would be a key dispute in the coming decades as the Romans became aware that a new 'sub-version' of Judaism had appeared: should such Christians be allowed (as was their parent-body, Judaism) to be absolved from emperor worship? Or, if they refused to worship the emperor, were they committing a Roman crime?

Gallio quickly saw, however, that the issues were bound up, not with Roman law, but simply with *Jewish* law. It was not about 'some misdemeanour or serious crime' (that is, against Roman law), but was rather just a matter of 'words and names and your *own* law' (Acts 18:14–15). Gallio recognized that nothing of criminal import was involved and immediately dismissed the case.

No doubt Paul was mightily relieved at this judgement – it meant his preaching work could carry on unabated. And Luke, with hindsight, saw it as very significant too. This was a ruling, not from a merely local official (as in Macedonia), but from a proconsul. It also set an important precedent in Roman law, which might prove useful in the future: according to Gallio, Christianity was not criminal; and, from a Roman perspective, it legitimately came under the umbrella of Judaism.



## Paul's ongoing work after his departure

Eventually Paul decided to move on. Going down to Corinth's eastern harbour (Cenchrea) he set sail for Ephesus, bound eventually for 'Syria'. Intriguingly at Cenchrea Paul had his hair cut 'because of a vow'. This sounds like a Jewish 'Nazirite' vow – perhaps made by Paul as a mark of thanks to God for fulfilling his promise to protect him in Corinth (Acts 18:9–10). If so, he may well have been heading not just for 'Syria' but also more specifically to Jerusalem, where he could complete the final requirements of this vow in Jerusalem's Temple. Even in Corinth, Paul was conscious of his Jewish roots and his links with Jerusalem.

No doubt Paul intended to come back to Corinth in due course. Yet he had long been interested in establishing a church in Ephesus and, when he left Aquila and Priscilla there in Ephesus, he expressly promised to return (Acts 18:21). This he did later that year (AD 52). So Paul's next dealings with Corinth were from Ephesus.

The communication lines between Paul in Ephesus and the church in Corinth seem to have been kept quite busy (during the sailing season, messengers could cross over the Aegean within three or four days). Paul needed to concentrate on his work in Ephesus, but he was still the apostle and pastor *in absentia* for the volatile church in

The *bema* (or tribunal) on the south side of the *agora*, where Paul was brought before proconsul Gallio.

Corinth. So he wrote several letters (some scholars suggest up to five: see p. 12); he also made at least one quick return visit. What was going on in the Corinthian church that demanded all this attention?

Intriguingly during those years after Paul left Corinth we know of several events in the city's life that will have caused problems for the new believers: the special provision of 'kosher' food for the Jewish community was discontinued (meaning that all meat had the potential of having been sacrificed on pagan altars); and there were some major food shortages, giving the Corinthians a real sense of looming crisis. So Paul had to give some new, further teaching to guide the young church (1 Corinthians 7–10).

Yet there were also other issues that needed urgent attention: some factionalism in the church, triggered by the arrival of another, gifted preacher called Apollos (1 Corinthians 1–3); and some confusion about marriage, 'spiritual gifts' and even about the physical resurrection of Jesus (1 Corinthians 7:12–14; 15). Moreover there was some unruly behaviour in their worship (1 Corinthians 10–11) and some

## Later news from Corinth

Discovering what happened in Paul's churches after he had left is often hard for us to determine at this distance in time. With Corinth, however, we are fortunate to have the text of a long letter sent to the Corinthian Christians around AD 96 by a man called Clement in Rome. Clement is regularly listed as the fourth 'bishop' of Rome (see, for example, Irenaeus, *Heresies* 3.3.4), but was also acting as a kind of 'secretary for external affairs' in this instance.

Perhaps not so surprisingly, the issue that now needs addressing 40 years later is one of church order: the Corinthians have dismissed their 'clergy' (referred to variously as 'deacons' and 'presbyters' or 'bishops') and replaced them with others. Clement writes at some considerable length, eventually rebuking them for this lack of discipline, which he sees as the result of envy and jealousy, and commends to them instead the goal of '*homonia*' (harmony):

*We cannot think it right for these men now to be ejected from their ministry, when, after being commissioned by the apostles... with the full consent of the Church, they have since been serving Christ's flock in a humble, peaceable and disinterested way... By all means be pugnacious and hot-headed, but about things that will lead to salvation...*

*Why must there be all this quarrelling and... dissension among you? Have we not all the same God and the same Christ? Is not the same Spirit of grace shed upon us all? Then why are we rending asunder the limbs of Christ and fomenting discord against our own body?*

*Read your letter from the blessed apostle Paul again... How truly the things he said about himself and Cephas and Apollos were inspired by the Spirit! – for even at that time you had been setting up favourites of your own... It is quite unworthy of the Christian training you have had that the loyal and ancient church of Corinth... should now be at odds with its clergy. Even those who do not share our faith have heard this report...*

**1 Clement 44–47**

It is remarkable how this picks up the themes outlined by Paul in 1 Corinthians: the church is Christ's body, so there should be unity among those who confess a Trinitarian faith; and it is a tragedy when those outside the church see Christians falling out with one another. Modern readers will sense on reading this that this has been repeated endlessly through church history, right up to the present day. And it is salutary to note Clement's diagnosis: the poison of envy and jealousy.

Some 80 years later (around AD 170), we hear of a letter going in the reverse direction – from Dionysius, bishop of Corinth, to the church in Rome. Eusebius, being interested in the martyrdoms of Peter and Paul in Rome, quotes from this letter at the point at which Dionysius is drawing attention to the fact that *both* Peter and Paul were involved in the early years of *both* their churches: 'both planted in our Corinth, and likewise taught us; and likewise they taught together in Italy and were martyred on the same occasion' (Eusebius, *Ecclesiastical History* 2.25). Dionysius himself seems to have been a person of some influence, writing letters to various churches (see Eusebius, *Ecclesiastical History* 4.23); regrettably, however, it is hard to discern much about life in the Corinthian church from the few excerpts that have survived.

instances of sexual immorality – in particular a believer was living with his father's wife (1 Corinthians 5–6). Almost certainly this last issue was what provoked the next series of heated exchanges and led to Paul's 'painful visit' (2 Corinthians 2:1). He also sent Timothy and Titus to check out this matter, who brought back some conflicting reports (1 Corinthians 16:10; 2 Corinthians 2:3, 13); and, at a later stage, the Corinthians were probably disturbed by another unhelpful delegation of 'Judaizers' claiming to have come from Jerusalem (2 Corinthians 10–13).



## The cost of ministry



All these things required Paul's urgent attention. The fact that Paul was prepared to go through such heartache might be interpreted by some as a sign of his over-meddling. More truly, however, it reflects an apostolic concern that to condone such compromise would lead to the unravelling of all his work. Sexual immorality, once tolerated in the church, would prove its undoing; so too would any attempt to impose Jewish demands on the new Gentile believers.

Dealing with Corinth's troubles clearly cost Paul heavily at a personal level. To read 2 Corinthians is to sense a man who is emotionally drained. Paul himself, however, would have seen it all as part of his apostolic responsibility not to leave a fledgling church in a vulnerable state. To use his own metaphors, he was not just a midwife, but also a 'mother' and a 'father' (he uses both terms in 1 Thessalonians 2:7, 11); and the Corinthians, partly because of the extraordinary nature of their city, really needed his 'parenting' and guidance.

Paul made his final visit to Corinth in or around January AD 57. He was there for three months, during which time the overt problems in the church were seemingly ironed out and Paul's relationship with the church was restored. This state of comparative peace may have helped him during these months to compose his major piece of theology – his letter to the church in Rome (see pp. 102, 112). Evidently he would have dearly loved to strike westwards and visit Rome, but his next task was to head back to Jerusalem with his collection of money for the saints (Romans 15:25–28). From Romans 16 we learn that the letter was dictated to a man called Tertius and then

View from Acro-Corinth, looking across the site of ancient Corinth towards its northern port, Lechaion, on the Corinthian Gulf.

despatched with a woman named Phoebe who lived in Corinth's port, Cenchrea; he also sends greetings from various believers in Corinth (such as Gaius, Quartus, Lucius, Jason, Sosipater and Erastus) as well as from Timothy, his 'fellow-worker', who had probably just arrived from Ephesus ready to join Paul on the trip to Jerusalem. It was time to leave.

But their long-laid plans got changed once again. Paul and his companions were about to set sail from Cenchrea, when news reached them of a plot against Paul's life on the boat they were about to use (Acts 20:3). They were also carrying a considerable amount of money, carefully collected, which had to be guarded with extreme care. Paul decided they must travel by land, painstakingly retracing their steps clockwise round the Aegean, even if it added several weeks to their journey. So they picked up their bags and walked northwards from Cenchrea across the narrow isthmus.

In some respects Paul may have been glad to turn his back on Corinth; it had certainly been for him a place of tears and stress. But, as he walked northwards, perhaps he remembered his feelings when he had first come south along that same road, not knowing what awaited him in this cosmopolitan city. He had been full of anxiety, resolving to 'know nothing except Jesus Christ and him crucified' (1 Corinthians 2:2). Now, some seven years later, he was taking his leave, but deeply aware of God's faithfulness to him during those intervening years.

And, although Corinth had taught him painfully what it meant to follow a crucified Lord, it had also taken him more deeply into Christ's resurrection-power: 'Jesus was crucified in weakness, yet he lives by God's power; likewise we are weak in him, yet by God's power we will live with him' (2 Corinthians 13:4). Corinth had knocked Paul's ministry into a *cruciform* shape. It was therefore perhaps only fitting that he was leaving Corinth bound, not without a new sense of foreboding, for that place of ultimate death and resurrection – Jerusalem.

## Corinth today

Corinth is a place whose history begins to make sense as soon as you see its geography. The ancient city occupied a unique location. Visitors approaching southwards from Athens first see the grey limestone massif known as 'Acro-Corinth' rising up in the distance beyond the ancient city. Then they cross over the modern isthmus canal, being able to see the sea on both sides and thus appreciate just how narrow this strip of land is at this point. Moreover, the ruins of ancient Corinth are not surrounded by a large urban area (there is only a small village adjacent to the main site), so there is a real opportunity to imagine Corinth as it was in Paul's day.

A good way to appreciate Corinth's location is to go first to the summit of **Acro-Corinth** (1,887 feet or 575 m above sea level). Surrounded today by the crenulated line of some Venetian fortifications, this was the site of the infamous temple to Aphrodite. Strabo claimed it had a thousand female priestess-prostitutes; but apart from a few foundation cuttings, little remains of this temple and archaeologists suggest it was not that large – perhaps just 33 by 52 feet (10 x 15 m). There is still a Hellenistic tower, but otherwise all that can be found here are some buildings from a later period (some mosques, a Frankish fort and a Byzantine cistern). What is impressive about the summit is its spectacular views.

Facing northwards, ancient Corinth is below you; the Corinthian Gulf comes in from your left, until it is blocked by the narrow land-bridge of the isthmus; to your right are the waters of the Aegean. Corinth itself was over a mile (2.5 km) inland, but was served by two ports, the general outlines of which can be seen even at this distance: Lechaion (on the Corinthian Gulf) and Cenchrea (on the Saronic Gulf of the Aegean).

At **Lechaion** excavations have unearthed one of the largest Christian basilicas in Greece (dating to the fifth century AD). At **Cenchrea** there is a small bay with a promontory marked by some ancient harbour foundations, so it can be worth a brief visit later. It is, after all, expressly mentioned as the place from which Paul sailed for Ephesus (Acts 18:18); also as the location of a small church that was home to a certain woman called Phoebe (Romans 16:1). More poignantly still, this was where Paul was about to board ship, headed for Jerusalem, only to discover there was a plot against his life, which forced him to travel instead by land (Acts 20:3). Sitting on the rocks beside this quiet bay, you can imagine the quick, quiet discussions that took place near here as Paul made his rushed, alternative travel arrangements.

The modern road that runs down from Acro-Corinth passes a host of small temples and sanctuaries (to Greek gods and mystery cults) that would have littered the hill-side in Paul's day – the most visible (just below the road) being one dedicated to Demeter.

The various shop-buildings surrounding the Temple of Apollo may have been used for selling meat previously sacrificed in temple rituals.

On approaching the **main site of ancient Corinth**, however, the most visible feature is the **Temple of Apollo**, with its seven Doric columns still standing and supporting the architrave. This is slightly ironic, since Corinth's atmosphere in Paul's day was far more Roman than Greek. In fact, little else survives from the Hellenistic city; this temple, however, though originally built around 550 BC, was restored by the Romans when the city was refounded in 44 BC.

To its north is **a line of shops** that gives a good idea of the many shops that will also be found once within the enclosed archaeological site. Commerce, after all, lay at the very heart of Corinth's existence. Noting the proximity between these particular shops and the ancient temple, we can sense the problems involved in buying meat already offered in pagan religious services: could one in good conscience eat meat that (however perfunctorily) had formed part of an idolatrous act of worship? The meat market and the temple, trade and religion, these were all inextricably intertwined. Sometimes special arrangements were made for *Jewish* residents, but what were *Christians* supposed to do?

The southern end of the Lechaion Road, ending in the steps that lead up to the forum; colonnaded arcades would have lined the street on either side.

Once inside the city, some visitors make straightaway for the southern end of the **Lechaion road**. Certainly great views can be found at this point, giving a good idea of what it would have been like to come up from the port at Lechaion en route for the main forum. This last stretch of the road is 35 feet (10 m) wide, surrounded on both sides by colonnades and shops, and covered with slabs that date back to around the time of Paul. On the right are various buildings (including the **'north basilica'**). The more impressive are on the left: some baths and latrines; then what is known as the **'precinct of Apollo'** (but which in Paul's day may have been the city's main meat-market); and, finally, the beautiful **Fountain of Peirene**, built over a natural spring which can still be found running today.

The Lechaion road comes to an end when it meets several steep steps that form the base of the grand **triumphal arch** (or *propylaea*) that led into the forum; chariots and other goods vehicles had to turn back at this point. The **Roman forum** was thus a large 'pedestrian zone', one of the largest in antiquity – about 600 by 300 feet (180 x 90 m). On the far side was the truly impressive **'southern *stoa*'** (its original dating back to the fourth century BC). Containing over 30 shops at ground level (each with a front and back room), topped by an upper storey, and fronted by 71 Doric columns, it was the longest such colonnaded arcade in the Roman empire. In the years prior to Paul it had been remodelled to cater for a string of **administrative buildings**, some of which can tentatively still be identified: some for officers associated with the Isthmian games; some for the Roman governor or the city's chief officials; and one (with its curved stone benches) that is almost certainly the city's council chamber (or *Bouleuterion*). To the left of centre there was also a marble fountain, behind which lay the large **'south basilica'**, probably used as the city's law courts.

Parallel with this *stoa* (indeed running through the very middle of the forum) was a further line of shops. In the centre of these was the tribunal (or *bema*), an elaborate raised platform where the proconsul would hear important civic cases. Almost certainly this is where Paul appeared before Gallio (Acts 18:12–17). Later Christians believed this to be the case, building a small tri-apsidal church over a rectangular stone in the ground in front of the *bema* – the place where the defendant would stand when on trial. Quite probably this is indeed where Paul stood. Intriguingly, almost exactly behind him there would have been an elaborate two-storey façade, which had some statues of barbarians being taken captive (now found in the Corinth Museum). On this occasion, however, Paul was not taken captive but instead given a remarkable verdict of freedom, being cleared of any crime.

At the shorter ends of the forum there were further civic buildings: on the east, the **Julian Basilica**, situated close to the starting-line of a former Greek race course; to the west a line of six small temples and the **Babbius monument**, put up according to its inscription by a local politician called Babbius Philinus – in honour of himself.

Another inscription, however, is of particular interest for New Testament studies. It concerns a different Corinthian politician named Erastus. Erastus is described by Paul as the 'city's director of public works' (Romans 16:24); he joins Paul in sending greetings to the Roman church – presumably because he himself was a Christian. Near the large Greek theatre there is a paved area with a first-century inscription that reads as follows: '*//RASTUS PRO AEDILE S.P. STRAVIT*'. When translated this means: 'Erastus laid [this



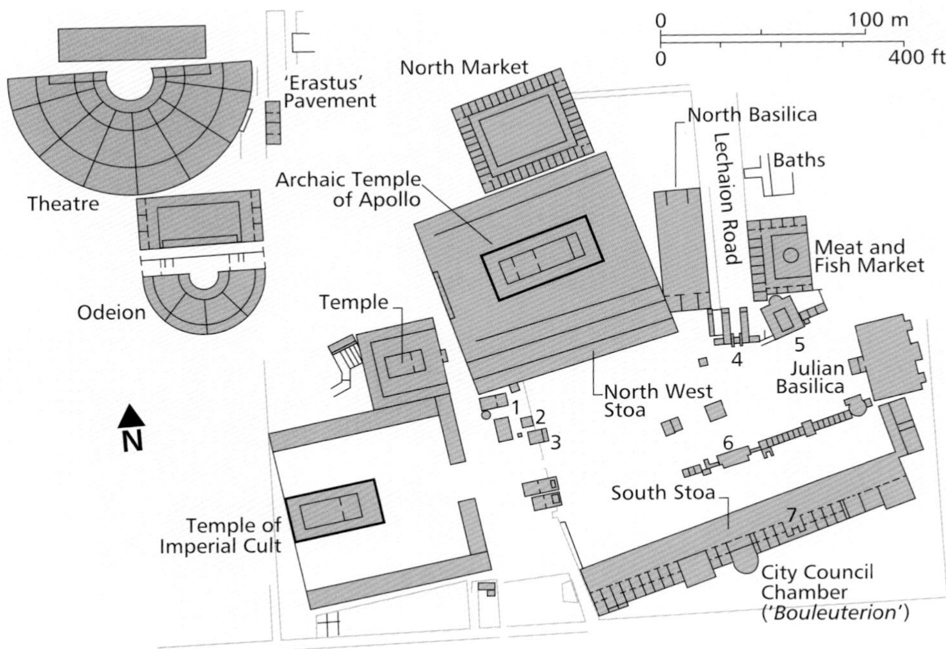


**Plan of ancient Corinth.**
1 Temple of Tyche
2 Babbius Monument
3 Fountain of Poseidon
4 *Propylaea*
5 Peirene Fountain
6 Speaker's Platform ('*Bema*')
7 Fountain House

pavement] at his own expense in return for his aedileship'. Corinth's city officials were known as *aediles*. So Erastus had made some election promises and then put them into practice after his successful election.

This inscription, expressly mentioning someone known from the New Testament, gives a fascinating window into Paul's world. Although 'not many' of the first Christians were from the wealthy classes (1 Corinthians 1:26), Paul's message evidently *did* reach some influential people. And Erastus provides an example of a Christian who was simultaneously committed to his local city, becoming one of its benefactors; his gift enabled 15,000 theatre visitors to walk on his pavement! In cultural terms, this may seem a long way from the hill-sides of Galilee, but somehow this message of Jesus' kingdom was beginning to span these two different worlds.

Other sites to see in ancient Corinth include: the 3,000-seater **Odeion** (just to the south of the theatre) and the **Corinth Museum**. This contains many of the clay figurines dedicated to Asclepius (the Greek demi-god of medicine and healing) in his nearby sanctuary, as well as some significant remains from Roman times – including a bust of the young Nero with a slight beard.

The 'Erastus' pavement near Corinth's theatre: the only surviving archaeological remains that name a Christian believer known to us from the New Testament.

No visit to the area is complete, however, without stopping near the **isthmus**. The **modern canal** is itself an impressive piece of engineering – being 3½ miles (5.5 km) long, up to 300 feet (90 m) deep in places, and 65 feet (20 m) wide at the bottom. Just after Paul's visit to Corinth this same Nero tried to build such a canal with slave labour, but in the centuries before dynamite it proved impossible. If he had succeeded, he would have saved those sailing round the Peloponnese an estimated seven days. It was certainly worth a try – shortening the journey by around 200 miles (320 km). Faced with this situation many centuries earlier the ancient Greeks had built a special road (known as the ***diolkos***), along which a wooden platform could be hauled (with small boats secure on the platform). Some of its flagstones (together with its two ruts) are still clearly visible in places.

Finally, some wish to visit **Isthmia**, the site of the ancient Isthmian games, located about 2 miles (3 km) to the south-east of the isthmus. Excavations have revealed several buildings, including a fifth-century temple of Poseidon (later rebuilt by Tiberius). Intriguingly, at the start of the track there are some line-markings in the slabs, showing exactly where runners were to stand when 'under starter's orders'. These two-yearly games were a key part of Corinth's life, probably taking place during Paul's visit (in AD 51). However, because of Jewish sensibilities concerning competitors performing naked, Paul probably never visited this games area himself. Even so, he was not opposed to using this athletic imagery to describe the Christian life, as seen in 1 Corinthians 9:24–25: 'Run in such a way as to get the prize.'

*'Run in such a way as to get the prize. Everyone who competes in the games goes into strict training. They do it to get a crown that will not last; but we do it to get a crown that will last for ever.'*

**1 Corinthians 9:24–25**

10

CHAPTER

# Ephesus and Miletus

*Paul took the road through the interior and arrived at Ephesus... Paul entered the synagogue and spoke boldly there for three months.... But some of them... publicly maligned the Way. So Paul left them. He took the disciples with him and had discussions daily in the lecture hall of Tyrannus. This went on for two years, so that all the Jews and Greeks who lived in the province of Asia heard the word of the Lord.*

*God did extraordinary miracles through Paul, so that even handkerchiefs and aprons that had touched him were taken to the sick, and their illnesses were cured and the evil spirits left them... A number who had practised sorcery brought their scrolls together and burned them publicly... In this way the word of the Lord spread widely and grew in power.*

*About that time there arose a great disturbance about the Way. A silversmith named Demetrius... called the craftsmen together and said: 'This fellow Paul has convinced and led astray large numbers of people here in Ephesus and in practically the whole province of Asia. He says that man-made gods are no gods at all... The great goddess Artemis... will be robbed of her divine majesty.' When they heard this, they began shouting: 'Great is Artemis of the Ephesians!'... the people rushed into the theatre. Paul wanted to appear before the crowd, but the disciples would not let him.*

**Acts 19:1, 8–12, 19–20, 23–30**

## Teaching and farewells

Paul's ministry in Ephesus began sometime around the autumn of AD 52. After Syrian Antioch (his sending church) Ephesus was perhaps the largest city on the Anatolian landmass – a vital and strategic place for a pioneer such as Paul. To be sure, it had been in his sights for several years, but divine guidance had seemingly closed the door up to this point (Acts 16:6). Now, after gaining valuable experience in a string of ever larger cities (from Philippi, through Thessalonica to Corinth), it was time at last to approach the largest of them all.

Travelling once more through the region of south Galatia, Paul took the road 'through the interior' (Acts 18:23; 19:1) and approached Ephesus from the east after a journey of over 500 miles (800 km) that would have taken over a month without stopping. (We cannot tell whether he travelled down the Lycus/Meander valley – passing places such as Colossae and Laodicea – or came along the north side of Mount

Messogis: see map on p. 84.) Fairly exhausted upon arrival, he no doubt searched immediately for Aquila and Priscilla, whom he had left there the previous spring when heading for Jerusalem.

Had the Christian message already reached Ephesus prior to Paul's arrival? Strangely, soon after his arrival Paul came across twelve 'disciples' who knew about the baptism preached by John the Baptist, but not about baptism in the name of Jesus (Acts 19:1–7). This is a very odd episode; yet the very fact that no one had brought them up to date with the teaching about Jesus may well suggest that there were few, if any, Christians in the area. If so, Ephesus was pretty much 'virgin territory' – an enticing challenge for someone like Paul whose 'ambition' was always to 'preach the gospel where Christ was not known' (Romans 15:20).

Paul would eventually spend three years here (the longest he spent in one place after starting on his travels) and then leave the work in the hands of Timothy. And it was work that would stand the test of time, with Ephesus becoming one of the major centres for the Christian faith in subsequent centuries.

View south-eastwards up Curetes Street, with the Temple of Hadrian on the left. The residential houses are up the hill to the right.

## A wonder of the world

Although the official capital of the province was Pergamum (some 90 miles or 145 km to the north), Ephesus was the major port in the province of Asia and, according to Strabo's *Geography*, the greatest trading centre west of the Taurus Mountains.

Originally just one of numerous Greek settlements established along this 'Ionian' coastline, Ephesus had become dominant both because of its strategic position (at the mouth of the River Caister) and also because of its reputation as the guardian (or 'temple warden') of the goddess Artemis. The vast Artemision Temple (about 1½ miles or 2.5 km to the north of the city) was one of the 'seven wonders' of the ancient world.

The city itself was enclosed by a five-mile- (8-km-) long wall that went up and down numerous hills. For those arriving by sea, the city centre was reached by a long colonnaded street that led eastwards towards a hill on which was built the city's vast theatre (with an estimated capacity of 25,000, serving a population of perhaps ten times that figure). In addition to its commercial prowess, the city also had a distinctive reputation for its interest in magic: 'Ephesian writings' was a phrase used in antiquity to describe documents containing mysterious spells and coded formulae. This city, famous for its pagan worship and magic practices, was about to encounter Paul's teaching about Jesus as Lord.

The goddess Artemis, as depicted in a 'life-size' statue (second century AD) discovered in the Prytaneion. Ancient visitors would have been able to purchase tiny replicas of this from the traders who took offence at Paul's preaching.

## Paul's strategic ploy

Some have estimated that there were up to 10,000 Jews in Ephesus in this period. Paul had visited one of the synagogues earlier in the year and received an open invitation to return, which he now did (Acts 18:20; 19:8). A period of comparative welcome lasted for 'three months', but then the familiar pattern of rejection developed (Acts 19:9).

This time Paul had a brilliant alternative venue in mind: a lecture hall associated with a teacher called Tyrannus (presumably 'Tyrant' was a nickname, given to him perhaps by his students!). According to a variant reading of the text of Acts, Paul used this each day from 'eleven in the morning through till four in the afternoon' – quite possibly during Tyrannus' 'siesta' time. Though hot work during the summer months, Paul kept this up for two years (roughly AD 53 and 54), during which time, says Luke, 'all the Jews and Greeks who lived in the province of Asia heard the word of the Lord' (Acts 19:10).

This is a pardonable overstatement, but perhaps not by much. Many would at least have heard *about* Paul's message and many may have dropped by to hear Paul directly. Perhaps it even 'caught on' as something that visitors did when they came to Ephesus from elsewhere in the province, and they then spread the word back home (almost certainly this is how the church in Colossae was born through a man called Epaphras: Colossians 1:7). Paul had struck on a strategic formula. Located in a key centre like Ephesus, he did not need to go out to the world – the world came to him.

## Paul's teaching

What did Paul teach during those 3,500 hours? Regrettably Luke was not with Paul in Ephesus, so he gives us no idea. Our only evidence for Paul's speaking in such

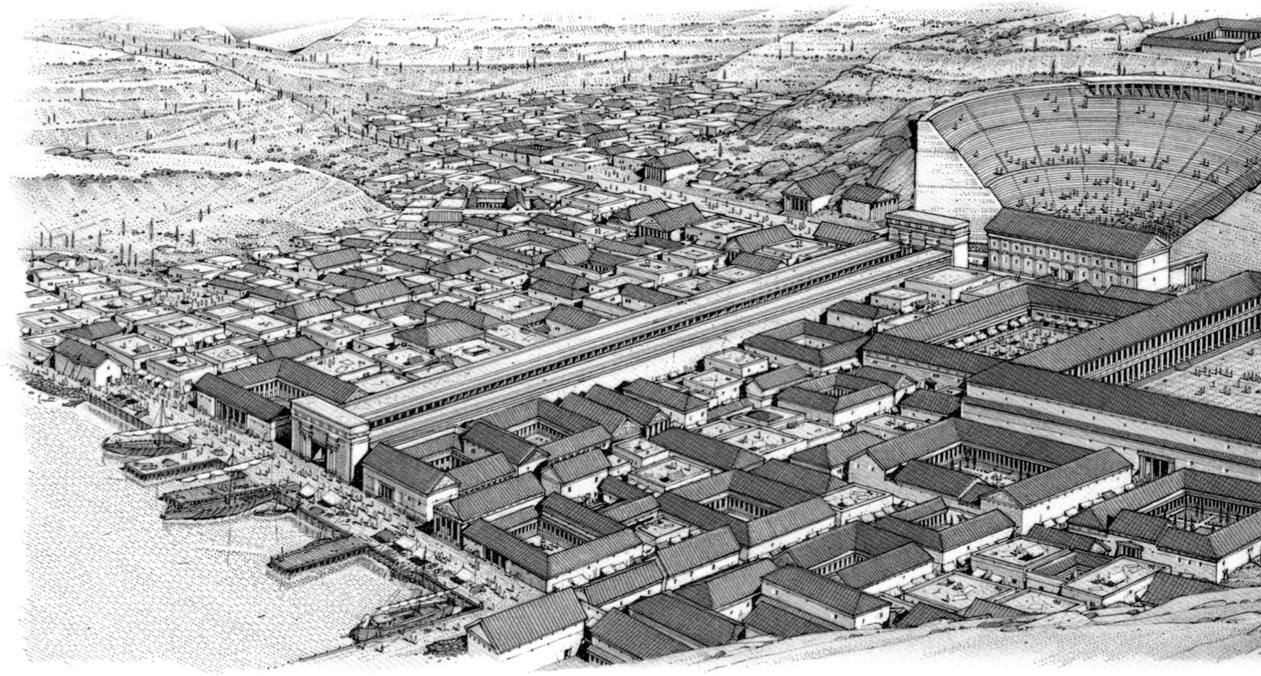

Artist's impression (as from the south-west) of ancient Ephesus, including (from left to right) its harbour, the Arcadian Way leading up to the theatre, and then the Commercial Agora.

evangelistic contexts comes instead in Luke's highly selective accounts of his speeches in Pisidian Antioch and Athens (see pp. 79, 109).

One key point, however, is that Paul would have ensured that new converts received as much material as possible that related to Jesus' own life and teaching. The fact that Paul in his *letters* does not endlessly quote what we now have in the Gospels does not mean that Paul in his *public ministry* did not know the more detailed tradition about Jesus' life and teaching. No, his letters often *presuppose* Jesus' teaching and assume that his readers have been well 'catechized'. Indeed this catechetical role may have been an important part of what Paul's colleagues did (in this instance, Aquila and Priscilla). Thus, if Paul was the pioneer evangelist who won people to faith, it was his colleagues who then passed on the Jesus-tradition to the new believers. Later on, Luke may have found himself in this vital role – which would nicely explain his interest in eventually publishing his collected material in a written Gospel.

Some confirmation of this point comes in Paul's later speech in Acts 20 when he summarizes his 'three years' of ministry in Ephesus. For at the end of his speech he gives the one quotation of Jesus that fails to appear in any of our four Gospels: 'it is more blessed to give than to receive' (Acts 20:35). We find ourselves dependent here on Paul, not the Evangelists, for preserving Jesus' original words. Evidently, then, Paul could not afford in his teaching *about* Jesus to depart recognizably from the teaching *of* Jesus. Both were needed; and, if we had been there in Tyrannus' lecture hall, we would surely have heard them both.

In fact, if we want an overview of what Paul's lectures were about, the clearest clue comes from this farewell speech of Paul in the spring of AD 57. In his haste to reach Jerusalem Paul decided to bypass Ephesus but summonsed the key leaders of its congregations to rendezvous with him at Miletus (some 25 miles or 40 km to the south). Here's how he described his Ephesian ministry:

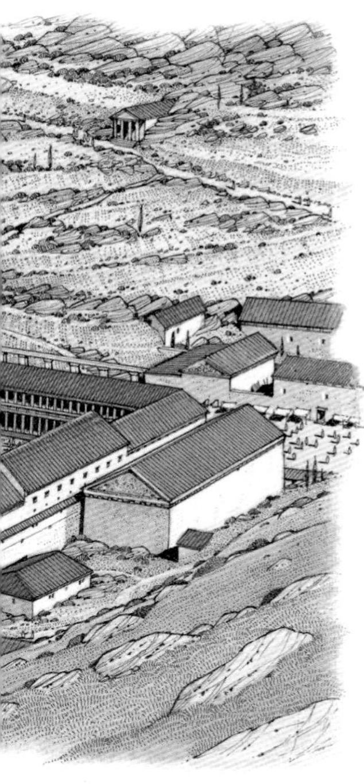

*I have not hesitated to preach anything that would be helpful to you, but have taught you publicly and from house to house. I have declared to both Jews and Greeks that they must turn to God in repentance and have faith in our Lord Jesus… I must complete the task… of testifying to the gospel of God's grace… [and] preaching the kingdom. I have not hesitated to proclaim to you the whole will of God. Remember that for three years I never stopped warning each of you night and day with tears.*

**Acts 20:20–21, 24–25, 27, 31**



The central themes are clear: God's will, his kingdom, his grace; the need for repentance and faith. Clear too is Paul's passion and commitment, not shrinking back but rather pursuing his teaching ministry relentlessly – 'night and day' and 'with tears'.

## Successes and struggles

So Paul's ministry here appears to have been not just influential, but fruitful. Conceivably, if we estimate that between 20 and 30 elders came out to visit him, this might suggest there were around 400 believers in Ephesus as a result of this ministry. This can only be speculation, however.

What else do we know about his time in Ephesus? Luke's account indicates that it was indeed a period of controversy, with some 'highs and lows'. On the positive side there was the episode when many of the city's magicians 'brought their scrolls together and burned them publicly' (19:19). In a city given to magic, clear evidence had emerged of the spiritual power that could be found only in the name of Jesus, and so these sorcerers destroyed their parchments worth an estimated '50,000 drachmas' – a quite enormous sum.

But there were low times too. In 1 Corinthians Paul says he wants to stay on in Ephesus 'because a great door for effective work has opened… and there are many who oppose me' (1 Corinthians 16:9). He also talks about 'fighting wild beasts in Ephesus' (1 Corinthians 15:32) – almost certainly a figurative way of speaking about the intense opposition. Some months later, in the opening chapters of 2 Corinthians, he is reeling from something far worse – a near-death experience:

*We do not want you to be uninformed about the hardships we suffered in the province of Asia. We were under great pressure, far beyond our ability to endure, so that we despaired even of life. Indeed in our hearts we felt the sentence of death.*

**2 Corinthians 1:8–9**

What this was, precisely, again we do not know: possibly a severe illness but (more likely?) acute opposition from some quarter. Paul refers in his address at Miletus to being 'severely tested by the plots of the Jews' (Acts 20:19); so one extended hypothesis is that Paul was accused by the Jewish community of 'temple-robbery'. This initially seems slightly bizarre but might have been based on the idea that Paul's proposed collection for the believers in Jerusalem was effectively undercutting the collection of the Temple tax (paid by all Jews everywhere for the annual upkeep of the Jerusalem Temple). If so, it is further suggested, then Paul may initially have been acquitted by the proconsul, Silanus, but then re-arrested after Silanus' assassination.

Though only a hypothesis, something severe like this may have hit Paul in his final months in Ephesus. Later he speaks of Aquila and Priscilla 'risking their lives' for him and two men, Andronicus and Junias, who had been 'in prison with me' (Romans 16:4, 7). Likewise in his list of his sufferings in 2 Corinthians he speaks of 'frequent' times in 'prison' (2 Corinthians 11:23). So was Paul thrown into prison? Did Aquila and Priscilla somehow engineer his rescue? Though Luke does not mention this, some such scenario is extremely possible.

## Key dates: Ephesus and Miletus

|  |  |
|---|---|
| c. 980 BC | First settlement on the Coressus acropolis by Ionian Greeks. |
| 560 BC | Croesus of Lydia builds the Temple of Artemis, relocating the Ionian settlement nearby. |
| c. 480 BC | Xerxes the Persian spares the Temple of Artemis in his campaign towards Greece. Silting up of the River Caister is already causing problems. |
| 431–404 BC | Though a member of the Attic League, Ephesus now sides with Sparta against Athens in the Peloponnesian War. |
| 356 BC | Artemision Temple destroyed in an arson attack by a man called Herostratus, which then required a total rebuilding. |
| 336 BC | Alexander the Great liberates the city from the Persians. |
| 319–281 BC | Alexander's general, Lysimachus, relocates the city, enclosing it in a 6-mile (10-km) wall and building the Sacred Way back to the temple site. |
| 189 BC | Seleucid rulers defeated by the Romans at the Battle of Magnesia. |
| 133 BC | Attalus III of Pergamum bequeaths Ephesus to the Romans. |
| 51–33 BC | Ephesus visited by key Romans: Cicero (51 BC), Julius Caesar (48 BC), Brutus and Cassius (44 BC), and Cleopatra with Mark Antony (41 and 33 BC), who arranges the murder of her sister, Arsinoe IV (41 BC). |
| 32 BC | Short-lived 'senate-in-exile' established by Romans in Ephesus in opposition to Octavian/Augustus. |
| 29 BC | Ephesus now becomes the seat of the Roman governor (instead of Pergamum); Strabo the geographer visits the city. |
| AD 51 | Paul's first (brief) visit to Ephesus en route to Syria (Acts 18:19). |
| AD 52–55 | Paul spends three years (on and off) in Ephesus (Acts 19). |
| AD 82 | Ephesus' promotion of imperial cult earns it the title *neokoros* (a 'temple guardian') due to its building a temple for the Flavian dynasty. |
| AD 96 | After the assassination of Emperor Domitian, this temple is rededicated to Vespasian alone. |
| AD 124–29 | Ephesus visited twice by Emperor Hadrian: the city becomes the 'imperial capital' of Asia; the harbour is dredged; work starts on a second imperial temple (the Olympeion). |
| AD 251–53 | Decian persecution affects Christians in Ephesus. |
| AD 262 or 263 | Ephesus suffers a major earthquake, leading to the Goths ransacking the damaged Artemision Temple. |
| AD 391 | The Edict of Theodosius (which made Christianity the state religion) leads to Ephesus' pagan temples being destroyed or Christianized (for example, the Olympeion and Artemision). |
| AD 395–408 | During his reign, Emperor Arcadius remodels the road from Ephesus' harbour to the theatre. |
| AD 431 | The third 'Ecumenical' Council meets at Ephesus to debate Mary's role as the mother of Christ. |
| AD 449 | Another synod, meeting in Ephesus, is denounced for its practices, earning it the name *Latrocinium* (a 'council of brigands'); the archbishop of Ephesus (John) is later given the title 'exarch' at the Council of Chalcedon (AD 451). |
| AD 500s | City relocates back to the area of the Archaic acropolis (modern Selcuk), with Justinian's new Church of St John becoming the city's cathedral. |
| AD 654 | First Arab attack on Ephesus. |
| 1090 | City occupied by Seljuk Turks. |
| 1390 | Ottoman Turks defeat the Seljuks. |
| 1869 | After searching for seven years a British railway engineer, J.T. Wood, discovers the Artemision Temple below Selcuk. |

## The riot in the theatre

What Luke does mention (which only confirms the heightening opposition to Paul) is the famous riot in Ephesus' vast theatre (Acts 19:23–41). It was triggered by a combination of economic and religious concerns – as seen in the remarks made by a silversmith called Demetrius. He saw Paul as posing a direct threat to the Artemis cult and to the craftsmen's trade (if true, this would be a tacit witness to the success of Paul's mission). Other craftsmen started shouting, 'Great is Artemis of the Ephesians!' This chant then got picked up by others who gradually converged as a great mob in the theatre, still chanting their slogan.

Two of Paul's companions were jostled into the theatre but Paul was persuaded to stay away by some of the local officials, known as 'Asiarchs' (Acts 19:29–31). That Paul wanted to face the angry mob speaks volumes for his courage; that the Asiarchs wanted to spare him a mob lynching (and also knew how to get a message through to him) tells us that Paul was well known and not without his supporters at the highest level.

Once again some in the Jewish community wanted to make trouble for Paul; one Alexander tried to speak to the crowd, presumably not just to join in Paul's denunciation but also to make it clear that the wider Jewish community wanted nothing to do with this Paul. An outburst of anti-Semitic rioting (as had recently occurred, for example, in Antioch: see p. 44) had to be avoided. But the crowd, realizing he was Jewish, prevented him from speaking. The 'city clerk' (*grammateus*), who was personally responsible to the Romans for preventing any riots, then spoke up. He agreed about the greatness of Artemis and Ephesus, but encouraged the traders to take the issue to the assize courts or else to a 'legal assembly'. Eventually the crowd calmed down. For Paul this commotion only signalled that his time in Ephesus had come to an end: he 'sent for the disciples… said good-bye and set out for Macedonia' (Acts 20:1). As far as we can tell, he never returned.

*'But this happened that we might rely not on ourselves but on God, who raises the dead. He has delivered us from such a deadly peril, and he will deliver us.'*
**2 Corinthians 1:10**

## Taking leave of Ephesus

At least this is the case if we accept the dating of the pastoral epistles outlined above (pp. 12–13). On this reading, 1 Timothy, for example, does not come from a later period of Paul's ministry back in Ephesus, but rather reveals how Paul needed to entrust this major work *almost immediately* to his 'right-hand man'. We then understand why Timothy, being still so young, needed guidance in this major assignment. Paul sets out to encourage him, giving clear instructions about his own conduct (chapter 4), about the worship and social programme of a local church (chapters 2 and 5), and about those suitable for leadership (chapter 3). Paul is passionate about the 'church of the living God' (1 Timothy 3:15), not wanting his work of church planting in Ephesus to be undone. And he expresses particular concern about false teachers who are promoting wrong doctrines and generally stirring up strife (1 Timothy 1:3–7; 4:1–4; 6:3–5).

Meanwhile in 2 Timothy (written perhaps four or five years later) Paul remembers with thanksgiving one Onesiphorus who had helped in 'many ways in Ephesus' (2 Timothy 1:18); and he sends greetings to Aquila and Priscilla who are back in Ephesus after some years in Rome. But he also remembers some individuals who have deserted the faith (2 Timothy 2:17), and the opposition of Alexander (2 Timothy 4:14). Indeed, he even feels that 'everyone in the province of Asia has deserted me'.

*'Alexander the metalworker did me great harm…'*
**2 Timothy 4:14**

## Aegean ports of call

Paul's route from Philippi (en route to Jerusalem) would have been frequented by many travellers. Spring was in the air, and people were once again travelling along this beautiful route, not sailing far out to sea.

The first part of the journey involved crossing over from Europe to Asia Minor, sailing from Philippi's port at Neapolis (see p. 103) to Alexander Troas. Interestingly the voyage, which a few years earlier had taken only two days (Acts 16:11), this time took five days (Acts 20:6) – presumably because of an easterly wind.

At Troas they met up with those who had sailed directly from Corinth (20:5). Troas was a major port that took its name from the ruins of ancient Troy further to the north. It was where Paul had first met Luke (Acts 16:8–10); Luke may have come here on medical business of some kind, or perhaps this, rather than Philippi, was his original home. Troas is the place where Paul spoke for so long that a young boy, seated in an upper window, fell asleep and fell to his death but was raised from the dead through Paul's prayers (Acts 20:7–12). The believers then 'broke bread' together. Since Luke records that this was also 'the first day of the week' (that is, Sunday), this may be our first indication of what believers did in their weekly Sunday worship services. Paul had been here before, when the Lord 'opened a door' for his preaching (2 Corinthians 2:12); so Paul was now reconnecting with people converted through his own preaching.

One of his converts was a man called Carpus. Later Paul would ask Timothy to visit Carpus and 'bring the cloak I left' and 'my scrolls, especially the parchments' (2 Timothy 4:14). Evidently, now that it was springtime, Paul no longer needed his heavy winter cloak. Nor could he trust his precious parchments (quite likely copies of *his own* letters) to the vagaries of sea travel. After all, this might be the last time he was in a port with known trusted friends.

TOP: The harbour town of Assos: here Paul rejoined his companions after walking across the headland on his own (Acts 20:13).

ABOVE: Patara was one of the ports Paul visited en route to Jerusalem.

Luke and the others then sailed round the headland to Assos. Paul however decided to go there by himself 'on foot' (Acts 20:13). The distance is not great (c. 30 miles or 50 km), but the picture we get of Paul is insightful: his physical robustness, and his preference to be on his own. There was little privacy on board ship, so would this be one of his last opportunities to be on his own before he arrived in Jerusalem? He needed space to think, to pray, to enjoy his freedom.

Once all together at Assos, the boat took them via Mitylene (on the island of Lesbos), to Chios and then Samos – the three, quite large, islands close to the coast of Asia Minor. Presumably they simply spent one night in each place and then moved on. At this point, however, they crossed back over to the mainland, to Miletus, where they seem to have stayed longer. At least there was time for Paul to send word to summons the church leaders from Ephesus (see p. 143–44). After their tearful farewells Paul's party then set sail, going past Patmos (where later the author of Revelation would be exiled) en route to Cos and Rhodes, and then rejoined the mainland at Patara, where they boarded a boat sailing to Syria.

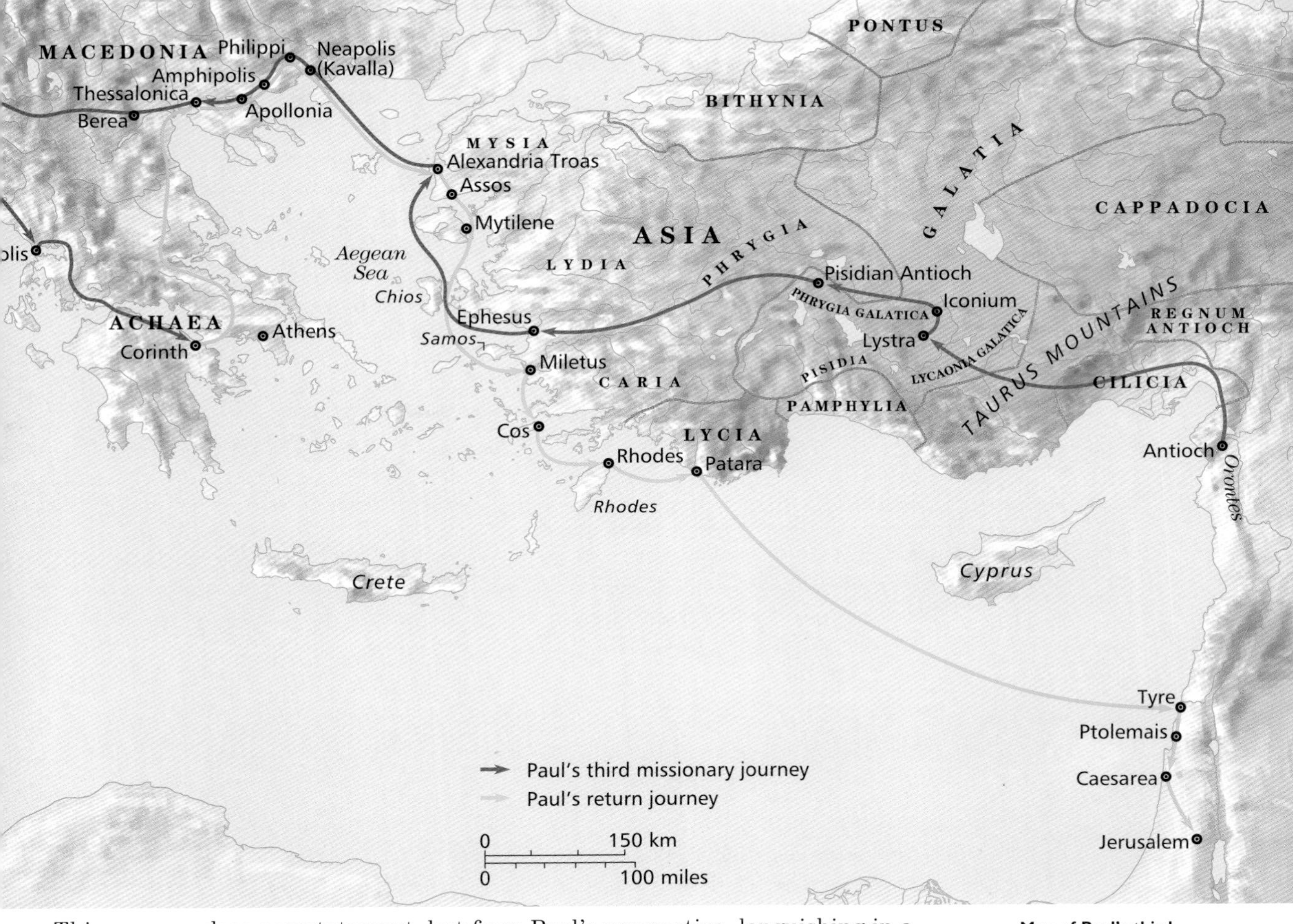


Map of Paul's third 'missionary journey'.

This seems a clear overstatement, but from Paul's perspective, languishing in a Roman jail and longing for some signs of solidarity and support, that is what it felt like. No wonder he wanted Timothy to leave Ephesus and join him in Rome, sending Tychichus to replace him (2 Timothy 4:9, 12).

This would be a depressing note on which to draw a close on Paul's great work in Ephesus. A more positive note would be to highlight the incredible *tour de force* which is Paul's letter to the Ephesians. Almost certainly this was a circular letter intended to go the rounds of the various churches in the province of Asia (see p. 147), so it does not tell us anything specific about the church in Ephesus itself. Yet its vision of the 'spiritual blessings' found 'in Christ' and of what it means then to 'live in the light' have inspired numerous church congregations ever since.

We close our story, however, by turning once more to Paul's speech to the Ephesian elders gathered at Miletus in May, AD 57. Paul is under no illusion that some of his labours may prove to have been in vain, yet he is also quietly confident:

*'You know how I lived the whole time I was with you, from the first day I came into the province of Asia. I served the Lord with great humility and with tears,*

*although I was severely tested. And now, compelled by the Spirit, I am going to Jerusalem, not knowing what will happen to me there...Therefore, I declare to you today that I am innocent of the blood of all... Keep watch over yourselves and all the flock of which the Holy Spirit has made you overseers... I know that after I leave savage wolves will not spare the flock. Even from your own number some will arise and distort the truth in order to draw away disciples after them. So be on your guard!... Now I commit you to God and to the word of his grace...'*

*When he had said this, he knelt down with all of them and prayed. They all wept as they embraced him. What grieved them most was his statement that they would never see his face again. Then they accompanied him to the ship.*

**Acts 20:17–32, 36–38**

For the Ephesian elders, this was such a poignant moment. Here on the beach was the man who, almost single-handedly, had brought them the good news about Jesus. Now he was leaving them for ever, entrusting his labours into their hands. Would they fail and let him down? And how would *he* cope with the traumas awaiting him in Jerusalem and beyond? It was enough to make one weep.

But Paul stepped resolutely into the boat. As the features of Miletus with its big theatre receded from view, Paul could look back and see the small group clustered on the beach, perhaps waving their hands or huddled in prayer. In them lay all his future hopes for the great city of Ephesus.

# Ephesus and Miletus today

The remains of ancient Ephesus are truly a site to behold. Remarkably, as late as the 1960s visitors could wander onto the site at leisure; nowadays, however, it is hard to find the site uncrowded. The best way to gain a sense of the ancient city is undoubtedly to take a seat somewhere high up in its vast theatre. From here you can see the main street (the 'Arcadian Way') making its way down to the site of the ancient harbour (now silted up), with the distinct slopes of Mount Coressus on the harbour's left. At the end of antiquity, when remodelled by the Emperor Arcadius, this street was one of only a few in the entire empire that was lit by torchlight each night – an impressive spectacle upon arrival in the harbour.

## Walking towards the Celsus Library

For practical reasons, however, many visits start back round at the south-eastern entrance to the site. Just inside this 'upper' entrance, there are a series of buildings situated around the long, rectangular **State Agora** (c. 525 x 190 ft or 160 x 58 m). As usual, this large market place, which served as the city's administrative district, was surrounded by various colonnaded *stoas* and civic buildings. Two are particularly interesting. One is the **Prytaneion** (or town hall), which contained the 'sacred fire' of *Hestia Bouleia* (the goddess of the hearth). Cult priests (known as *curetes*) were responsible for ensuring that the eternal flame, which symbolized the city's life, never died out. This building, also used for civic banquets, was the place where the famous statue of Artemis was discovered in 1956. Next door (to the right) is the **Odeion**, a semi-circular concert hall that could seat around 1,500 people (built c. 150 AD). Here one can call to mind the 'lecture hall of Tyrannus' (see p. 137); we know neither the location nor the shape of that lecture hall, but if it was even half this size, one can readily see how so many got to hear Paul's preaching.

Moving westwards the visitor passes various monuments, especially the **Pollio Fountain**, built to honour this benefactor shortly before Paul's time, and the (slightly earlier) **Memmius monument**, built to honour a grandson of the Roman general Sulla. Not to be ignored (though it dates to after Paul's time) is the large terrace on which was built the **Temple of Domitian**. The emperor Domitian expressly proclaimed himself as 'Lord and Saviour' and instigated severe persecution of Christians. Fear of this persecution may have inspired the writer of Revelation to encourage the seven churches in this region, including that of Ephesus, to be faithful (Revelation 2:1–7). After Domitian's assassination, however, his memory was officially condemned, so this temple reverted to its original purpose – to honour his father, Vespasian. Inside the temple were vast statues of the emperors (some now on display in the Ephesus Museum) – a telling sign of the promotion of the imperial cult in Asia. As a reward for building this temple to the divine emperor Ephesus was given the title of *neokoros*. This oppressive environment of emperor-worship was growing apace, making Ephesus a tough place for Paul's message about a crucified Jew being the true 'Lord and Saviour' to be received.

Returning to the main street, one walks down the marble-slabbed **Curetes Street**

The famous Celsus Library, originally dating from the second century AD but reconstructed in the 1970s by Austrian archaeologists, with its statues of the four 'Virtues'.

(a modern name derived from several columns relocated here that had originally listed the *curetes* in the *Prytaneion*: see p. 144). The view from here down towards the Celsus Library is justly famous. After passing the **Fountain of Trajan** (built c. AD 103) and the **Temple of Hadrian** (built c. AD 130, with its relief in the centre of the arch to Tyche, the goddess of fortune), one comes first to the **public baths** (renovated much later, in the fourth century AD, by a Christian woman called Scholastica) and then to the **latrines**.

Ancient latrines, modern tourists...

As in Salamis and elsewhere, the modern visitor is made aware at this point that ancient views about privacy were quite different from our own. Such places were quite probably where Paul and the early Christians conversed with their fellow-citizens, sometimes 'gossiping the gospel' – as confirmed by the story about the apostle John entering one of Ephesus' bath-houses (see p. 147). Intriguingly, one word for latrines (*paidiskeion*) could also be used of a 'brothel', which explains why another building next to the latrines (where this word is found in an inscription) has often been identified as a **brothel**. This identification, though popular with tour guides, may be mistaken (especially if the inscribed stone was relocated here from the latrines). Yet it reminds us that daily life required from the first Christians an attitude of continual watchfulness if they were to 'live as children of light' (Ephesians 5:8).

Around the time of Paul a new *stoa* was being built along the south side of Curetes Street, with shops and living quarters above for the shop owners (the fine mosaics visible here date to the fifth century AD). Behind the *stoa*, going up the hill, was a **residential area** made up of numerous terrace houses constructed around various courtyards. The recent excavations here (though subject to an extra admission charge) are well worth a visit: mosaics, frescoes and ornate carvings indicate that this was a wealthy quarter. Also on this south side, further down Curetes Street, there is an **octagonal monument**; a skeleton of a young girl (aged around fifteen) was found underneath in a marble sarcophagus, so this is quite probably a memorial for Cleopatra's young sister, murdered by Mark Antony (see p. 140). A little further down is the large **Gate of Hadrian**.

At this point, however, the main spectacle is the truly impressive **Celsus Library** (built to honour a proconsul who served around AD 105). Originally a three-storeyed building, this would have been one of the largest libraries of its day until it was destroyed

**Below: Plan of ancient Ephesus.**
1 Monument of the Four Evangelists
2 Harbour Gymnasium
3 Basilica Stoa
4 Temple of Hadrian
5 Latrine and so-called brothel
6 Gate of Hadrian
7 Baths of Scholastica

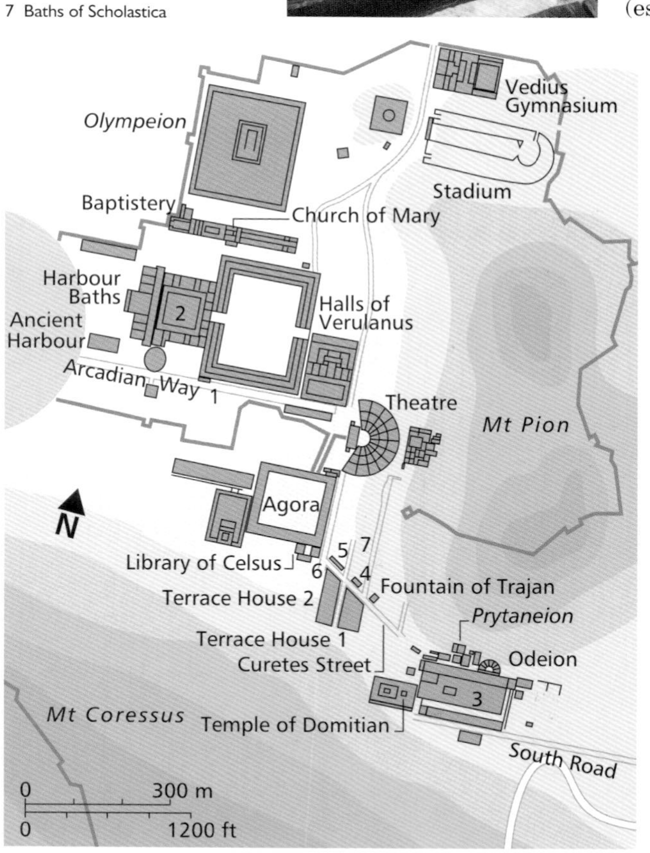

## Ephesus and the two Johns

When Paul said goodbye to the Ephesian elders at Miletus in the spring of AD 57, he was clearly anxious about how the church would fare after his departure. So what happened next in Ephesus?

Encouragingly, the church seems to have continued to grow. We next hear of it in the book of Revelation (written, almost certainly, after AD 70, perhaps as late as the AD 90s). The author, known to us as 'John the divine' (or 'seer'), conveys some words of Christ to seven churches in Asia Minor, the first of which is Ephesus (Revelation 2:1–7). In this letter Christ commends the church for its 'perseverance' amid hardship and for resisting the practices of a group (unknown to us) called the Nicolaitans; but he chides the believers for 'forsaking their first love'. Evidently the intervening years since Paul's departure have been tough in many ways, but they have held on, needing now just to recapture what they had in those early years under Paul: 'do the things you did at first' (v. 5).

The other churches in Revelation 2–3 (Smyrna, Pergamum, Thyatira, Sardis, Philadelphia and Laodicea) form a circle, arching round clockwise from Ephesus, and may reflect the route used by couriers in Asia Minor. Paul never visited these cities (though he mentions Laodicea in Colossians 4:16); but the church's existence there may be the fruit of his own pioneering work in Ephesus, as believers travelled back to their homes with the message of Christ.

The history of the church in Ephesus in this period, however, is traditionally associated with a second John named 'John the apostle'. Almost certainly this leading disciple of Jesus emigrated to Ephesus – probably around the time of Jerusalem's destruction in AD 70, if not before. In the light of his promise to look after Jesus' mother (John 19:27), some wonder if he travelled here with Mary; but there is no firm evidence of this.

The evidence for John's relocation to Ephesus comes both from Eusebius' *Ecclesiastical Histories* and from Irenaeus, the bishop of Lyons in Gaul around AD 190. Irenaeus states that he himself in his 'early youth' had met Polycarp (bishop of Smyrna, martyred in AD 156), who in turn had met as a child the elderly apostle John in Ephesus (Irenaeus, *Against Heresies* 3.3.4). There was a link here spanning three generations.

So Ephesus may be the place where John's Gospel was first produced. Seen by many as the mature reflections of Jesus' 'beloved disciple' (John 13:23), this Gospel was perhaps finally published by John's own followers around the time of the apostle's death.

We can also glean something about the early church in Ephesus from reading John's three short epistles (1, 2, 3 John). In particular he warns against a movement which is now known as 'docetism' – a variant of Christian faith which asserted that Jesus was so fully divine that he only *seemed* to be human. That some in Ephesus were espousing this belief does much to confirm that there had clearly been strong teaching previously which underscored the divinity of Jesus.

John was also opposed to a sect led by a man called Cerinthus. On one occasion the elderly apostle went into Ephesus' bath-house and was horrified to find himself in the presence of Cerinthus:

> *'He rushed out of the bath-house without bathing, exclaiming, "Let us fly, lest even the bath-house fall down, because Cerinthus, the enemy of truth, is within..."'*
>
> **Irenaeus, *Against Heresies* 3.3.4**

John's traditional burial place is in the church in Selçuk, near Ephesus. Although its precise authenticity cannot be established, it is fitting, when gathered in its main apse, to read out verses from John's Gospel and hear again the power of his words somewhere in the vicinity of where they were first written.

The slightly 'furred' water-pipes (TOP) near Laodicea explain why the water, after flowing for over a mile through such pipes, was 'lukewarm' (see Revelation 3:16). The triple-ached entrance way (BOTTOM) is the western entrance into the ruins of ancient Hierapolis (nearby modern Pamukkale).

From Ephesus' vast theatre there are great views down the Arcadian Way to the ancient harbour area (now silted up), with the shadows of Mount Coressus visible to the left.

by an earthquake in the mid-third century AD. Its façade was restored in the 1970s allowing us to appreciate its slender Corinthian columns and the four (plaster cast) statues, which represent the four virtues (from left to right: wisdom, character, judgment and expertise). Once inside, the niches in the walls give a good idea of how the many scrolls would have been stored.

## The theatre and the Church of Mary

The main street now makes a right-angled bend, going northwards towards the theatre. It is worth a detour to the left, however, going into the large **Commercial Agora**

(c. 370 square feet or 34 square metres) through a gate that was built around 4 BC in honour of Augustus' family. As usual the *agora* would have been surrounded on all four sides by colonnaded *stoas*. The best view of it, however, is from the **theatre**. This vast structure, which was expanded in the centuries after Paul's time, could seat up to 25,000 people in its heyday. In Paul's day the second and third tiers of seating had not been added, but we can still imagine the uproar of the crowds as they chanted incessantly, 'Great is Artemis of the Ephesians!' Despite what many tour guides say, Luke is quite clear that Paul himself did *not* enter the theatre to address the crowd (Acts 19:30). It was left to the city clerk to quell the impending riot.

Because there is little to see down in the area of the former harbour, many visits effectively end at this point. Yet there is at least one more site that should be seen, if at all possible. Starting down the Arcadian Way and then detouring along some dirt tracks to the north, one comes to the Byzantine **Church of Mary**. The whole structure is very long and thin; it turns out to be a remodelling of an earlier *stoa*, which originally had formed the southern edge of a large temple complex (the *Olympeion*) dedicated to the worship of the emperor Hadrian (called *Zeus Olympios*). Sometime around AD 400 this pagan building was destroyed (its structures being burnt to lime) and Christians took over its southern porticoes to build a church.

Quite possibly this work was under way when the Third Ecumenical Council of bishops gathered to resolve the proper ways of referring to the Virgin Mary (AD 431). In due course the church was indeed dedicated to Mary, and then at a later period divided into two separate areas (with the bishop's home and offices in the eastern section). Even if the precise archaeological dating is uncertain, one can easily imagine the bishops gathered from around the empire for this historic meeting. And visiting the church's baptistery (on the north side) gives a good sense of how Byzantine Christians were admitted into the church family: facing eastwards (turning their backs on the west and renouncing the arena of 'darkness'), they went down a few steps into some shallow water, there to be baptized by the clergy sprinkling water over their heads, and then came up the steps on the other side (facing the arena of light) to receive their new baptismal clothes.

*'You stopped your ears against the pernicious seed these visitors were sowing'; 'faith is the beginning and love is the end'.*

**Ignatius, *Letter to the Ephesians* 9, 14**

For those willing to wander off the beaten track there are many further hours of exploration to be had within the main archaeological site: near the harbour on the Arcadian Way is a sixth-century monument with four columns, thought to have been decorated with statues of the four Evangelists; there are more **bath-complexes and gymnasia**, for example, some down near the harbour, others at the very end of the site, back up near the remains of the **Magnesian Gate**. There are also the clearly identifiable contours of Ephesus' **stadium** (expanded during the reign of Nero), now some 200 yards (180 m) outside the main entrance. But there are still other sites nearby that must be explored, which are essential visits for those interested in the New Testament.

## Neighbouring Selçuk

Selçuk is the Turkish name of the town now situated some 1½ miles (2 km) to the north-east of ancient Ephesus. When Ephesus' harbour finally silted up beyond repair, the town effectively relocated here. Yet, even in ancient times, this was very much part of the wider 'Ephesus area' – not least because this was the location of Ephesus' magnificent **Temple of Artemis**. The sad remains of this vast structure can now be seen on the left of the approach road to Selçuk. The first (quite tiny) temple on this site was built back in the eighth century BC, apparently marking the site of a meteorite's landing, believed to have come from the gods. This was replaced by a mammoth temple (built entirely from marble in the sixth century, and rebuilt in the fourth century on a higher platform to avoid flooding), which deservedly ranked as one of the 'seven wonders' of the ancient world. Over 370 feet (110 m) in length, with some 117 columns rising nearly 60 feet (18 m) into the air, it must have been an awesome sight. It was a major tourist attraction, functioning both as the 'credit bank' of the province and as a place of asylum and refuge for those seeking 'sanctuary'. No wonder Demetrius and the city clerk spoke of the temple in such glowing terms (as recounted in Acts 19:25–27). Now there is but a solitary column (itself reconstructed in 1973) standing up in a field that is normally under water. And instead of the rallying cries of the craftsmen, one is more likely to hear the taunting, repetitive croaks of the site's many frogs.

*'I came to a big stagnant pond... The frogs which haunt it by the million set up their* brekekekekex co-ax *until the air rang as if a hundred invisible rattles were being whirled. The croaking shaped itself in my mind... "Great is Diana... Great is Diana of the Ephesians." For this stagnant pond is the site of the Great Temple of Artemis – Diana of the Ephesians – once one of the Seven Wonders of the World.'*

**H. V. Morton, describing the site of the Artemision**

Overlooking the site is Selçuk's acropolis (known as 'Ayasoluk'), on the southern slopes of which is housed a church built in memory of Paul's fellow apostle, John – the **Church of St John the Theologian**. There are early Christian traditions that clearly link Jesus' 'beloved disciple' with Ephesus. During the fourth century this site was selected for a church; there is no extant evidence that the memory of a particular grave had been preserved, so perhaps the site was chosen for other reasons. Later in the sixth century, however, Justinian ordered the building of a massive cross-shaped basilica with six domes (compared by some to the great Hagia Sophia in Constantinople), which in due course became the cathedral church when the city relocated here.

The church's ground plan gives another fine example of Byzantine church architecture: a treasure-room, an octagonal baptistery, and a large outdoor courtyard to the west. The domes, however, have all collapsed. Even so, John's apostolic witness comes powerfully to mind. Standing round the central area in the apse (with its mosaics and slender columns dating from the middle Byzantine period), people can read out some words from John's writings, sensing the power of his words and the lasting legacy he left within Ephesus and far beyond. During excavations three graves were found in the crypt below, one of which presumably had been identified as John's tomb at some point before the church's construction. So there is still a distinct, even if

The temple of Artemis ('Artemision') was one of the seven wonders of the ancient world; but the site is now frequently marshy and under water. In the distance are the fortifications of Ayasoluk, Selçuk's acropolis.

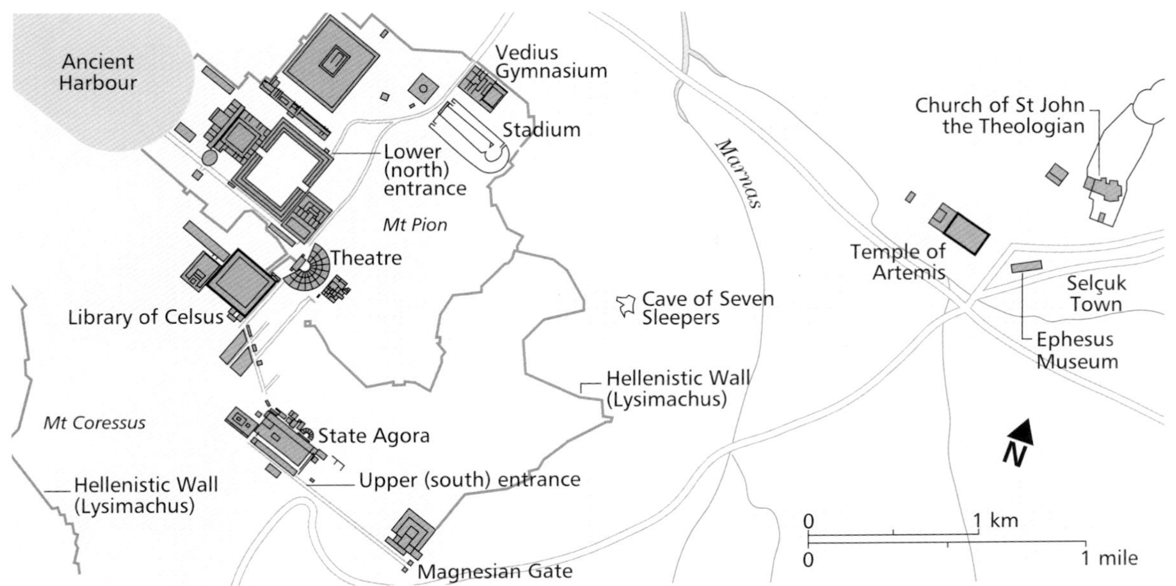


Plan of the wider Ephesus area.

LEFT: The Church of John the Theologian in Selçuk, near Ephesus: a view from its central apse down the nave, with the four columns covering the area of the tomb associated with the apostle.

ABOVE: The font into which baptismal candidates would step down, coming up the other side (facing east) having been sprinkled with water.

small, possibility that this does indeed mark the final resting place of Jesus' 'beloved disciple'.

Nearby is the important **Ephesus Museum**, with some of the many artefacts discovered in ancient Ephesus: domestic items, statues, grave monuments and inscriptions. There is a remarkable wall-painting of Socrates; some remains of the massive statue from the temple of Domitian (now identified with Titus, not Domitian); as well as the two famous statues of Artemis (first discovered in the *Prytaneion*), which remind us vividly of Artemis' association with fertility (see p. 137). Evidently, promoting and depicting 'Artemis of the Ephesians' was big business; so it is a remarkable testimony to the power of Paul's preaching that after such a short time the silversmiths and other artisans began to sense a potential downturn in their sales.

Many also visit the so-called **House of Mary**. There is a tradition that Jesus' mother emigrated with John to Ephesus. This appears to have been largely an inference from a passage in John's Gospel in which, in response to Jesus' dying instructions, John is said to have taken Mary 'from that time on into his home' (John 19:27). In the nineteenth century, a German Catholic nun described a house, supposedly belonging to Mary, that she had seen in a dream. A house, matching that description, was soon discovered, high up in the hills south of Ephesus. It turned out to be a house built in the Middle Ages, but conceivably on the site of an earlier dwelling (which may date back even to the first century AD?). There is, of course, no means of verifying this tradition. The same goes for the tower (originally a part of Ephesus' Hellenistic wall-fortifications) which, since the seventeenth century, has been referred to as **St Paul's Prison**. What these buildings do signify, however, is something of the lasting impact that the first generation of Christians, including Paul, had on this vibrant city, the metropolis of Asia.

Finally an excursion out to **Miletus** (20 miles or 32 km to the south) completes the tour, being the place to which Paul summonsed the elders from Ephesus. In Paul's day Miletus had been a major port and centre of culture for more than 600 years. Yet the River Meander would eventually silt up its harbour for good. Thus Miletus' large **theatre**, which once was set immediately between the city's two harbours, is now stranded miles from the coast.

The theatre had recently been rebuilt by the Romans with vaulted tunnels for access to the upper seats. Intriguingly, one of the seats still has an inscription

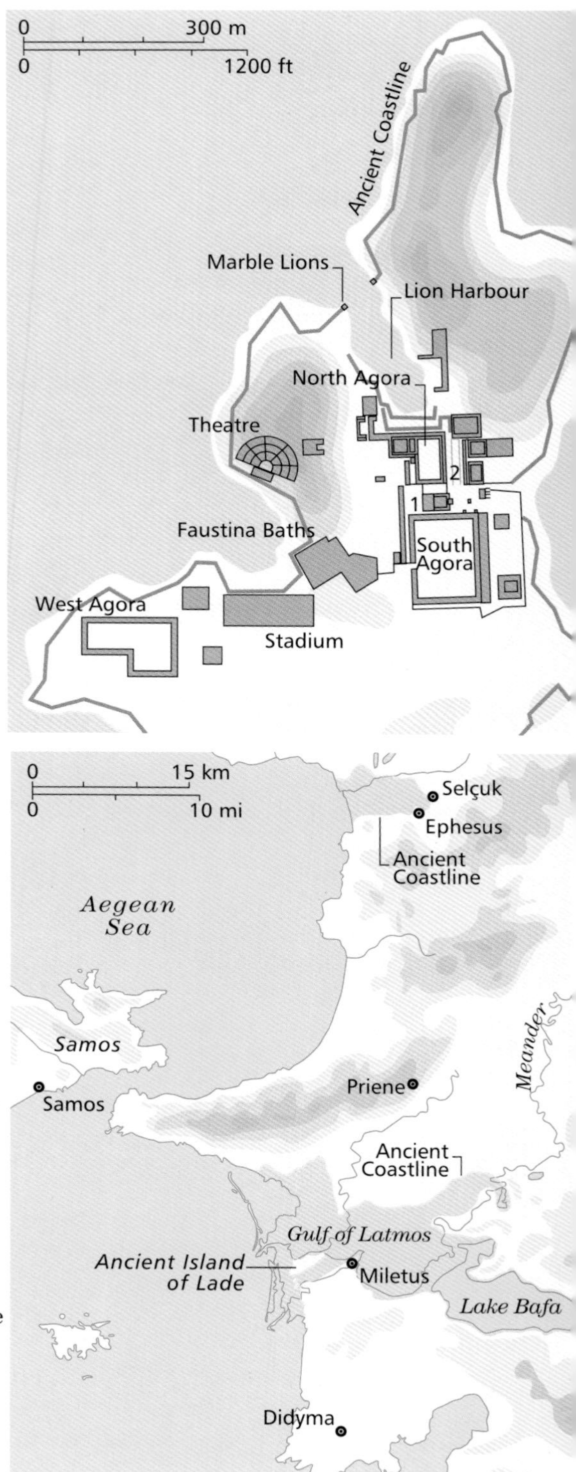


**Top: Plan of Miletus' harbour area**
1 Council Chamber
2 Sacred Way

Below: Changes in the coastline around Ephesus and Miletus from ancient to modern times.

Top: The theatre at Miletus, set into the hill that separates the city's two harbours.

Below: A Greek inscription from one of the rows in the upper tier of the theatre, suggesting these were seats to be used by 'God-fearers'.

identifying it as being for use by the 'God-fearers' (see p. 80). From behind the theatre at the top, there are good views of the rest of the site, much of which is quite marshy: the South Agora, the council house, the three-storeyed Fountain House, for example. Given the changes, it is hard to imagine this as a bustling port; but somewhere near here, Paul spoke to the Ephesian Christians and then walked down to the ship, where he said farewell to Ephesus and its church for ever.

11
CHAPTER

# Jerusalem

*A prophet… named Agabus took Paul's belt, tied his own hands and feet with it, and said: 'The Holy Spirit says, "In this way the Jews of Jerusalem will bind the owner of this belt and will hand him over to the Gentiles."'*

*We pleaded with Paul not to go up to Jerusalem. Then Paul answered, 'Why are you breaking my heart? I am ready to die in Jerusalem for the name of the Lord Jesus.'*

*When we arrived at Jerusalem, the brothers received us warmly. The next day Paul and the rest of us went to see James, and all the elders were present.*

**Acts 21:10–13, 17–18**

## In the Master's steps

Paul arrived in Jerusalem just in time for Pentecost (25 May) in the year AD 57. Paul knew the city well: he had been 'brought up in Jerusalem' in his younger days and had visited it at least three times since his conversion (see pp. 32, 45, 48). Yet he knew this visit would be different: he came carrying a gift of money from his Gentile mission; he came more willing than ever to suffer for Jesus' sake, if need be, in this city where

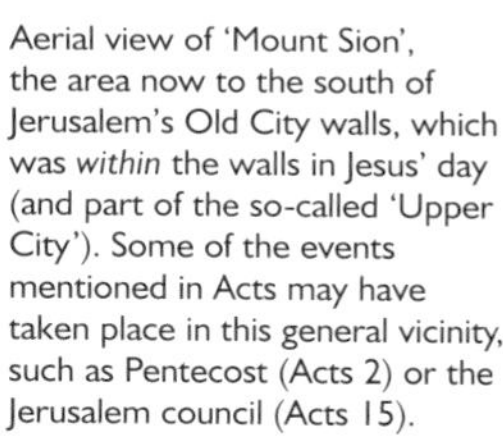

Aerial view of 'Mount Sion', the area now to the south of Jerusalem's Old City walls, which was *within* the walls in Jesus' day (and part of the so-called 'Upper City'). Some of the events mentioned in Acts may have taken place in this general vicinity, such as Pentecost (Acts 2) or the Jerusalem council (Acts 15).

## The collection for Jerusalem

Paul's missionary journeys can be seen as journeys *to and from Jerusalem*. Although Antioch was his home church, which commissioned him on his first expedition (Acts 13:3), Paul evidently tried to visit Jerusalem too whenever he was in the eastern Mediterranean (though disputed, the reference in Acts 18:22 to his visiting 'the church' probably refers to the church in *Jerusalem*, not Antioch). Indeed there is a sense that Jerusalem effectively may have acted as a 'launch-pad' for his journeys – as though each visit to Jerusalem only gave him the courage (or mandate) to go yet further away in the cause of the gospel.

If so, this shows the importance that Paul ascribed to keeping in touch, if possible, with the original 'mother' church. At the same time, Paul was not uncritical of Jerusalem. His scathing comments in Galatians 4:25 ('the present city of Jerusalem is in slavery with her children') certainly suggest that, theologically, he had abandoned his former devotion to the city. And for many years he was given much trouble by the antics of Judaizing Christians emanating from Jerusalem (see pp. 47, 84). So why did Paul put so much energy into gathering this 'collection' for the Christians in Jerusalem? At the least it revealed his generosity of spirit and his refusal to take any revenge on those who had hindered his ministry.

Evidently the project had been on his mind for several years. Paul had been talking about it to both the Galatian and Corinthian churches around AD 53/54 (1 Corinthians 16:1–4) and then, a little later, to the Macedonians (2 Corinthians 8–9). The disputes in Corinth, however, had caused him to wonder if they might renege on their promise, and, despite various visits by Titus, Paul probably decided he needed to visit Corinth in person to check things were in order – quite probably pushing the schedule back by a further twelve months. Writing from Corinth early in AD 57, Paul is then pleased to confirm that both 'Macedonia and Achaia' are now fully behind this project, which he describes as a 'service' or 'contribution for the poor among the saints in Jerusalem' (Romans 15:25–26).

Paul had a heart for the poor and had been to Jerusalem before to offer famine relief (Galatians 2:10; Acts 11:28–30); yet he clearly saw this particular project in more than strictly financial terms. Thus, although he desired a greater level of financial 'equality' (2 Corinthians 8:14), he also saw a special significance in his (largely) *Gentile* congregations assisting *Jewish* believers: 'if the Gentiles have shared in the Jews' spiritual blessings, they owe it to the Jews to share with them their material blessings' (Romans 15:27). So this collection was a way of expressing the essential solidarity that existed between his Gentile converts and the mother-church in Jerusalem. Conceivably Paul was also influenced by Old Testament passages that spoke of Gentile nations being 'gathered in' to Israel and bringing their gifts to Zion. The word of the Lord had indeed 'gone forth from Zion' (Isaiah 2:3), but now there was some fruit to show for it.

It was also, of course, a tacit witness to the fruitfulness of Paul's own ministry. Those who received it would have to acknowledge this; hopefully, as a result, they would now stop criticizing him and recognize the good work he was doing. This then explains why Paul needed all to go well and also for the situation in Corinth to be sufficiently sorted out beforehand. It would have been pointless to go up to Jerusalem a year earlier with no money from this leading church, or with everyone aware of the problems in Corinth. His critics in Jerusalem would have been able to use this as powerful evidence against him.

So Paul had waited until he himself had been to Corinth. He also put together a strong team of companions: Luke, Sopater, Aristarchus and Secundus (from various parts of Macedonia); Gaius and Timothy (originally from Galatia), and Tychichus and Trophimus (from Asia). The eight of them set off from Corinth in March AD 57. Almost certainly Titus (who strangely is never mentioned in Acts) was deliberately not included – precisely because someone had to 'hold the fort' in the Aegean region while these key personnel were absent. Titus had already been to Jerusalem anyway; and seemingly he was Paul's toughest 'trouble-shooter' (more so than Timothy), who could be relied upon to keep things steady while they were away.

We do not know how much money they carried with them, but it may have been a significant amount if some congregations had been collecting money on a weekly basis for some time (1 Corinthians 16:2). The very fact that Paul took eight companions strongly suggests that they were carrying between them quite a large sum. Travelling by boat could be particularly dangerous (as indicated by the plot on Paul's life before they set sail: Acts 20:3); but major sections of the journey simply *had* to be by sea if they were ever to get to Jerusalem in a reasonable time.

And so they arrived in Jerusalem, but with some anxiety: how would people react to this group of Gentiles? And would the local believers receive or rebuff their gift?

Jesus himself had suffered; and, almost certainly, he came knowing this would be his last visit. For, if he ever got out of the city alive, his sights were now set on further missionary work in the West, from where such return visits to Jerusalem would be increasingly difficult or simply unnecessary.

## The believers' response to Paul's gift





*'I am on my way to Jerusalem in the service of the saints there... Pray that I may be rescued from the unbelievers in Judea and that my service in Jerusalem may be acceptable to the saints there.'*
**Romans 15:25, 31**

Paul did get out alive – but only just. Paul's words in Romans 15 reveal that he was acutely anxious about his forthcoming visit to Jerusalem, and events proved his fears to be well founded. His obvious concern was about the hostility he could reasonably expect from Jerusalem's Jewish residents. But he was also anxious about his financial collection for the believers (what he calls his 'service'): would they gratefully receive this or would it be rejected?

How Paul's collection was received, we do not know. One's initial presumption would be that this act of generosity was warmly welcomed. However, when describing the official reception party on the first morning after their arrival, Luke fails to mention the handing over of this gift (Acts 21:17–25). Is this a sign that things did not go so well, and that it had been an embarrassing fiasco?

In fact, there is an oblique reference to the collection later in Acts, when Paul mentions in his speech before Felix that he had gone up to Jerusalem 'to bring my people gifts' (Acts 24:17). So Luke was not totally silent on the issue. His comparative quietness on the issue, then, may have been for some quite different reason – for example, if Paul's collection had indeed led to his being accused of 'temple-robbery' (see p. 140), Luke may not have wanted Paul's motives to be misconstrued or even somehow used against him when later on trial.

On the other hand, the Jerusalem church leaders were evidently seriously anxious about how 'thousands' of their local church members would respond to news of Paul's arrival (Acts 21:20). If this was the atmosphere on the ground (and any gift from Paul would be tainted politically with his problematic reputation), then maybe the leaders could not accept this gift straightforwardly – at least not on that first day. In fact this may explain why they came up immediately with the slightly strange request that Paul should publicly fulfil a purification rite in the Temple that lasted seven days (Acts 21:23–24). This was intended precisely to allay the fears of those church members. Perhaps, then, this became effectively a condition of their receiving the gift: *only after* Paul had done this could they be seen to accept it. Yet, if so, the fact that Paul was arrested *before those seven days had elapsed* probably means that Paul himself never got to hand over the money – it all had to be sorted out by Paul's companions *after* Paul's speedy exit from the scene. So, even if it was later gratefully received, there were aspects of this extravagant gesture that had clearly backfired.

Behind this issue of Paul's collection stands that of Paul's previous relationship with the Jerusalem church, which had been problematic for several years (see pp. 46–49). For among the believers in Jerusalem there were evidently a good number of those whom we refer to now as the 'Judaizers' or the 'circumcision party' – that is, people who believed all Gentile converts should be circumcised. These Judaizers had dogged Paul's steps on his journeys and, even though the Jerusalem Council had ruled against them back in AD 49 and had tried to prevent their activity causing problems *elsewhere*, they would still have been a major force to be reckoned with *in Jerusalem*. As a result, James, as the emerging leader of the Jerusalem believers, would have had an almost impossible task as he tried to affirm the Gentile mission while acknowledging the concerns of these strict Jewish believers – not least because in Jerusalem they were all being closely watched by ardent Jewish nationalists quick to criticize this new messianic movement for being treacherously anti-Jewish. In Jerusalem persecution was in the air.

However, the issue had another layer to it as well (not perhaps fully resolved at the Jerusalem Council): what was to be expected of *Jewish* converts? In Jerusalem many would presumably have continued to be observant of *other* aspects of the Jewish Torah (such as the food laws, not just circumcision). Yet such observance became increasingly problematic in Gentile surroundings, especially when Jewish and Gentiles believers could not share the same food. In response Paul saw this issue of a 'shared table' as a critical matter that challenged the fundamentals of the faith (see p. 48). He, though himself a Jewish convert, was now convinced that all foods were 'clean' (Romans 14:14). In a spirit of flexible pragmatism, however, he urged people of his conviction to be patient with those with 'weaker' consciences (1 Corinthians 8:1–13; Romans 14:1–4).



But now news reached the elders of the Jerusalem church that Paul was coming up to Jerusalem for Pentecost. It would have sent a flurry of questions through their minds. How could they control the reactions of these Judaizers, who were all 'zealous for the law'? Worse still, they had been informed that Paul was not just working among Gentiles but was also encouraging *Jews* in the Diaspora to 'turn away from Moses, telling them not to circumcise their children or live according to our customs' (Acts 21:20–21). How would these Jewish believers react when they heard that this Paul was in town?

Jerusalem, ever a place where issues of obedience to the Jewish Torah are keenly felt; here a *bar-mitzvah*, focused on a Torah-scroll, is celebrated at the Western Wall.

## Stage-managing Paul's visit

The elders came up with a three-point plan:

- First, Paul and his Gentile companions would be accommodated in the house of Mnason. This man, originally from Cyprus, was a Jewish believer, but one with a Hellenistic (or Greek-speaking) background; he was not one of the (Aramaic-speaking) Hebrew believers, who had the most difficulty with Paul's approach to the Torah (Acts 6:1).
- Next, on their first morning they would be given a private meeting with *all* the elders of the various Jerusalem congregations. There was to be no repeat of what happened back in AD 45 when some major sections of the Jerusalem church only discovered too late what others had privately agreed with Paul (see p. 46).

- Thirdly, Paul would be asked to join four of these local believers in fulfilling a Nazirite vow associated with the Temple. Thus, when news of Paul's arrival percolated out to any concerned Hebrew believers, they would simultaneously learn that Paul was performing an act that showed his obedience to the Torah. Of course, if Paul refused to comply, then that would only show that the rumours were all too true; but hopefully Paul would accede to their request.

Thankfully Paul had no hesitations on this third, crucial point. It was a symbolic gesture that demonstrated his solidarity with his Jewish brothers and sisters. Moreover, it was fully in accord with his own principles, as articulated in 1 Corinthians. When in Jerusalem, he might have said, do what the Jerusalemites do. The problem was that the strict Jewish believers might interpret Paul's Temple vow as a sign that Paul was *always* observant of the Law, when in practice this was not so. For the other side of Paul's principle was, we might say, 'When in Rome, do as the Romans do.' This was the issue left, tantalizingly, unresolved.

*'To those under the law I became like one under the law...; to those not having the law I have become like one not having the law... I have become all things to all people...'*
**1 Corinthians 9:20–22**

Quite probably Paul was content to leave the matter thus. For, if Jesus' words of warning about the Temple and Jerusalem were true (Luke 21:20–24), then in the not-too-distant future historical events might soon overtake this whole debate. All these thorny issues relating to the Temple and the Torah would look very different when the Temple was no more and when the Gentile churches no longer had any church in Jerusalem to which they owed an allegiance.

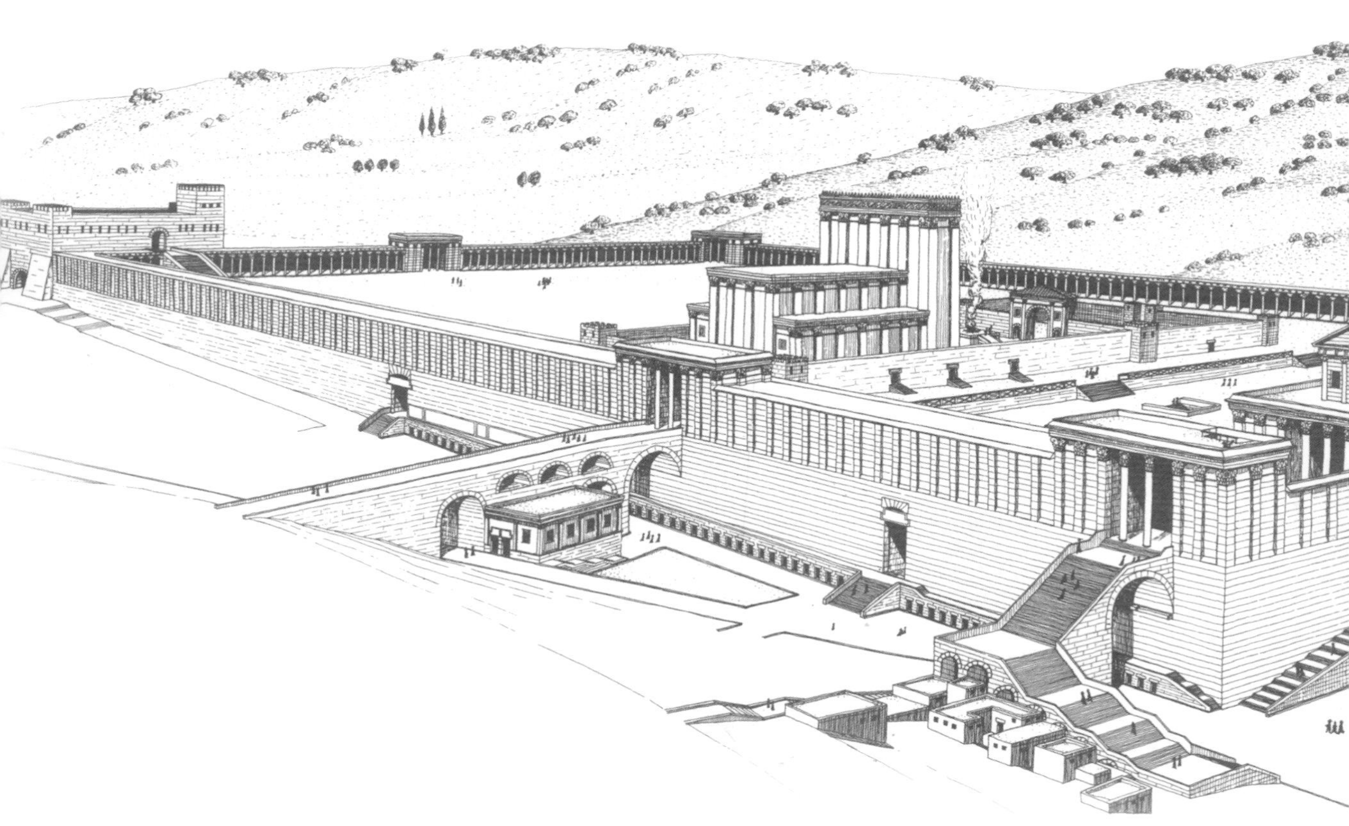

## Paul in Jerusalem's Temple

So Paul joined in the purification rites of these four men, as requested, and paid their expenses. Yet things did not turn out as everyone had hoped. For, when Paul went into the Temple later that week, it provoked a riot.

Almost certainly Paul would have gone into the Temple in any event. After all, it was here that over twenty years before he had received a vision of Jesus telling him to go to the Gentiles (described later in Acts 22:17–18). Conceivably, then, on *all* his subsequent trips to Jerusalem, Paul made a point of going back into the Temple – to be reminded of his calling and to bring back, as it were, an account of his apostleship.

Yet, equally, Paul would have entered the Temple with very mixed feelings. Jesus' prophetic words meant that its future was precarious. Moreover, the Temple promoted a hard-line distinction between Jews and Gentiles: any Gentile who ventured through the low fence that surrounded the inner Court of Israel would be lynched. But Paul believed this division between Jews and Gentiles had been removed by Jesus' death, and all people could now have access to Israel's God. So the Temple was all part of an old system that the gospel was now undermining at its very foundations. And Paul, when wandering through its courts, would be praying that his own people would come to focus not on this Temple but instead on their Messiah.

Even so, when Paul reached this low partition-wall, he would clearly have left his Gentile companions (such as Sopater or Luke himself) in the outer 'Court of the Gentiles' – even if reluctantly. If not, they would have been dead within minutes. Yet this was precisely what Paul was now accused of doing. Among the international

*'When you see Jerusalem being surrounded by armies, you will know that its desolation is near. Then let those who are in Judea flee to the mountains, let those in the city get out, and let those in the country not enter the city. For this is the time of punishment in fulfillment of all that has been written... There will be great distress in the land...'*

**Jesus' prophetic words, as recounted in Luke 21:20–24**

Artist's impression (from the south-west) of the Temple in Paul's day, with the Mount of Olives in the distance. Note (from left to right) the Romans' Antonia Fortress, the tall inner sanctuary (including the Holy of Holies), and the inner 'boundary wall' (*soreq*) which prevented Paul from taking his Gentile converts into the sanctuary. The first Christians may have congregated in Solomon's Colonnade (on the far side); the Sanhedrin may have met in the two-storeyed building on the right (when they interrogated Peter and John in Acts 4 and Paul in Acts 23).

INSET: The inscription warns Gentiles in Greek that they themselves will be responsible for their own deaths if they trespass beyond the *soreq* wall into the Court of Israel.

visitors for Pentecost there were some Jews from Asia who recognized Paul (quite possibly including the Alexander mentioned by Paul as a fierce opponent: see p. 141). They had seen Paul walking around with Trophimus (a Gentile convert known to them from Ephesus). So, as soon as they saw Paul in the Temple, they charged him with having brought Trophimus into the inner sanctuary.

There was no basis for this charge at all, but they knew it would provoke the crowd immediately. Paul was quickly thrown out of the inner sanctuary (its gates being closed after him) and molested by the mob, who tried to kill him. Fortunately the Roman soldiers looking over the Temple precincts from the Antonia Fortress rushed down to intervene; and the Roman commander, Claudius Lysias by name, had Paul put in chains and man-handled into the barracks.

## The opportunity to testify

In all the commotion the Romans had not established what the fuss was all about. Initially the commander thought Paul was the Egyptian Jew who a few years earlier had led a revolt on the Mount of Olives (Acts 22:37–39); so he was surprised when Paul started speaking fluent Greek. Amazingly, he then gave Paul permission to address the crowd – positioned safely on the fortress' steps and presumably handcuffed between soldiers. This was the moment Paul had long been waiting for – his 'once in a lifetime' opportunity to speak to his fellow-Jews in the heart of Jerusalem and to 'testify to the gospel of God's grace' (Acts 20:24). He had made it quite plain that he was willing to 'die in Jerusalem for the name of the Lord Jesus' (Acts 21:13) – if death was to come, what better place than in the city where Jesus himself had died for him? So it was now or never.

*'Woe to me if I do not preach the Gospel!'*
**1 Corinthians 9:16**

Paul probably realized he would have only a few minutes at most. How could he get across the gospel message without immediately causing offence? He chose to speak in Aramaic and simply to tell his own story, emphasizing things with which they might identify: his own zeal for God, his training under respected Gamaliel, his initial hatred of the 'Way' (Acts 21:40 – 22:21). Yet the message about Jesus also came through increasingly clearly: Paul's encounter with this 'Jesus of Nazareth' on the Damascus road, whom Paul then repeatedly identified as 'the Lord'; and Paul's being baptized to wash away his sins. The good news was being proclaimed in Jerusalem.

The audience, however, began to grow restless. The opportunity was fast slipping away. He carried on, but when he mentioned Jesus' calling him to preach to 'the *Gentiles*', that one word was enough to send the crowd into a frenzy once more: 'Rid the earth of him; he's not fit to live!' (Acts 22:22). Paul was promptly rushed inside the barracks, this time to be interrogated under torture. At this critical point Paul made clear that he was by birth a Roman citizen (Acts 22:25). The Roman commander, slightly alarmed, now needed urgently to find out what exactly this Roman citizen was being charged with. The only option, then, was to let the Sanhedrin assemble the next day (probably in the Royal Stoa on the south side of the Temple courts), to bring their charges against Paul (brought there under heavy guard).

A panoramic morning view of Jerusalem from the Mount of Olives, looking across the Kidron Valley towards the site of the ancient Temple (now with the golden Dome of the Rock in its centre). 'Mount Sion' is just out of view to the left (or south-west).

## Investigations, plots and a night-time escape

So the next day Paul was brought before the Sanhedrin. Paul had only finished his first sentence when Ananias, the high priest, had someone strike him on the mouth. The proceedings were clearly going nowhere, so Paul shrewdly opted for a tactic that would throw things into confusion along long-standing party lines.

The Sanhedrin had a majority of Sadducees, but with a vociferous minority of Pharisees: the latter believed in God's ability to raise the dead, the former did not. Paul simply identified himself as a Pharisee who believed in the resurrection. Paul, of course, was implicitly referring to the unique resurrection of *Jesus*, but his fellow Pharisees now rallied round to his side, thinking that someone who was so sound on this point could not be a total rogue! Once again a total uproar ensued, and once again Paul was whisked away. The poor commander was left none the wiser as to what this Paul had done to provoke such animosity – not just from the Temple crowds but now also from the Sanhedrin.

Meanwhile there were those who were not going to let this matter rest. More than 40 of them took a corporate vow not to eat or drink until they had killed Paul: if the Sanhedrin could be persuaded to ask for a further hearing (perhaps this time in a more remote part of the city), then they would ensure that Paul was ambushed and murdered on the way (Acts 23:12–15).

At this point, quite intriguingly, Paul's nephew appeared on the scene (see p. 35). Somehow this young man (still in his teens?) had heard about this plot. Was this quite by chance? Or was it because he and his family moved in the same circles as the conspirators (indicating perhaps that Paul's wider family were known to be themselves strongly opposed to Paul's message)? Either way, he evidently did not want his uncle lynched to death; so he was determined to get the news through to Paul himself and then to the commander (Acts 23:16–22).

Claudius Lysias was now clearly out of his depth. The case had to be heard by the Roman governor in Caesarea and Paul needed to be removed immediately from

Jerusalem. Thus it was that Paul, little over a week since he had first arrived in the city, found himself being led out of the city by cover of night surrounded by a mammoth Roman escort. No fewer than 200 soldiers and 200 spearmen were ordered to accompany him on a 37-mile (60-km) march to Antipatris, at which point it was felt safe to leave Paul to cover the remaining 27 miles (43 km) to Caesarea under the ongoing protection of the 70 cavalry.

It was a dramatic end to Paul's visit. Paul had fled numerous cities in his time (starting with Damascus, when he was dropped over the city wall hidden in a basket) but nothing quite compared with this: hounded out of his mother-city, the Jewish apostle to the Gentiles began his long journey towards Rome in the company of no fewer than 470 Roman soldiers! There would, however, be no similar fanfare to greet him at the other end; and, for Paul, this was now truly farewell to Jerusalem. After this, no one – not even Paul himself – would be able to countenance his return to the city. Paul was just 'too hot to handle' in Jerusalem and the best thing was to keep him as far away from there as possible.

## Key dates: Jerusalem

|  |  |
|---|---|
| c. 1000 BC | David makes Jerusalem his capital. |
| c. 970 BC | Solomon's building of the Temple to the north of David's city. |
| 587/6 BC | Destruction of the Temple by the Babylonians. |
| 515 BC | Rebuilding of the Temple on a smaller scale. |
| 63 BC | Jerusalem brought under Roman rule. |
| c. 15 BC | Herod the Great expands and renovates the Temple. |
| AD 30 | Probable date of Jesus' crucifixion (April 7); first preaching of Christian message by the apostles in Jerusalem and its Temple courts (Acts 3–4). |
| c. AD 31 | Stephen stoned to death outside Jerusalem's walls, witnessed by Paul (Acts 7:59 – 8:1). |
| c. AD 35 | Paul, returning from Arabia and Damascus, spends a fortnight in Jerusalem meeting Barnabas, Peter and other Christians (Acts 9:26–30). |
| AD 41–44 | During the reign of Herod Agrippa, Jerusalem expands northwards (with the construction of a 'third' wall), possibly incorporating the site of Jesus' crucifixion and burial. |
| AD 42 | Peter, having escaped from prison in Jerusalem, leaves Palestine for missionary work elsewhere (Acts 12:17). |
| c. AD 45 | Paul and Barnabas visit Jerusalem to offer famine relief, also meeting Peter, John and James (Acts 11:29–30; Galatians 2:1–10). |
| c. AD 49 | 'Apostolic' Council in Jerusalem (Acts 15:1–33). Clashes with the Romans lead to the massacre of nearly 10,000 people in the Temple courts (Josephus, *War* 2:12). |
| c. AD 54 | An Egyptian Jew, gathering troops on the Mount of Olives, prophesies the collapse of Jerusalem's walls and Rome's defeat; but he vanishes when attacked by governor Felix (Josephus, *War* 2.261). |
| AD 57 | Paul, Luke and their companions travel to Jerusalem with the Gentile collection (late May). Paul is arrested in the Temple and eventually removed from the city (Acts 21:17 – 23:31), having appeared before the high priest Ananias (described as a 'glutton' and 'embezzler' by Josephus, *Antiquities* 20.205–207). |
| AD 62 | James (Jesus' brother) is martyred, thrown down from the Temple Pinnacle by members of the Sanhedrin, during a handover between Roman governors (Eusebius, *Ecclesiastical History* 2:23). |
| c. AD 70 | Romans under Titus destroy the Temple (August); city of Jerusalem burnt to the ground (September). |
| c. AD 135 | Emperor Hadrian refounds the city as 'Aelia Capitolina'. Much of the Upper City now left *outside* the walls of Hadrian's 'camp'. |
| AD 324 | Constantine comes to power in the East, and commissions the building of several churches in and around the city. |
| c. AD 340 | Construction of the 'Upper Church of the Apostles' on 'Mount Sion'. |
| AD 638 | Arrival of Islam. |
| 1099–1185 | Crusader control of the city. |
| c. 1335 | Franciscan rebuilding of Sion as a monastery (the Cenacle). |
| c. 1517 | Suleiman the Magnificent builds the 'Old City' walls. |
| 1948 | Declaration of State of Israel (East Jerusalem coming under Jordanian control). |
| 1967 | Six Day War, resulting in Jerusalem being under Israeli control. |

# Jerusalem today

Those visiting Jerusalem today have many other things on their minds. Only a few come with an express interest in finding the Jerusalem known by Paul. Paul lived in Jerusalem as a young man and revisited it many times, but the only place we know Paul certainly visited was the Temple – during his visits in AD 35 and AD 57 (as described in Acts 22:17–21; 21:27). So that will be our main focus here.

## The Temple and the Antonia Fortress

The **Temple** itself in Paul's day would have been virtually identical to that known by Jesus – though some parts were still under construction. It is mentioned several times in Acts, in connection both with Paul and with other believers.

Some have wondered if the events of Pentecost should be associated with the Temple in some way – certainly this was an easy place for crowds to gather, and the ritual baths by its entrance would have been useful for any baptisms (Acts 2:41). However, a more natural setting is a 'house' (Acts 2:2), perhaps somewhere in the Upper City and opening out onto a crowded street.

Thereafter the first believers used the Temple to meet and to pray. Peter's healing of a paralytic took place near a 'Gate called Beautiful' (Acts 3:2) and the first disciples gathered in 'Solomon's Colonnade' along the Temple's eastern side (Acts 5:12). How long this continued is unclear. They soon attracted the criticisms of the Temple authorities and, in any event, Jesus himself had spoken out unequivocally against the Temple, predicting its destruction in due course. So believers might well have had mixed feelings about it.

A model of Jerusalem's Temple, looking down westwards into the Court of the Women (with its four large candelabra) and then the Court of Israel surrounding the Holy of Holies (with the altar of sacrifice to the left of the main entrance).

On the other hand, James and others continued to be involved in some Temple rituals and it was when James requested Paul to do the same that Paul was arrested – falsely accused of ignoring the warning signs, which forbade Gentiles from trespassing into the inner sanctuary (Acts 21:23–28).

Today Jerusalem's Temple Mount is under Muslim control, so access to these sites is not always possible. Indeed, artists' impressions can yield more insight than trying to gain access to the precise locations. Yet, once on the Temple Mount, visitors are aware just how vast this area was. By going to the north end of the site, they can also sense how close was the Roman Antonia Fortress, from which the soldiers came to sort out the commotion caused by Paul's accusers.

The site of this fortress is well established,

View from the Temple steps on the southern side of the Temple, showing the (now bricked in) Huldah Gates (the main entrance up into the Temple).

being immediately to the north and west of the Temple courts. Indeed some of its stonework is still preserved in the walls of the **Umarraya School**, which overlooks the Temple platform. There is also evidence of the secure passageway that soldiers used to enter the Temple precincts at speed. The Antonia is unlikely to have been the place of Jesus' trial, but this is certainly where Paul gave his defence to the crowds (Acts 22). Thus the excavations visible under the nearby **Ecce Homo Convent** (even if dating to the second century AD) can be seen in a new light – as being on the site, not of Jesus' trial in AD 30, but of Paul's arrest in the summer of AD 57. So those who choose to read out Paul's speech in Acts 22 when standing in the roof garden of the Ecce Homo can rest assured that they are only yards away from where Paul himself had stood.

Easter decorations outside the small cathedral of St Mark in the Old City.

## Elsewhere in the city

Where else Paul visited in Jerusalem must remain conjecture. Paul had come here to study under Gamaliel, but we do not know the location of Gamaliel's 'school'. After his conversion Paul tried to debate with Hellenistic Jews in their synagogues (Acts 9:29); but we do not know where these synagogues were. Paul visited the apostles on at least three occasions, but where such meetings occurred we cannot tell. The only venue mentioned in Acts as a meeting place for believers is the home of John Mark (Acts 12:12). No tradition about its location was preserved in the early church, but presumably this would have been one of the larger houses in the wealthier Upper City, so the Syrian **Cathedral of St Mark**, though lacking a firm tradition, may be in the right general vicinity.

What early tradition there is suggests that the first Christians may also have congregated during that first generation somewhat further to the south – on the site now marked by the **Cenacle**. At least this is where Christians in the fourth century AD remembered the event of the first Pentecost. After Jerusalem's destruction in AD 135, this site was abandoned and found itself to the south of the refounded town. Yet it remains statistically possible that the first Christians met in this area. If so, even though the Cenacle now offers only a Crusader reconstruction of the upper room where the Last Supper was held, its prime significance may instead be that this was the location of the first Christian church. If so, was this where Paul visited the apostles? Indeed, was this where the apostles gathered for their apostolic conference (Acts 15)?

## Paul at the cross

Finally, did Paul ever choose to visit the site of **Golgotha**? When preaching far away from Jerusalem, Paul was often trying to portray Jesus' death to his hearers (Galatians 3:1). So it would only be natural if Paul himself went there occasionally to ponder what Jesus had done for him in that unique location. However, the site may have been transformed out of all recognition in the early 40s AD, as the city expanded north-westwards and houses were built in the vicinity. The unquarried rock formation, now associated with Golgotha and visible within the **Church of the Holy Sepulchre**, was left untouched and the nearby tombs ritually cleansed, but the overall aspect of the place might have been considerably altered.

Even so, it is intriguing to imagine Paul in the vicinity of Golgotha. Did he come here on his first visit after his conversion in AD 35? Did he return here on later visits to find the place quite altered? And what prayers did he pray, maybe under his breath, when standing in the very place where Jesus had died, so he believed, for him? Perhaps he made fresh resolutions to proclaim this message faithfully or quietly uttered his famous dictum: 'May I never boast except in the cross of our Lord Jesus Christ' (Galatians 6:14).

*'I have been crucified with Christ and I no longer live, but Christ lives in me. The life I now live in the body, I live by faith in the Son of God, who loved me and gave himself for me.'*
**Galatians 2:20**

12

CHAPTER

# Caesarea

*'Get ready a detachment of two hundred soldiers, seventy horsemen, and two hundred spearmen to go to Caesarea at nine tonight.' So the soldiers, carrying out [the commander's] orders, took Paul during the night and brought him to Antipatris... When the cavalry arrived in Caesarea they delivered the letter to Felix the governor... [who] ordered that Paul be kept under guard in Herod's palace.*

*Five days later the high priest Ananias came down to Caesarea with some elders and a lawyer, and they brought their charges against Paul before the governor... Felix, who was well acquainted with the Way, adjourned the proceedings... [and] ordered the centurion to keep Paul under guard, but to give him some freedom and permit his friends to take care of his needs... When two years had passed, Felix was succeeded by Porcius Festus; but because Felix wanted to grant the Jews a favour, he left Paul in prison.*

*Festus... convened the court. When Paul appeared, the Jews who had come down from Jerusalem stood around him, bringing many serious charges against him, which they could not prove... Festus said to Paul, 'Are you willing to go up to Jerusalem and stand trial before me there on these charges?' Paul said, 'I am now standing before Caesar's court, where I ought to be tried. I have not done any wrong to the Jews, as you yourself know very well... I appeal to Caesar!'*

**Acts 23:23, 31–35; 24:1, 22–27; 25:6–7, 9–11**

The artist's impression (RIGHT, TOP) shows how far Herod's grand harbour came into the sea; passengers came through its narrow entrance (facing north-west) and then, once disembarked, faced the large Temple of Augustus. On the headland to the south (right) was Herod's Palace, the seat of the Roman governors, where Paul was possibly kept under guard. The aerial view (BELOW) shows the remains of the buildings between Herod's Palace and the impressive semi-circular theatre.

## Place of waiting

So Paul arrived back in Caesarea, under arrest, and was placed in the palace of the former King Herod, the new headquarters of the Roman administration. It was early June in AD 57. What Paul could not know at the time was that he would now be stuck in Caesarea for a further two years – through to the early autumn of AD 59. Paul's journeys around the Mediterranean now come to a grinding halt.

### A tale of two cities: old and new

'Caesarea Maritima' breathed a completely different atmosphere from that of Jerusalem. One was ancient; the other entirely modern. One was up in the hills, somewhat off the beaten-track; the other, located on the flat coastal plain, was already a vital hub of communication, lying on the main road from Egypt to Damascus and well connected by sea with the empire. One was a numinous, religious city, centred on the

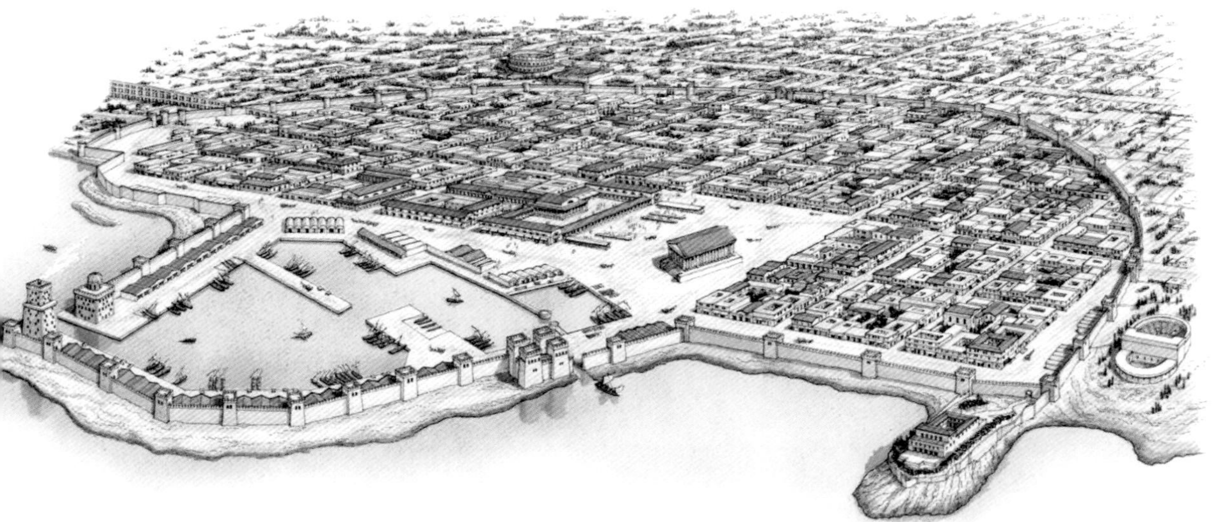



Temple and at the heart of Jewish life; the other a pagan, commercial city, focused around the harbour and government buildings. With hindsight, then, the rise of the one would, almost inevitably, spell the demise of the other. For in some ways Caesarea represented everything that Jerusalem most disliked – the pagan empire, commercial trade, the far too 'modern' world – and it quickly became established as the provincial capital of 'Palestina'.

Herod the Great had needed an alternative political capital; but Palestine also desperately needed a decent harbour. Its coast, washed up with silt from the Nile Delta, was almost entirely smooth (apart from the bays found at modern Haifa to the north and Joppa to the south). Here at Caesarea there had been a tiny harbour, called Strato's Tower, but effectively Herod was building entirely from scratch.

His builders did an incredible job. They built two mammoth harbour walls reaching out far into the sea, using massive cut stones joined together by a recently invented setting agent – concrete. They built a sluice to prevent the harbour from getting silted up. They devised a sewage system which, taking advantage of the tides, flushed away the city's waste

twice a day. And they ensured fresh drinking water reached the city, brought by tunnel and aqueduct from springs beneath Mount Carmel. The whole city, surrounded by a wall and laid out on a grid system, comprised about 8,000 acres (3,200 ha) and included impressive buildings such as a theatre, an amphitheatre, and a temple to Augustus. The initial population was probably entirely Gentile – the Roman army, the imperial administrators and others in commerce – though in due course some small groups of Jews and Samaritans settled in this alien environment.

Luke's account in Acts portrays Caesarea in just this light – as a Gentile place of maritime trade and provincial administration. Earlier in his narrative he devotes nearly two chapters to the story of Peter's encounter with Cornelius, a Roman centurion in Caesarea (Acts 10 – 11:18). He also describes an incident relating to Herod's grandson, Agrippa I, who, having been flattered as a 'god' by an audience of traders, suddenly died – 'eaten by worms' (Acts 12:19–24). Throughout his account we note how several of the tensions between Gentiles and Jews come pointedly to the surface in Caesarea; and we sense how Caesarea and Jerusalem represent two very different worlds (Acts 11:1–18; 21:10–16).

Paul, the apostle to the Gentiles, had learnt to straddle these two worlds. Though trained in Jerusalem, he had been born in a commercial maritime city not unlike Caesarea and, through his missionary travels, he had grown increasingly accustomed to life in such Gentile, secular cities. In other circumstances Paul might have been quite comfortable with being in Caesarea, but he arrived here now under arrest.

## Paul the defendant

Inscription found at Caesarea in 1961, referring to 'PILATUS' – the first archaeological evidence for Pontius Pilate, the procurator at Jesus' trial in Jerusalem.

Soon after his arrival a delegation came down from Jerusalem (including Ananias the high priest) to press their charges on Paul before the Roman governor, Marcus Antonius Felix. Felix had already established a reputation for his tough response to the emerging liberationist movement known as the *sicarii*. Now he had to make a decision about Paul. Was he too some kind of political rebel?

The Sanhedrin delegation, after suitably flattering Felix, described Paul as a 'troublemaker, stirring up riots among the Jews all over the world'; and as 'a ringleader of the Nazarene sect' who had 'tried to desecrate the temple' (Acts 24:5–6). Similar things had been shouted to the crowds back in the Temple: 'this is the man who teaches people everywhere against our people and our law and this place [the temple]' (Acts 21:28). Paul's reputation around the Jewish Diaspora had clearly got back to Jerusalem. There was no denying that his teaching often led to riots; what was less clear was the precise sense in which his teaching was supposed to be critical of those three great bulwarks of Jewish faith – the elect nation of Israel, its Torah and its Temple.

*'Felix exercised the power of a king with the mind of a slave.'*
**Tacitus, *History* 5.9**

Naturally such matters of theology would hold little sway with Felix – hence the Sanhedrin's primary focus on Paul simply as a rebel and riot-monger. Precisely the same tack had been taken with Jesus before Pilate (Luke 23:5). And, as in Jesus' trial, so here the initial charge (of posing some challenge to the Temple) proved impossible for his accusers to support. No witnesses were brought who could speak directly to the charge that Paul had taken Gentiles into the Temple's inner courts – as Paul was quick to point out.

At this point Felix could have closed the case in Paul's favour. Instead he adjourned the proceedings, pending the arrival of Claudius Lysias, the commander who had sent Paul to him from Jerusalem. It proved to be the start of a long period of procrastination. Felix came back with his young Jewish wife (Drusilla was under twenty) to hear Paul speak about his Christian faith, but then stopped him when Paul's preaching became too personal. Luke records that Felix then continued to meet Paul 'frequently' but that he was probably motivated simply by the hope of a bribe. This went on for two whole years (Acts 24:22–26).

Throughout this time, Paul was under guard but was given some 'freedom', with 'his friends' being allowed to 'take care of his needs' (Acts 22:23). This probably refers to Aristarchus and to Luke himself (both mentioned later in Acts 27:2), while Paul's others Gentile companions returned to their various assignments (for example, Timothy, who went back to Ephesus?). Luke almost certainly decided to travel around Palestine to pursue his research on Jesus' ministry; if so, then when back in Caesarea Luke and Paul could conceivably have begun formulating a first draft of what we now know as Luke and Acts. As a result, these two years, though doubtless a very frustrating time, may still have been quite productive. And, given Felix's generally favourable attitude, this time of waiting was not necessarily filled with great anxiety.

*'My accusers did not find me arguing with anyone at the Temple, or stirring up a crowd in the synagogues; and they cannot prove the charges they are now bringing against me… I was ceremonially clean when they found me in the Temple courts. There was no crowd with me, nor was I involved in any disturbance. But there are some Jews from the province of Asia who ought to be here before you and bring charges if they have anything against me…'*

**Acts 24:12–13, 18–19**

Suddenly, however, Felix was summonsed back to Rome – probably to defend himself for the violent way he had quelled some rioting (caused by local Jews demanding an equal right of citizenship within Caesarea). Felix was replaced by Porcius Festus, at which point things for Paul began to look much bleaker. This new governor had no Jewish wife and was quite inexperienced in matters relating to the Jews. One of his first acts was therefore to try to establish good relations with the Sanhedrin, but the Sanhedrin immediately took this as an opportunity to re-ignite the issue of Paul. Coming down to Caesarea they urged that Paul be brought back up to Jerusalem to face trial there (Acts 25:1–3).

Paul's position was now precarious in the extreme. Faced with being returned to Jerusalem (which would almost certainly have led to his death), Paul opted bravely – as was his right as a Roman citizen – to appeal instead to the emperor in Rome. To this Festus replied, perhaps with a measure of relief: 'You have appealed to Caesar; to Caesar you will go' (Acts 25:12).

This is a defining moment in the book of Acts. Paul, who had longed to visit Rome for many years (see Acts 19:21; Romans 1:13, 15:23), now reckoned his best way of getting there was as a Roman prisoner. Yet, as Luke notes ironically, Paul might have walked free, if only Festus had had the courage to clear him of his charges. As the young Herod Agrippa II said to Festus a short while later after hearing Paul speak, 'This man could have been set free if he had not appealed to Caesar' (Acts 26:32).

## The reasons behind his appeal

What drove Paul to this crucial step? Partly it was because the threat was so real that he would be ambushed en route to Jerusalem, or else lynched once he got there. Compared with that, facing the emperor might have seemed the safer option – not least

## Key dates: Caesarea

This Caesarea was often referred to as Caesarea Maritima ('Caesarea by the sea') to distinguish it from Caesarea Philippi, the city developed as the capital of Gaulanitis by Herod's son Philip.

|  |  |
|---|---|
| 22 BC | Herod the Great founds Caesarea on the site of Strato's Tower. |
| 10 BC | Caesarea is dedicated in honour of Caesar Augustus. |
| AD 6 | Caesarea officially recognized as the capital of the Roman province of Palestine. |
| c. AD 38 | Influenced by a vision received while in Joppa, Peter visits the household of a Roman centurion, Cornelius, in Caesarea (Acts 10:9–48). |
| AD 44 | Death of Herod Agrippa II in Caesarea (Acts 12:19–23) |
| AD 52–59 | Marcus Antonius Felix serves as procurator of Palestine. |
| AD 57–59 | Paul is removed from Jerusalem to Caesarea, where he remains in prison for two years (Acts 23:23-25:12); Luke has opportunities to conduct research work around Palestine. |
| AD 59–62 | Porcius Festus serves as procurator of Palestine. |
| AD 66 | The Romans support Syrians against Jews in riots in Caesarea; the 'First Jewish Revolt' spreads from Caesarea throughout Palestine. |
| c. AD 115 | Caesarea suffers damage from a major earthquake. |
| AD 220 | Origen arrives from Alexandria to study and preach in Caesarea; he founds an important library and works on commentaries, establishing a reliable text for the Old Testament in consultation with local rabbis. |
| AD 251–53 | Persecution of Christians under Emperor Decian. |
| AD 313 | Eusebius becomes the bishop of Caesarea and Metropolitan of Palestine; his writings (between c. AD 290 and his death in AD 339) include his *Church History, Martyrs of Palestine, Onomastikon, Preparation and Demonstration of the Gospel* and his *Life of Constantine*. |
| AD 303–310 | Persecution leading to several martyrdoms in Caesarea (see Eusebius, *Martyrs of Palestine*); during one court trial Firmilianus, the Roman governor in Caesarea, indicates he has never heard of a place called 'Jerusalem'. |
| AD 324 | Constantine becomes emperor in the East, encouraging a resurgence of Christian interest in the Holy Land. |
| AD 325 | Eusebius, attending the Council of Nicaea, promises Constantine 50 copies of the Bible (to be produced in the library at Caesarea). |
| AD 325–450 | Significant expansion of Byzantine Caesarea, including new city walls; Caesarea's bishops, however, are gradually eclipsed in relation to the increased significance of Jerusalem within the church. |
| AD 637 | Muslim armies take over Caesarea, leading to its gradual decline. |
| 1101 | The arrival of the Crusaders means the city then changes hands frequently. |
| 1251 | Louis IX of France builds the impressive Crusader walls in the harbour area. |
| 1265 | Sultan Baibars destroy Caesarea. |
| 1878 | Bosnian Muslims take refuge here. |
| 1953 | Underwater archaeology commences, with subsequent excavations of the site by Italian, American and Israeli teams. |
| 1961 | 'Pontius Pilate' inscription is discovered. |

because the rumours circulating about the young Nero during his first five years as emperor were all so positive (see p. 189). Moreover, he had received a favourable verdict from Felix here in Caesarea and from Gallio, the proconsul in Corinth, eight years earlier (Acts 18:14–16). Hopefully this could now be confirmed once and for all by the emperor himself.

Unknown to Paul, however, Nero was becoming unpredictable. Moreover, these previous rulings (that the dispute was simply an *intra*-Jewish matter) were inevitably going to be contested soon as the rapidly expanding church became a visibly Gentile phenomenon. Perhaps Paul was fully aware of this, and so was offering himself deliberately as the ultimate 'test case'. Even if it led to his martyrdom, was this not all an integral part of his calling to be an apostle to the Gentiles?

In any event, as Paul waited in Caesarea, he would have sensed how this cosmopolitan city sat very much at the interface of two worlds. One can almost imagine Paul looking out on the Mediterranean through the windows of his prison cell – an apostle longing to be free, longing to escape the troubled waters of Palestine. This good news about Jesus, although it was a story rooted in Jerusalem, could not be confined to this one 'corner' of the world (Acts 26:27). Indeed this message had to avoid being drowned in the political turmoil that was so evidently brewing back in Jerusalem. If Jesus' predictions were correct, Jerusalem's days were numbered, which meant the message about Jesus *had* to be securely established in other parts of the empire before those stones came tumbling down. So Paul resolved to turn his back on Jerusalem and set his face resolutely towards Rome – even as a prisoner.

Even though he was turning his back on Jerusalem, however, Luke insists that Paul remained totally loyal to his Jewish heritage. Paul claimed to 'worship the God of our ancestors, believing everything laid down in the Law and the Prophets'; to have committed no 'offence against the law of the Jews, or against the Temple'; and to share with his Jewish adversaries the 'same hope of our ancestors' (of resurrection) (Acts 24:14–15; 25:8). But that was precisely the point. The disagreements were 'about a certain Jesus, who had died, but whom Paul asserted to be alive' (Acts 25:19). The cross and resurrection of the Messiah had truly occurred, and together they formed the defining moment of God's purposes towards Israel and the world. The time had now come, Paul insisted, when all the world must be told of what God had done for them. To Rome he would go.

So, though no doubt frustrating, Caesarea was still for Paul a place of powerful proclamation. He did not abandon his hope, or his role as an apostle. His convictions about Jesus only deepened, and strengthened his resolve. And so, in due season, Caesarea became for Paul a point of embarkation and departure into the unknown – the launch pad of his journey to the destiny awaiting him in Rome.



Herod's aqueduct brought water into Caesarea from Mount Carmel. To meet the demands of the expanded city, Hadrian had to build a second aqueduct immediately adjacent to this one (around AD 135).

Floor mosaics from a Byzantine church, located at the southern end of Herod's amphitheatre (and hippodrome).

## Caesarea today

As the capital of Roman Palestine, but long since deserted, Caesarea is a brilliant site to visit. Few modern buildings have been built here and indeed the vast majority of the site, going inland, is covered by sand dunes, undeveloped and unexcavated. Scattered historical remains poke up eerily above the sand; the shape of the Byzantine hippodrome, for example, can be seen in what is now a field. Along the coastline, however, there are several major sights to see (not least the aqueduct, the crusader walls and the theatre) and excavations during the last 40 years have uncovered major finds from under the sand: a Byzantine street, mosaic floors, numerous store-houses and other buildings.

Naturally the site of this large city is quite spread out. Many people visit it in three stops, starting first with the **aqueduct** in the north. This impressive construction, set picturesquely close by the beach, now breaks off about 330 feet (100 m) north of the Byzantine wall. The long section that remains rises up impressively above the sand dunes, offering great views of the Mediterranean through its arches. Closer inspection reveals the remains of *two* aqueduct channels, simply joined side by side: the original built under Herod the Great, the second one by the emperor Hadrian (around AD 130). It is comparatively easy to work out which is which, since the pointed decorative edging of Herod's aqueduct (on the right) is now embedded into Hadrian's (on the left). The combined volume of water (brought from springs 6 miles or 10 km away underneath Mount Carmel) would have been vast – a clear sign of how much Caesarea was expanding through to the Byzantine era (reaching an estimated population of up to 30,000).

The majority of the sites, however, are back near the harbour. Here there is the broad **Byzantine street**, which marks the line of one of the north–south streets in the original first-century plan. The large sloping **Crusader walls**, perhaps because they are so impressive, can cause the casual visitor to lose a sense of how much larger the city was even by the time of Paul. Standing on an observation point just to the north of the Crusader's Cathedral of St Peter, you gain a good view of the modern harbour. The remains of this cathedral stand on the same small hill where once stood the vast **Temple of Augustus** – estimated at some 100 by 165 feet (30 by 50 m) in size. This spectacular building would have dominated the vision of anyone disembarking – a clear indication of pagan and imperial dominance in the province. In the Byzantine period it was replaced by a *martyrium* church (marking the burial site of the martyred Procopius), and later still by a mosque. Nearby numerous first-century **storerooms** can be seen, built to cater for all the cargo. Sometime in the third century AD one of these rooms was seemingly adapted into a **Mithraeum** (a place for worshipping the god Mithras).

It is difficult for visitors to gain a sense of the sheer extent of Herod's royal **harbour** (known as 'Sebastos'). Little of it is immediately obvious above the water line, but aerial photography can reveal quite clearly the submerged lines of Herod's breakwaters, and underwater archaeology has revealed the intricacies of its work. The southern breakwater – measuring over 200 feet wide by 2,000 feet long (60 x 600 m) – had at its end a large tower, quite possibly a lighthouse. The Romans had recently discovered that, if volcanic ash rather than sand was used, then concrete would harden even under water. So these sea walls were founded on concrete blocks, created by pouring concrete into massive wooden frames. There was another, smaller harbour, along the coast further to the south, which sailors preferred because of cheaper fees.

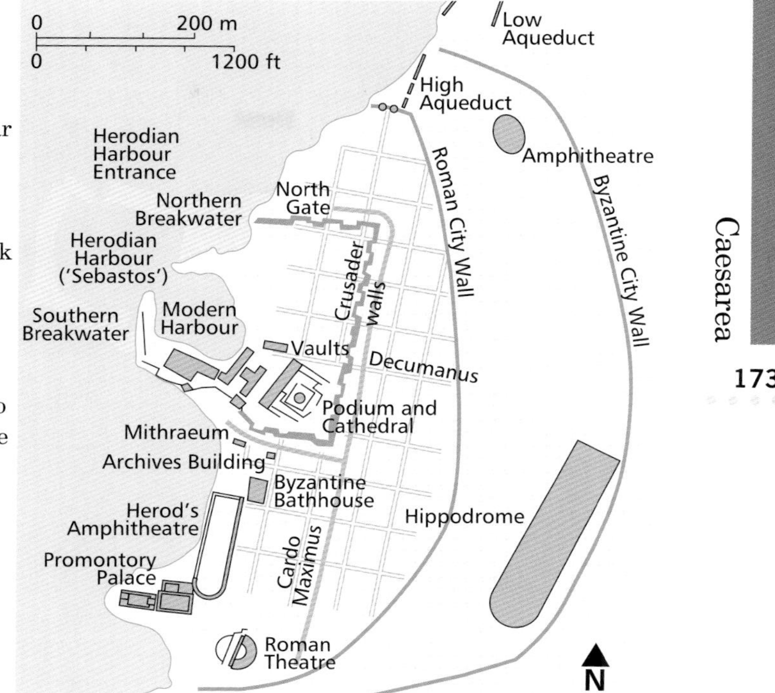

TOP: Plan of Caesarea Maritima.

BELOW: The Crusader ramparts around the harbour area (built by Louis IX of France in 1251).

Herod's royal harbour, however, seems to have ceased operating around the start of the second century AD.

Moving to the south of the Crusader walls, there are some **mosaic floors;** in two different rooms there is a text from Paul's letter to the Romans, encouraging obedience to the state and payment of taxes. Some wonder if this might mark the site of Origen's famous library; more probably this may be a treasury building from the Byzantine period. Either way, one wonders how Paul might have felt to know that his words were now being quoted in Caesarea's floor decorations! The man who had been in prison nearby was now, 300 years later, being vindicated and his words being used to buttress the position of local civic authorities.

From here southwards visitors can witness the fruit of recent excavations, which have brought to light further Byzantine offices and bath-houses, as well as Herod's large **amphitheatre**. Though later used in other ways, this was initially a hippodrome, offering 15,000 spectators a view of the horse and chariot races. Conceivably this was the venue for the story Luke recounts about Herod Agrippa I, just before his death, when he 'sat on his throne and delivered a public address to the people' (Acts 12:21).

'Do you want to be free from fear of the one in authority? Then do what is right and you will receive praise from him.' Paul's words in Romans 13:3, later inscribed in floor mosaics at Caesarea.

Jutting out into the sea is the so-called **'promontory palace'**, with its rectangular ornamental pool. Pottery finds suggest this could well have been the palace of Herod the Great, subsequently used by Roman governors such as Pontius Pilate – hence the location here of the plaster cast of the **column** (originally found in the theatre) which refers to Pilate. To the east there is also an upper terrace containing another courtyard garden and storage areas. Luke expressly says that Paul was 'kept under guard in Herod's palace' (Acts 23:35). So was it somewhere near here that Paul was held prisoner? And was this the place where he made his various defences before governors Felix and Festus?

Finally there is the **theatre**, which stands so impressively after all these years. Sitting in one of its curved-back seats, looking down at the stage with the backdrop of the Mediterranean beyond, one senses why Caesarea feels so different from Jerusalem. It looks away from the Holy Land to the wider world. When Luke and Paul came here from that wider empire, they found themselves in a city not so different from the ones they knew elsewhere. No wonder, as Paul looked out on the waves from his prison, he longed to travel far away to Rome.

# Malta

CHAPTER 13

*When it was decided that we would sail for Italy, Paul and some other prisoners were handed over to a centurion named Julius… We boarded a ship from Adramyttium about to sail for ports along the coast of the province of Asia, and we put out to sea. Aristarchus, a Macedonian from Thessalonica, was with us.*

*The next day we landed at Sidon… From there we… passed to the lee of Cyprus… When we had sailed across the open sea… we landed at Myra in Lycia. There the centurion found an Alexandrian ship sailing for Italy and put us on board… When the wind did not allow us to hold our course, we sailed to the lee of Crete… and came to a place called Fair Havens.*

*Much time had been lost, and sailing had already become dangerous because by now it was after the Fast. [However] since the harbour was unsuitable to winter in, the majority decided that we should sail on, hoping to reach Phoenix…*

*Before very long, a wind of hurricane force, called the 'northeaster', swept down from the island… so we gave way to it and were driven along.*

**Acts 27:1–9, 12, 14–15**

# Haven from shipwreck

When Paul left Caesarea, he knew the future was full of risks; headed for trial before Caesar, he was not expecting an easy ride. He knew that his two-year imprisonment in Caesarea might prove to be only the 'calm before the storm'. What he did not know was that this storm was going to manifest itself in such a brutal, literal way.

For within a few weeks of leaving the relative security of Caesarea, Paul and his companions found themselves on a cargo ship adrift in the middle of the Mediterranean – buffeted along for two long weeks under dark skies with absolutely no idea of where they were. Paul's fate seemingly hung in the balance; and Luke's story about him looked in danger of itself being drowned at sea.

## Luke's emphases

One whole chapter in Acts is devoted to describing this horrendous experience. No doubt this was partly because it was so traumatic for Luke himself. Paul, we learn from elsewhere (2 Corinthians 11:25), had been shipwrecked on at least three previous occasions – even once spending a full 24 hours afloat on the open sea. For Luke, however, this may have been quite beyond anything he had previously experienced. He lived to tell the tale, but only just.

## Ancient sea travel

As biblical commentator F. F. Bruce notes, Luke's account of Paul's voyage and shipwreck in Acts 27 has rightly been called 'one of the most instructive documents for the knowledge of ancient seamanship'.

The ancient Hebrews were not a seafaring people and tended to view the sea in fairly hostile terms. The few references to the sea in the Old Testament emphasize its dangers. By contrast their Phoenician neighbours were famous for their sea journeys and established colonies along the coast of North Africa, and in Malta and Sicily.

Piracy had been a major problem through much of the second and first centuries BC (see pp. 34, 38), but the *Pax Romana* now meant that the Mediterranean was opened up for easier travel to and fro. It was like a 'Roman lake' – hence their referring to it as 'our sea' (*mare nostrum*). The most vital trade route was between Rome and Alexandria, which effectively supplied Rome's urban population with all its grain. There were thousands of ships involved in this trade and they would often travel in large convoys. Since the prevailing winds were north-westerly, the southbound journey could take less than fifteen days; the return journey from Alexandria, however, often required an extensive detour along the shores of the eastern Mediterranean and was marked by a continuous process of 'tacking' into the wind.

The world of the New Testament is evidently one in which people moved around a great deal. Many Jews in the Diaspora tried to visit Jerusalem frequently, and those present on the day of Pentecost included people from places as far apart as Pontus, Asia, Egypt, Cyrene and Rome (Acts 2:9–11) – most of which would have required a sea journey of some kind. In the next few years all the apostles went their separate ways; and people such as Priscilla and Aquila evidently travelled frequently – we hear of them in Rome, then Corinth, then Ephesus, and later back in Rome. One of the amazing things about Luke's account in Acts 27 is the detail that the total number of people on board the sinking ship was 276. Travel in the ancient world was, then as now, big business.

Sailing on the open seas could be dangerous – not so much because of storms, but because cloudy weather made it impossible to fix one's location with any accuracy. So far over 600 wrecks of Roman ships have been found off the shores of Europe. And the boats were not even safe once they were moored: thus Tacitus (*Annals* 15.18) records that in AD 62 (just two years after Paul arrived in Rome) some 200 corn ships sank in a bad storm while harboured in Ostia (Rome's port on the Mediterranean).

The 'safe' sailing season was reckoned to be from 27 May to 14 September. The closed season was from 11 November until 10 March. Travel at other times (in early spring and late autumn) was deemed risky, but not impossible. This explains what we find in the books of Acts: for example, Paul's travelling across land (not by sea) at the start of his second 'missionary journey' in the early spring of AD 52; his wintering in Nicopolis and Corinth (in AD 56/57) and then rendezvousing around mid-March (AD 57) to set out for Jerusalem; and the fact that of the three Jewish festivals in Jerusalem, it was Pentecost (in mid-summer) that was the one most frequented by international visitors (Acts 2:1–11).

Judging from Luke's statement that the Day of Atonement (which fell on 5 October in AD 59) had already passed when they were in Crete, we can calculate that *all* of Paul's voyage towards Rome, even from Caesarea, must have taken place in the risky season. The sailing from Myra was especially hazardous, since it inevitably involved crossing the open sea at the south of the Aegean and by now it was late September.

Yet there is some evidence that the emperor Claudius (trying to prevent a repeat of some of the disastrous grain shortages in Rome) had given to owners of large cargo ships some financial incentives, which then encouraged them to risk more voyages out of season. The vessel Paul boarded at Myra is described by Luke as an 'Alexandrian ship' and so may have been in this category. Some estimate that it was a two-masted vessel, weighing about 250 tons (254 metric tonnes). Such boats regularly had four or more anchors (Acts 27:29) but did not require a vast crew. There would have been other cargo on board (Acts 27:18) which they threw overboard first, but the most valuable (the grain) was kept on board until the very last minute (Acts 27:38).

Finally, some telling confirmation of Luke's accuracy in recording the shipwreck comes from modern navigational calculations: a ship will normally drift at about 1.5 miles (2.5 km) an hour, which tallies closely with the distance over fourteen days from Cauda to Malta (see map on p. 178). Secondly, calculating the amount of angle that a boat could give to the north-easterly breeze yields a figure of 8 degrees above west, which again precisely matches the direction from Cauda to Malta.

Turkish fishing boats in the harbour at Myra, where Paul changed ships en route to Rome (Acts 27:5).

Luke may have had other reasons, however, for giving this episode the coverage he does. Throughout Acts he had wanted to emphasize the sufferings that Paul went through for the sake of Christ. Yet there was also much to learn here from how Paul conducted himself in such adverse circumstances, buoyed up by trust in his God. And then there was the deeper theological point about the overarching providence of God: despite the worst attempts of nature to thwart his purposes, God was faithful to his servant Paul and to the promises he had given him (both in Jerusalem and in the midst of the storm: Acts 23:11; 27:23) that Paul *would* indeed reach Rome and stand trial before the emperor. Despite the storms of life, God's word was a reliable anchor.

Some have even suggested that Luke was also drawing an intended parallel with Jesus' own experience. For, just as Jesus went through the valley of the cross before emerging into the light of the resurrection, so his servant Paul had to pass through this perilous storm before his own experience of rescue on Malta and then arrival in Rome. Be that as it may, the whole episode adds considerable drama and suspense to Luke's narrative. The reader is reasonably confident that all will work out well in the end – not least because it is written in the first person plural by the writer who had evidently survived to tell the tale! Yet the story is filled with suspense. And it certainly makes the moment when Paul eventually arrives in Rome all the more climactic – because we know all the traumas that Paul has been through in order to reach that final destination.



## Setting sail under guard

The story certainly bears retelling. Paul has to travel as a prisoner under guard. Luke travels with him, perhaps offering his services as the ship's doctor. Aristarchus (who had come up with the collection to Jerusalem: Acts 20:4) is also travelling with them – either as Paul's 'servant' or perhaps (for some unknown reason) under guard as well (he is later described by Paul in Colossians 4:10 as his 'fellow-*prisoner*'). There were a handful of other prisoners with them, all of them placed under the supervision of a centurion called Julius, who puts them on board a ship returning to its home port of Adrymyttium (on the Aegean, near Assos).

Julius is with them all the way to Rome. One of the features we can detect in Luke's account is the sense of mutual respect that becomes established between Paul and this centurion. Thus, within 24 hours of leaving Caesarea, Julius allows Paul to go on shore to meet his Christian friends in Sidon. Later he includes Paul in the debate about where to winter. And just before the moment of shipwreck he takes Paul's advice, when warned by Paul that the sailors are about to jump into the only lifeboat. So, when a little later some soldiers plan to kill all the prisoners (as they were technically supposed to do, to prevent them swimming to freedom), we read that 'the centurion wanted to spare Paul's life and kept them from carrying out their plan' (Acts 27:42–43). Something about Paul had impressed Julius. Perhaps initially this was simply a recognition that this was no ordinary prisoner – a man of learning, who was also accompanied voluntarily by a personal friend of some distinction (who claimed to be both a doctor and a historian!). As time went by, however, perhaps as he saw Paul praying and sensed his courage, he began to recognize something deeper still.

Julius belonged to the 'Imperial Regiment' and may have been a *frumentarius*, one of those who supervised the safe passage of the vital grain ships from Alexandria to

Rome. This is quite possible, for when they eventually reach Myra (one of the key ports on this grain route) Julius finds an 'Alexandrian ship sailing for Italy' (Acts 27:6). But from Myra onwards it is now a race against time. The (north-westerly?) winds have already been against them en route to Myra and they then spend 'many days' close to the coast of Asia Minor as they make their way slowly past Rhodes towards Cnidus. At that point they are unable to land and so are blown southwards towards Crete. They successfully round Cape Salmone (on its eastern end) and so are able to enter the calmer waters to the south of Crete, docking at a small harbour known (aptly enough) as 'Fair Havens'.

By now the time of sailing on the open seas has clearly passed. Luke writes that it was now 'after the Fast' – the Jewish Day of Atonement, which in AD 59 fell on 5 October. They are clearly not going to reach Rome and will need to spend the winter somewhere on Crete. But where? Paul urges them to stay here in Fair Havens (perhaps eager too to see if he can make contact with any of the new believers on Crete). The majority, however, think it is worth trying to go round to the much larger port of Phoenix, further to the west. Encouraged by the arrival of a gentle southerly breeze, the crew weigh anchor. But as they round Cape Matala they are greeted by a 'wind of hurricane force', coming down the slopes of Mount Ida – a fearsome north-easterly wind known to the locals as 'Euraquilo'.




## Storm at sea

There is now a real danger that they will be blown all the way down to the Syrtis sandbars near the coast of Cyrene (on the north coast of Africa). So the crew take advantage of some final calm in the lee of a tiny island known as Cauda (23 miles or 37 km to the south of Crete): they haul in the lifeboat (normally towed astern), undergird the hull with ropes, jettison some of the ship's tackle and cargo, and set the sail in such a way that, by presenting the starboard side of the boat to the wind, they can hold a course of about 8 degrees north of west. This keeps open the possibility, if

**Map of Paul's final journey towards Rome (AD 59–60).**

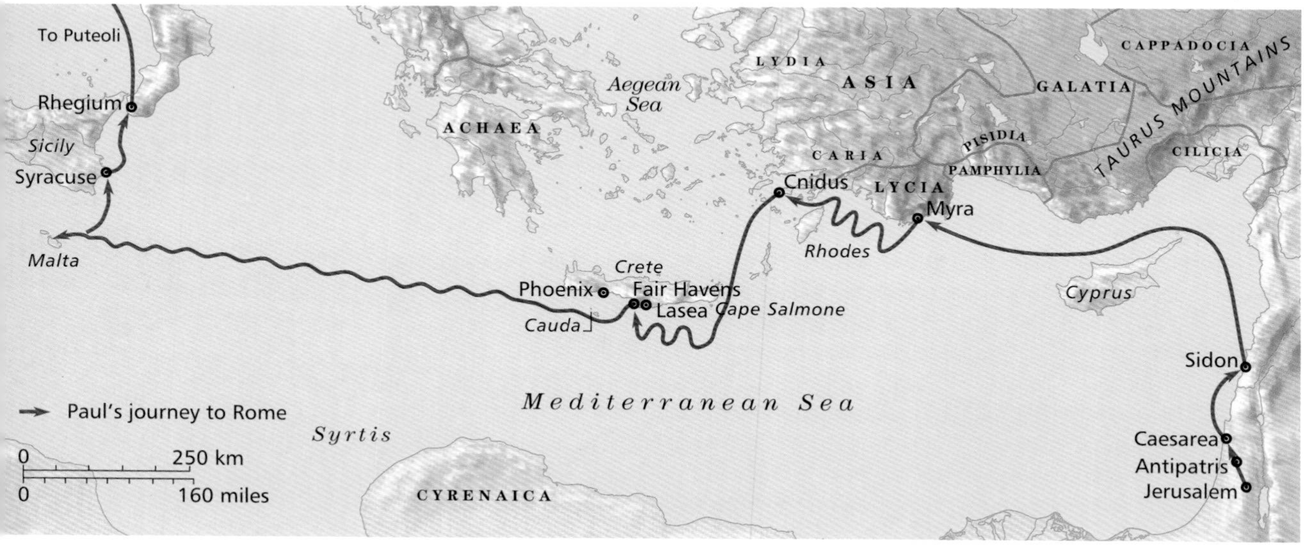

only the wind will die down, of their eventually reaching Greece or Italy – as long as they keep in the northern half of the Mediterranean (a section known at that time as the 'Adria', to the south of what we now call the 'Adriatic').

The storm, however, does not die down. After fourteen long days and nights, they are still at sea. Without any sun or stars, they are unable to get any clear idea of where they are. Then around midnight the sailors sense they are near land, take soundings that confirm this, and drop some anchors in the hope that this will prevent the ship from being dashed on any rocks in the darkness. Just before dawn Paul urges everyone to eat, speaking again about the promise he has received in a dream from God that not one of them will die and reminding them of his earlier prediction that they would run aground on some island. So he breaks bread (not unlike Jesus himself, when facing his earlier 'storm' in Jerusalem) and gives thanks to God 'in front of them all' (Acts 27:35). And then they all wait, eyes fixed on the western horizon, for some daylight. Will it ever come? What will they see? What will each have to do to survive?





## Land in sight

When daylight comes, the crew see a 'bay with a sandy beach' and aim to run the ship aground, but as they head towards the beach the ship runs aground on a sandbar. The storm is still blowing and the 'pounding of the surf' causes the ship's stern to start breaking in pieces. It is time to abandon ship. The centurion orders all those who can swim to jump overboard. Then the non-swimmers are told to take a plank of wood from the sinking ship and use that to cling onto as they too jump into the water. No fewer than 276 people, heads all bobbing in the surf, make for the shore. Amazingly, not least after two weeks of suspense and sheer exhaustion, everyone reaches the shore in safety.

They discover they have landed on an island 'called Malta' – quite possibly a place that Luke and Paul had never even heard of. The local inhabitants speak neither Greek nor Latin – hence Luke's (technically correct) description of them as 'barbarians' – but they make them welcome. Everyone is chilled to the bone, so the inhabitants build a large fire for them all. It was an act, comments Luke with his memory of how they all felt on that rainy November morning, of 'unusual kindness'.

And even then, the drama that surrounds Paul is not over. Picking up some brushwood for the fire, he also picks up a snake, which then clings to his arm. Paul shrugs it off into the fire, but the locals imagine he must be a murderer whom Justice will bring to his death – if not by shipwreck, then by poison. But Paul lives on, much to their surprise. Instead of dying, Paul becomes in the coming days an agent of healing – first to an old man suffering from dysentery (the father of Publius, the 'chief official of the island', who had welcomed the ship's survivors onto his nearby estate for three days) and then to the 'rest of the sick on the island' (Acts 28:1–9).

*'Others went out on the sea in ships… They saw the works of the Lord, his wonderful deeds in the deep. For he spoke and stirred up a tempest that lifted high the waves. They mounted up to the heavens and went down to the depths. Then they cried out to the Lord in their trouble, and he brought them out of their distress. He stilled the storm to a whisper; the waves of the sea were hushed. They were glad when it grew calm, and he guided them to their desired haven.'*

**Psalm 107:22–30**

## Luke and Paul on Malta

It is a gripping story, recounted by Luke in fine detail. Though some (bizarrely) think Luke's account is a literary fiction, everything suggests instead that the detail comes from Luke's own, painful, first-hand experience. Indeed it may be not too far-fetched to imagine just what this meant for Luke himself – struggling to keep his few wrapped

Excavations behind the Church of San Pawl Milqi: these first-century remains may mark the site of Publius' villa, where he welcomed the shipwreck's survivors (Acts 28:7).

possessions safe above the waterline, knowing that in them were his precious manuscripts and historical notes that would one day form the basis for his Gospel. His survival, their survival, Paul's survival – *the whole thing was an utter miracle*.

And when, with modern hindsight, we add the fact that the Maltese islands span only 20 miles (32 km) from north to south, we realize there was a very high probability of the ship bypassing the islands completely. To use a phrase (culled from a more modern form of travel), the 'angle of re-entry' was exceedingly narrow; a few degrees either way and Paul would have been last seen with his companions, helpless and adrift, starving and bound for death, heading off towards the coast of modern Tunisia.

So Paul and Luke would have seen their time in Malta – both their safe arrival and then their winter lodging there – as a sign to them of God's gracious provision and providence. No survivor from that ship, not even the centurion Julius, would even consider setting sail again until the spring (normally soon after 10 March). Getting the prisoners to Rome would simply have to wait. And, given that they were on an island from which there was thus no escaping, Julius may have given Paul a reasonable amount of freedom. Perhaps the whole island became a kind of 'open prison'. Was Paul allowed to preach his message about Christ in any local synagogues? Did his healing ministry lead to some conversions (including that of Publius) and the founding of a small church on the island? Luke does not tell us. He simply notes that they were on Malta for 'three months' and that the islanders 'honoured us in many ways', eventually furnishing them with the necessary supplies for their onward journey (Acts 28:10–11).

For Paul, Luke and Aristarchus, then, this time on Malta would have given them much-needed space for recovery, both physically and mentally. And surviving the shipwreck, far from discouraging Paul about what awaited him in Rome, may only have served to bolster his confidence that he was in the centre of God's will, strengthening his determination to see the matter through to its end. 'Do not be afraid', he had heard in the storm; 'you must stand trial before Caesar' (Acts 27:24). So, even if that trial proved to be yet another storm, there was nothing that could be thrown at him now that would prevent him from reaching his goal.

# Malta today

The three Maltese islands (of Malta, Gozo and the tiny, almost deserted, Comino) have a combined square area of some 122 square miles (316 sq km) and are home to around 400,000 residents, making them one of the most densely populated areas in Europe. Located 58 miles (92 km) to the south of Sicily and 180 miles (288 km) to the east of Tunisia, they have a warm climate as well as a distinctive culture – coloured by the various empires and rulers who have been interested in these small, remote islands with their quite strategic location. These have included over the centuries: Phoenicians, Carthaginians, Romans, Byzantines, Arabs, Normans and Spaniards; more recently, the French, Italians and British; and, for well over two hundred years, the distinctive Knights of St John. The local language, Malti, reflects all this, showing signs of Arabic and European influences; almost all the place names in Malta, for example, are Arabic in origin, reflecting the era when Malta was under Islamic rule.

The Maltese speak of living on a 'small island with a great history'. Yet reading Maltese guidebooks or attending a presentation such as 'the Malta Experience' (in Valletta), one can receive the distinct impression that Paul's visit in AD 59/60, though so brief, was one of the most important events to occur in the nation's long and varied history. Paul never intended to visit, but his three-month-long stay on the island is remembered keenly. Statues or paintings of him greet you frequently on many a street corner. One guidebook lists over 50 churches on the island that in some way develop this link with Paul.

## Key dates: Malta

|  |  |
|---|---|
| c. 3600–2500 BC | The Copper Age, when megalithic temples, the oldest surviving free-standing structures in the world, are built. |
| c. 800–450 BC | Island influenced by Etruscans and Greeks, but especially Phoenician traders. |
| c. 450–250 BC | Influence of Phoenicia's chief colony in North Africa, Carthage. |
| 218 BC | The Romans gain control of the islands during the Second Punic War (218–201 BC); the main island is named 'Melita' (Latin for 'honey'), as is its capital – located in the area of (later) Mdina. |
| AD 59 | Paul shipwrecked en route to Rome (November/December), probably at the north-eastern end of the main island. |
| AD 60 | Paul sets sail for Rome (late March?). |
| AD 395–800s | Malta administered from distant Constantinople. |
| AD 870 | Malta falls into Arab hands. |
| 1090 | The Norman count, Roger Guiscard, defeats the Arabs; subsequent colonization by both Germany and Spain. |
| 1249 | Final departure of Muslim residents. |
| 1530 | After losing Rhodes in 1522–23 to the Turks, the Knights Hospitallers of the Order of St John of Jerusalem are given Malta by the Holy Roman emperor, Charles V; they settle in Birgu (now Vittoriosa) to the south of the Grand Harbour. |
| 1565 | Suleiman the Magnificent orders the 'Great Siege' but is repulsed by the Knights under Jean de la Vallette. Subsequent building of Valletta's massive battlements, its aqueduct and its two main churches: St John's Co-Cathedral and the Church of St Paul's Shipwreck. |
| 1798 | Napoleon Bonaparte on Malta for six days (June), imposing French administration, leading to revolts. |
| 1800 | Nelson (returning from the Nile) delivers the islands, leading to Malta becoming a British 'Crown Colony' in 1814. |
| 1818 | Pope Pius VII donates to the Church of St Paul's Shipwreck some of the pillar on which by tradition Paul was beheaded in Rome. |
| 1921 | Maltese Council established for domestic affairs. |
| 1940-42 | Second 'Great Siege' by Axis forces; King George VI of England awards Malta the George Cross for its brave resistance. |
| 1964 | Full independence from Britain. |
| 1974 | Establishment of Maltese 'Republic'. |

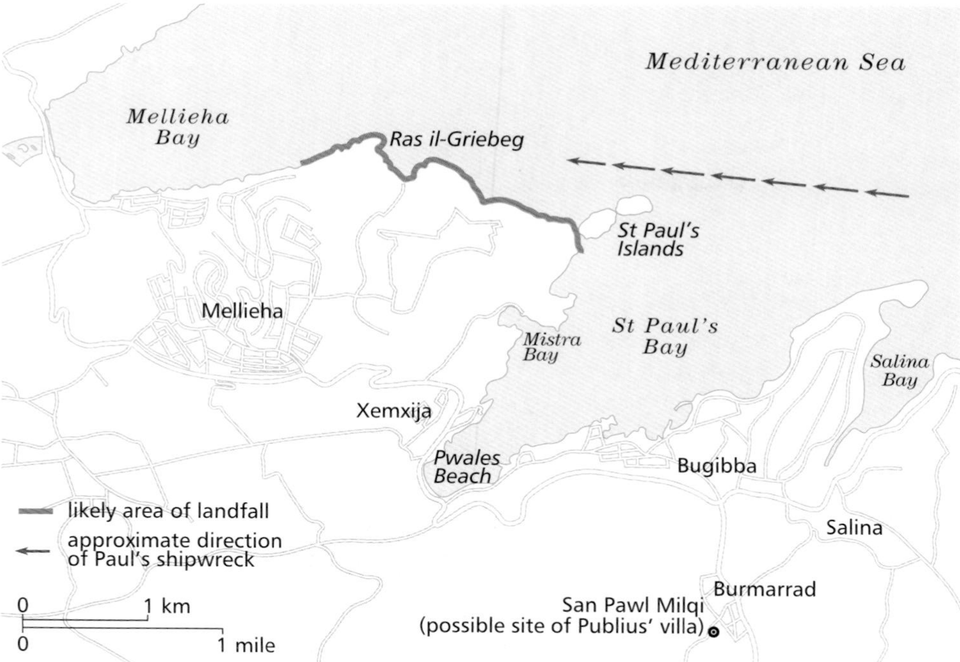


Plan of St Paul's Bay (north-east Malta).

This is perhaps hardly suprising, given that for centuries Malta has been a strongly Catholic country (a recent census showed that 52 per cent of the population still saw themselves as regular church-goers). So Paul is portrayed as founding the Christian church on these islands, with Publius (the Roman official whom he healed) being commemorated as a saint and even as Malta's first 'bishop'. Pope Paul VI referred to Malta simply as the 'island of St Paul'.

So visitors on the Pauline trail have several sites to see. From a New Testament perspective the priority must be to see the area on the north-east of the island where, by tradition, Paul's ship ran aground – the area of **St Paul's Bay**. Luke's narrative is not very specific, indicating only that the sailors saw a 'bay' with what looked like a 'sandy beach' but were not able to run the ship up on to the sand because it first hit a sandbar. In fact there are very few sandy beaches on Malta's eastern coast – much of it is marked by shallow limestone cliffs. So the traditional focus on the two larger bays at the north of the island (now known as Mellieha Bay and St Paul's Bay) makes good sense. Between them there is also a remote hilly promontory which also has some shoreline that, despite some low cliffs, might still be termed 'sandy' because of the predominant yellow limestone.

For whatever reason the southern bay has been identified over the years as the more precise site, with a town on its southern shore now called 'St Paul's Bay'. Meanwhile, at the entrance to the bay (on its northern side) are a couple of small, deserted outcrops of rock which have been called **'St Paul's Islands'**. On the larger one, only 30 yards (27 m) from the mainland, there is a statue of St Paul (built in 1845). His back is turned as he looks out to sea – as if to welcome (or is it to warn?) those sailing into the bay. About 100 yards (90 m) further to the north, there is a reef of rocks going out eastwards into the sea. In low water or rough weather the resultant line of surf could well give the impression of the sea being divided in two – which

'St Paul's Islands' at sunset on a winter's day. Paul's landing-point may have been in this small bay, or a little further to the left (north).

might be what Luke means when he describes the place as *diathalassos* (Acts 27:39).

Good views of the general area can be had from across the bay (driving from Qawra through Bugibba towards St Paul's Bay). For a closer view of St Paul's Islands, keep on Route 1 through Xemxija and then take a left fork onto a lane that doubles back under the main road and takes you north-eastwards along the shoreline, past the attractive small Mistra Bay. The tarmac ends at the 'Pinto Redoubt', from where a 20-minute walk (across rough but manageable terrain) brings you out opposite the statue of Paul. Looking northwards along the coast you can see the soft yellow limestone formations that may have looked like a beach from out at sea. Somewhere near here was the place where Paul and Luke, wet and exhausted, landed on that November morning.

In our Pauline travels this is one of the few places that has been left unchanged over the centuries. So it is a great place in which to imagine the events of that distant morning: nearly 300 people struggling in the water, some swimming, some clutching to pieces of the broken boat, but all eventually reaching dry land, their long nightmare over. In the summer season there are boat trips out to the area of St Paul's Islands, with opportunities to see the remains of two other (modern) vessels that sank near this rugged shoreline.

In the first century AD this whole area would have been a remote place – just a few fishermen's homes here and there – so it may have taken a while for news of the shipwreck to spread; and, given the large number of passengers, it was not surprising that they soon had to be accommodated on Publius' estate. Presumably this estate was inland, on one of the nearby hills. A possible site lies a couple of miles to the south, marked now by the small seventeenth-century **Church of San Pawl Milqi ('St Paul Welcomed')** above Burmarrad. Around the church there are some excavations revealing a large Roman villa and farm – in an ideal location between some terraced hills and the coast. Was this where Paul healed Publius' father? Did he and Luke continue to stay here for several weeks?

Other traditional sites in the area may only reflect subsequent conjecture: the **Apostle's Fountain** (Ghajn Rasul, near the head of St Paul's Bay), where Paul supposedly baptized his first converts; and the seventeenth-century Church of **St Paul's Bonfire** (though there is some evidence of a Norman church on this site, possibly itself on the site of an earlier foundation). Both of these feature in local celebrations in honour of Paul: on 10 February (the festival associated with his shipwreck) and 29 June (the festival of Peter and Paul), when people go out in fishing boats to hear Mass conducted on St Paul's Islands. Despite the February date for commemorating the shipwreck, however, it is reasonably clear from Luke's narrative that it occurred much earlier in the winter, probably in November.

Other sites are 'Pauline' more by way of extension. For example, there are several good places of an archaeological nature that give a good sense of life in Malta during the Roman period: the **Roman Villa** in Rabat (with its delightful mosaics and some statues of Claudius and his family, dating back perhaps to the very decade of Paul's visit); the **Roman Baths** to the west, just inshore from Golden Bay; and the **Maritime Museum** in Vittoriosa, with some anchors dating back to the era of Paul's shipwreck.

In Mdina and Rabat, which together mark the site of the island's ancient capital (known in Roman times as Melita), there are some further sites of interest. **St Paul's Cathedral** in Mdina is built, according to tradition, over a small fourth-century church that marked the supposed site where Paul converted Publius to the Christian faith. A Norman church was also built on this site in Paul's honour. The present church has some impressive paintings depicting Paul's life, including the *Conversion of St Paul* by Mattia Preti.

In Rabat, **St Paul's Grotto** (beneath the parish church of St Paul) contains a couple of caves which, according to tradition, were places where Paul lived and preached during his stay. There is no knowing when this tradition began and, of course, no sure knowledge that Paul ever stayed in the island's capital (though it is not unlikely). What we are seeing here, however, replicates something encountered more frequently in the Holy Land, whereby rock caves (being fixed, natural phenomena that clearly were *in existence* in the New Testament period) later attract a tradition of having been *used* in the New Testament period. There was no reason at all for Paul to use a cave for his home or for any meetings with fellow-believers, but this immobile cave is our one sure link back to the time of his visit.

Nearby (about 150 yards or 137 m along some narrow streets) there are **St Paul's Catacombs** (and also St Agatha's Catacombs). The names date from a much later period, but these impressive tombs give a chilling insight into the patterns of burial in the later Roman period (from the third to the fifth centuries AD). This was a chief burial area for the island's capital, so those buried here would have included many non-Christians (there are grave markings showing Jewish menorah, for example, as well as some Christian 'Chi-Ro' symbols); but it gives a clear reminder of the way the ancients faced death with their varied hopes of an afterlife.

Finally, a visit should be paid to the impressive **Church of St Paul's Shipwreck** in Valletta. Originally designed by the same Gerolamo Cassar responsible for the nearby Co-Cathedral of St John the Baptist, it describes itself as a 'hidden gem'. Facing onto one of Valetta's narrow streets and normally approached through a side-entrance in another, narrower street, it is indeed hidden and could be easily missed.

Inside there is a series of paintings depicting Paul's eventful stay on Malta (done by Palombi in the early twentieth century). There is also the brightly-coloured gilded wooden statue of Paul made in 1659 (with its unambiguous Latin title *Praedicator Veritatis*: 'the preacher of the Truth'), which is carried in procession around the city every year on 10 February.

More poignantly there is also in the southern transept a reliquary containing what is claimed to be some of Paul's right-hand wrist-bone (donated to the church in 1823) and a section of the pillar on which by tradition Paul was beheaded. The latter was donated to the church by Pope Pius VII in 1818, being cut away from the remainder of the pillar still housed in Rome in the Church of St Paul Outside the Walls. With its top now covered by a silver representation of Paul's severed head, it is a slightly gruesome reminder of what eventually was the fate of Jesus' apostle to the Gentiles – once he left the sanctuary of Malta and reached the empire's capital in Rome.

14

CHAPTER

# Rome

*After three months we put out to sea in a ship that had wintered in the island – it was an Alexandrian ship with the figurehead of the twin gods Castor and Pollux. We put in at Syracuse… then arrived at Rhegium… and on the following day we reached Puteoli. There we found some believers who invited us to spend a week with them. And so we came to Rome. The believers there had heard that we were coming, and they travelled as far as the Forum of Appius and the Three Taverns to meet us. At the sight of these people Paul thanked God and was encouraged.*

*When we got to Rome, Paul was allowed to live by himself, with a soldier to guard him. Three days later he called together the local Jewish leaders… and they came in even larger numbers to the place where he was staying.*

**Acts 28:11–17, 23**

# The goal at the centre

Every day, as spring returned, Paul knew his time to leave was growing closer. Julius, the centurion, would not wait beyond the middle of March. Another Alexandrian ship, wintering on Malta with passengers and grain cargo, was also waiting for the start of the sailing season. The day came when it was time to go.

## From Malta to Rome

The route was pretty much fixed: just over 90 miles (146 km) north to Syracuse (an ancient Greek colony, the main city of Sicily); then onwards to Rhegium, sailing carefully through the narrow straits of Messina (between Sicily and the 'toe' of Italy); and then to Puteoli (modern Pozzuoli) in the Bay of Naples. At that point the ship (which would be too large to moor at Rome's shallower harbour, Ostia) would need to transfer its grain cargo to a smaller vessel. As this would take some time, Julius decided the remainder of the journey would be overland. So Paul, together with Luke and Aristarchus, was granted a seven-day stopover and found that, even here in Puteoli, there was a small group of Christian believers.

These believers would straightaway have sent a message to the believers in Rome: 'Paul has arrived and is on his way!' Paul had last been seen alive the previous September (boarding a ship at Myra), so there may not have been a single Christian in the empire who knew where he was. Now here he was, alive and well!

This relief and excitement can be sensed too in the way some Roman Christians then came out to meet him along the Appian Way. After all his struggles and his long-held desire to see Rome, it must have meant so much to Paul to be approaching the city – albeit on foot and under guard – and now to be met by this welcoming party. 'At the sight of these men,' writes Luke with some emotional restraint, 'Paul thanked God and took courage' (Acts 28:15). According to Acts 19:21, Paul had first expressed his desire to visit Rome in the early 50s AD; but now ten years later – at long, long last – Luke and Paul were entering through the gates of the imperial capital. 'And so we came to *Rome*'!





## Upon first arrival

Soon after their arrival, Paul hosted a meeting with the leaders of the local synagogue (28:17–27). After all, the gospel was 'for the Jew first' (Romans 1:16). They initially responded in an open way, assuring Paul they had not heard anything negative about him from Jerusalem. This was good news for Paul: if he feared that the Jerusalem hierarchy had warned the Roman synagogue about him (perhaps seeking their support in prosecuting him), they had not yet done so. Paul had managed to reach Rome ahead of any negative press.

However, the Roman synagogue leaders *had* heard about this new movement that proclaimed Jesus as Messiah: 'people everywhere are talking against this sect' (Acts 28:22). Indeed their own temporary expulsion from Rome under Claudius may have been triggered by the rioting that had ensued as people in the synagogues debated the nature of Jesus' messiahship. If so, these synagogue rulers knew all too well that this new teaching was an explosive issue. To their credit, they decided to listen to Paul – this was a man with evident standing within this new movement – but understandably the result was soon divisive: some were convinced, others not, and they left in vigorous disagreement.

As Paul saw this all too familiar spectacle, he quoted from Isaiah about God's people being 'ever hearing but never understanding' (Isaiah 6:9 in Acts 28:26): 'God's salvation has been sent to the Gentiles, and they will listen!' (Acts 28:28). For Luke this episode epitomizes the whole pattern of Paul's ministry: the Jewish teacher, frequently rejected by his own people, who was now the apostle bringing good news to Gentiles. So Luke concludes his narrative:

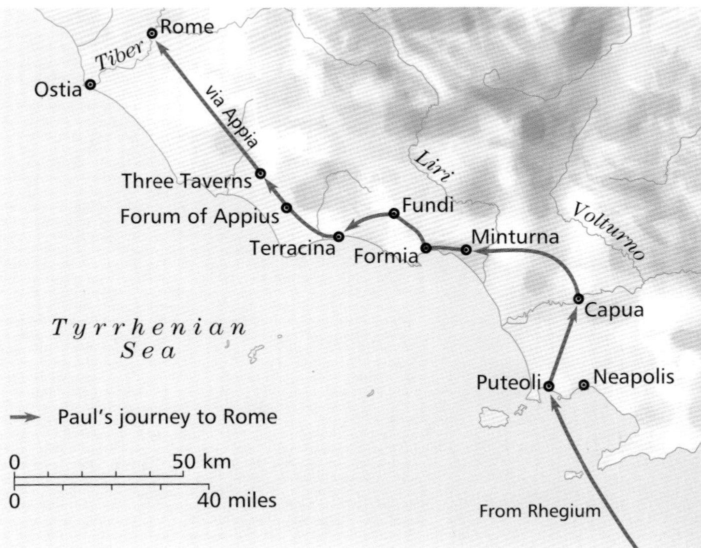


**Map of Paul's final approach (overland) to Rome in the spring of AD 60.**

*For two whole years Paul stayed there in his own rented house and welcomed all who came to see him. Boldly and without hindrance he preached the kingdom of God and taught about the Lord Jesus Christ.*

**Acts 28:30–31**

These are Luke's last recorded words. After two volumes, his final picture is this positive one of Paul being able to meet people and talk about Christ – not abandoned to solitary confinement in some dark cell. But Luke's words leave us with a string of questions: why has Paul's trial not taken place after two years? Did he *ever* stand trial before Caesar? Was he ever released from Rome, even on some kind of parole? How did Paul's life come to an end? And they leave questions too about Luke himself: why did he close his narrative at this point? Did he (and his readers) know all too well what happened next? If so, why did he not mention it (even as an epilogue)? The narrative has been building up to a climax (of Paul appearing before Caesar), but it never comes.

In the following we will offer a likely sequence of events, based on the evidence of Paul's letters from Rome and later accounts of his death (see pp. 194, 201). Although some of our reconstructed narrative remains conjecture, it may help us to engage imaginatively with what really took place.

## Reconstructing Paul's last days: a suggested narrative

Paul, we suggest, arrives in Rome exhausted. Both he and Luke, his 'beloved doctor' (Colossians 4:14), are not as young as they once were. So it comes as a great relief when Paul is given *libera custodia* – a form of imprisonment that does not involve incarceration. The authorities realize this prisoner is determined to stand trial and will not be trying to escape. So, although he is still kept in chains and guarded by a rotation of Roman soldiers, Paul is able to rent his own apartment and welcome visitors.

So far so good. But soon Paul realizes he will be waiting some considerable time. He is given an initial hearing (perhaps merely a registration of his name and the charges involved), but nothing can be done if his prosecutors prove slow in coming from Jerusalem to press charges. There is also now a considerable backlog in the system. Nero began his reign promising he would speed up the trial system by hearing cases himself *in person*; now, however, five years on, Nero is less predictable and is only hearing cases on a whim. So Paul, having braced himself for the worst, is now placed 'on hold'. And waiting is sometimes almost worse than the real thing – enough to fray the nerves of the strongest fighter.

Moreover, this news about Nero's altered character is particularly alarming. When first appealing to Caesar back in Palestine, Paul had heard glowing reports about the young emperor; but now Nero is rumoured to be mentally unhinged. What if Nero, wishing to clear his backlog, simply sentences him to death, giving him barely a chance to open his mouth? Paul's vision of witnessing boldly to Christ (even if it leads to his death) looks likely never to happen.

So Paul has to come to terms with the fact that he may be on 'death row' for several years. Worse still, it might prove at the end to be a little pointless. He now sees the complexity of vast imperial Rome and perhaps senses the darkness at the empire's heart. It is all somewhat unnerving and enough to make anyone feel acutely conscious of how small they are.

*'When he [Nero] was asked according to custom to sign the warrant for the execution of a man who had been condemned to death, he said: "How I wish I had never learned to write!"'*

**Suetonius, *Life of Nero* 10:15, describing the promising signs at the start of Nero's reign**

## The response of local Christians

Yet there may have been worse to come. What if the welcome of the local Christians proved less than warm? We can imagine something of the scenario. Yes, that small number had welcomed him out on the Appian Way, but even as they chatted on the road, perhaps it became clear that not everything in the Roman church was well.

In particular, ever since the return of the Jewish believers (with the general return of the Jews in AD 54), there have been tensions between them and the Gentile believers: some Gentiles are arrogantly dismissive of the Jewish believers; in return, some Jews are embarrassed about associating with Gentiles. Paul's own letter to the Romans was an attempt to ease the situation (with its balanced teaching about Jew and Gentile both praising God together); but some in Rome may not have appreciated Paul's vision or seen it as workable. So the arrival of this Jewish 'apostle to the Gentiles' may only serve to pour some oil on the flames. Which 'side' will he back?

Moreover, there are real fears in both groups that Paul's brazen determination to face Caesar will effectively 'blow the whistle' on their delicate relations with the Roman authorities. Remember that, until now, the young Christian movement had remained

LEFT: Model of Rome in the era of Constantine (c. AD 325), viewed from the north. From right to left in the middle distance we see the River Tiber, the semi-circular Theatre of Marcellus, the Jupiter Temple (on the Capitoline Hill), the clustered buildings of the ancient Forum and eventually the Colosseum. Beyond (TOP) is the Circus Maximus; on the other side (MIDDLE) the colonnaded *fora* built by Julius Caesar and Augustus.

undercover through being associated in the public mind with the Jewish synagogue. In Roman eyes Judaism was a permitted religion (*religio licita*) and Jewish people were exempt from sacrificing to the gods or emperors. But what will happen once the Roman authorities recognize that this Christian movement is now predominantly Gentile and increasingly disowned by mainstream Judaism? The situation in Rome itself is particularly delicate. The synagogues are beginning to re-gather momentum (after their period of exile) and may soon be able to persuade the authorities that they are distancing themselves from these odd 'Messianics'.

Into this tense situation comes Paul, ready to make a stand on behalf of Gentile believers, quite willing himself apparently to pay the ultimate price. But what if his coming 'blows their cover'? Frankly, many believers in Rome would much rather Paul did *not* appear before Caesar. And some secretly wish he had only stayed away.

For Paul this is enough, at least on a bad day, to get him down. For, even if he does get his opportunity to appear before Caesar, some of the very people for whom he is doing this will be acutely ungrateful. Being a martyr is hard enough, but doubly so if some people will never understand what you have done or why.

## Paul's response

Paul responds in various ways. In one of his letters he frankly acknowledges that his coming has caused division among believers; yet he sees this in a positive light, noting that other believers instead have a renewed confidence and that, either way, 'Christ is preached' (Philippians 1:18). In other letters he ensures that his Gentile readers, even though far away from Rome, sense that what he is going through is *on their behalf*; thus, even if there are some unappreciative believers in Rome, at least there will be Gentiles elsewhere who will value his stand.

RIGHT: Plan of ancient Rome before and after Paul's time.

A third response (which we cannot substantiate here in any detail) is that Paul encourages someone else to write to the Jewish believers in Rome the letter we now know as 'Hebrews'. In this letter the Jewish believers, fearful of being seen as separating from Judaism, are exhorted not to lapse back into the synagogue but to share in the disgrace of following a crucified Jesus (Hebrews 13:13). Very probably this was written to the church in Rome by someone who knew them well but was currently travelling outside 'Italy' (Hebrews 13:24). Paul himself may have had nothing to do with it, but it remains possible that he was involved somehow in its commissioning, recognizing that the local Jewish believers, even if they might not listen to him, might listen to a trusted former member of their community.

Finally, we see Paul's response in the sheer honesty shown in his personal letter to Timothy (2 Timothy). In this intimate letter, probably written soon after Paul's arrival in Rome (see p. 12), Paul evidently feels isolated and let down by local believers, and he has heard some news that leaves him feeling deserted by 'everyone in the province of Asia' (2 Timothy 1:15). So twice he urges Timothy to come soon – certainly before the coming winter, if possible (2 Timothy 4:9, 21). And, if Timothy cannot come (was Timothy himself in prison?), Paul asks that, unlike some of those in Rome, Timothy should not be 'ashamed' of him. Here we see Paul at his lowest. Despite all the strength his letter manifests, there are clear signs that for Paul life in Rome is tough: isolation, together with feeling deserted by some local believers, has struck him down.

## Joy amid sorrow

The good news is that Timothy responds positively, arriving in Rome a few months later. For we find him named as the co-author of Paul's next letters: Colossians and Philemon. In fact, the arrival of Timothy, his closest associate, probably gives Paul just the boost he needs. Soon, inspired by this young friend, his thoughts once more begin to soar on eagles' wings. Thus to this period probably belongs too his visionary letter to the Ephesians: guided by Timothy's recent knowledge of the situation in Asia, the apostle responds to any departure from his teaching by setting out a positive and compelling vision of the many blessings believers have in Christ (Ephesians 1:3–14).

*'Do not be ashamed of me the Lord's prisoner... only Luke is with me... everyone deserted me...'*
**2 Timothy 1:8; 4:11, 16**

During this time Paul is buoyed up by other visitors (Colossians 1:7; Philemon 13). Evidently people in the east have learnt not only that Paul is safe, but also that he is likely to be in Rome for some time, and is able to receive visitors. For a while, however, Paul hears nothing from Philippi, which bothers him; but then, to his delight, Epaphroditus arrives. In his response (Philippians, perhaps Paul's last letter) he speaks of desiring to die and 'be with Christ' (Philippians 1:23); of having learnt

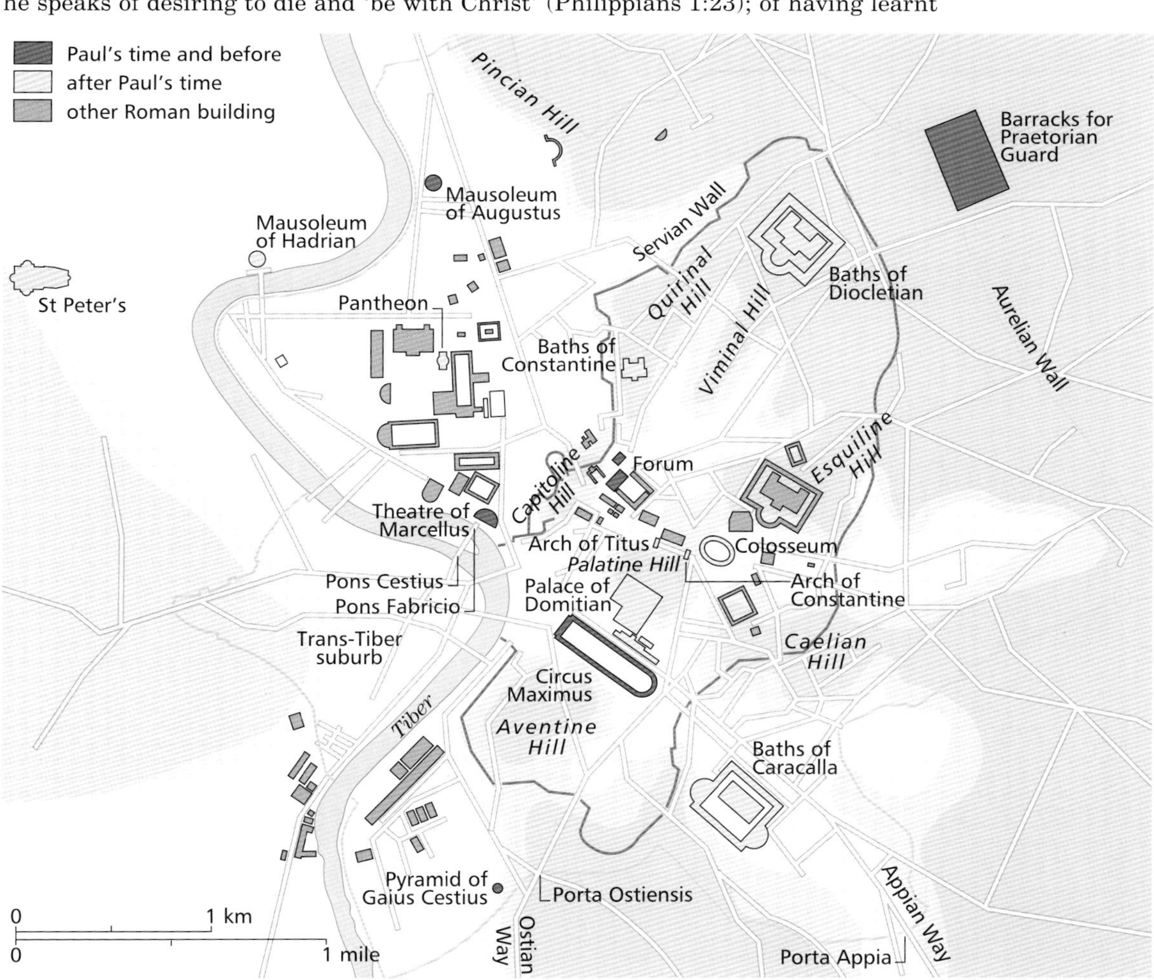

'contentment' in all circumstances; and of being able to do everything asked of him through Christ's strength (Philippians 4:13). His main command, however, repeated at the end, is simply to 'rejoice in the Lord' (Philippians 3:1; 4:4). Truly Paul's joy has returned.

Within Philippians, however, there is a small phrase that may solve another of our historical puzzles. For he writes of his relief that Epaphroditus' illness did not lead to his death; through this God spared Paul from experiencing 'sorrow upon sorrow' (Philippians 2:27). This seems to imply that Paul has recently experienced a 'sorrow', added to which this second 'sorrow' would have been almost unbearable. Is this Paul's way of referring to the death of his great travelling companion, the 'beloved doctor' Luke?

If so, Luke's slightly unsatisfactory ending to the book of Acts would make eminent sense. He did not proceed to give details about Paul's trial (let alone his martyrdom), because he, Luke, *died before Paul*. What he had written, he had written, and no one had the temerity to add to this brilliant work, which was his unique bequest to the church.

## Key dates: Rome

|  |  |
|---|---|
| 753 BC | Traditional date for the founding of Rome under King Romulus. |
| 27 BC–AD 14 | Augustus as Caesar. |
| AD 49 | Emperor Claudius expels all Jews from Rome because of violent riots caused 'at the instigation of Chrestus' (Suetonius, *Life of Claudius* 25.4) – possibly a confused reference to Jesus as the Messiah ('*Christos*'). |
| AD 54 | Start of Nero's reign: Jews return to Rome (including Aquila and Priscilla?). |
| AD 60 | Paul, walking along the Appian Way, arrives in Rome (late March). He stays under 'house arrest' for at least two years (Acts 28:30), writing his 'prison epistles'. |
| AD 63 or 64 | Death of Paul (beheaded on the Ostian Way) and of Peter (crucified upside down and buried near Nero's new circus on Vatican Hill); alternative date is no later than AD 67. |
| AD 64 | Great fire of Rome (18 July), for which Nero blames the local Christians. |
| AD 72 | Vespasian commissions the Colosseum (completed in AD 80) to replace Nero's Golden Palace. |
| AD 96 | Clement, a presbyter in Rome, writes to the church in Corinth (1 Clement). |
| c. AD 108 | Ignatius of Antioch is brought to Rome and martyred. |
| AD 120 | Hadrian reconstructs the Pantheon. |
| AD 150–60 | Justin Martyr writes his two *Apologies* for the Christian faith to Emperor Antoninus Pius, but is eventually martyred in Rome. |
| AD 210 | Hippolytus, a presbyter in Rome, describes the eucharistic liturgy used in Rome. |
| AD 257–58? | Severe persecution of Christians; bones of Peter and Paul may have temporarily been stored in catacombs (later known as San Sebastino). |
| AD 270 | Building of Aurelian's walls. |
| AD 312 | Constantine wins the Battle of Milvian Bridge and enters Rome, claiming to have conquered through using a sign of Christ; Arch of Constantine erected. |
| AD 324 | Constantine commissions two new churches over the tombs of both Peter and Paul (completed over twenty years later). |
| AD 390 | A vast new church, commissioned by Theodosius, is consecrated over Paul's tomb. |
| AD 400s | Church built at Tre Fontane (possible site of Paul's execution). |
| AD 410 | First sack of Rome by Alaric and the Goths. |
| AD 422 | Founding of St Sabina by Peter the Illyrian. |
| AD 440–61 | Leo the Great as Pope, agreeing to the teaching of the Council of Chalcedon (AD 451). |
| AD 475 | Fall of western Roman empire; transfer of power to Byzantium. |
| 1506 | Pope Julius II lays foundation for a new St Peter's Basilica. |
| 1626 | New Basilica of St Peter's consecrated. |
| 1823 | 'St Paul outside the Walls' is destroyed by fire (15 July). |
| 1870 | Unification of Italy. |
| 1929 | Lateran treaty creates a separate Vatican state. |
| 1962 | Second Vatican Council begins. |

## Paul's final years

If so, then Luke-Acts cannot help us figure out what eventually happened to Paul for the simple reason that *at the time of writing the author himself did not know*. Even so, there are clear hints in Acts that Paul was determined to stand trial before Caesar and was willing to be martyred. The historical presumption, then, must be that this indeed came to pass. If not, one might have expected a host of early witnesses and traditions to arise to set the matter straight.

Seen in this light, the few hints in the ancient sources that perhaps Paul was released and had another season of ministry away from Rome seem fairly weak. Almost certainly these arise in part from ancient authors such as Eusebius trying, like their modern counterparts, to find a possible setting for the pastoral epistles in the mid-60s AD (for an alternative setting, which removes the need for this, see p. 12). Partly too they stem from a misreading of Clement's words (quoted on p. 194, which were written around AD 96). Some see his reference to a *terma* (often translated as 'end') as referring to Spain (Romans 15:24). Yet Clement's wording evidently implies that this *terma* was identical with the place where Paul 'bore testimony before the rulers and departed this world' – which was clearly Rome. So *terma* might better be translated as Paul's 'goal'. The likelihood, then, is that Paul never again left Rome. He had reached his 'goal'.

In all probability, then, Paul was eventually brought before Nero in AD 63 or 64, after a period of some three years waiting for trial. Conceivably a delegation from Jerusalem arrived, determined to press charges in person. Josephus (*Antiquities* 20.9) informs us that Jewish leaders in Jerusalem took advantage of the interregnum resulting from the departure of Festus in AD 62 to kill James, Jesus' brother; so there may have been a parallel attempt to get rid of Paul. They decided the time was right.

What happened when Paul eventually appeared before Nero? We simply have no idea. There would hardly have been a Christian sympathizer in the courtroom. Almost certainly Nero heard Paul proclaim Christ as the true Lord of the world – which is what Paul had emphasized so clearly in his last letter to the Philippians (2:10–11). And it is not hard to imagine how the paranoid emperor would have responded. After a few moments, Nero would have had enough. Almost certainly it was a mockery of a trial – as was Jesus'. And Paul – again like his master before him – found himself condemned to death and led out of the city gate. The only difference was that, as a Roman citizen, Paul was spared the indignity of crucifixion.

And so, somewhere outside the city to the south-west (on or near the Ostian Way: see pp. 199–200), some duty-soldiers followed their orders. Not knowing the import of what they were doing, they beheaded this strange Jewish man. The journey that had begun, so strangely, outside the city gates of Damascus some 30 years previously had now come to its end, so bravely, outside the city gates of Rome.

## In conclusion: Paul and Peter leading the flock

*Nero substituted as culprits a class of men, loathed for their vices, whom the crowd styled 'Christians'. Christus had been executed by the procurator Pontius Pilate… and the pernicious superstition was checked for a short time, only to break out afresh, not only in Judea, the home of the plague, but in Rome itself, where all the horrible and shameful things in the world find a home... A huge multitude was convicted, not so much on the ground of incendiarism as for hatred of the human race. Their execution was made a matter of sport: some were sewn up in the skins of wild beasts and savaged to death by dogs; others were fastened to crosses as living torches...*

**Tacitus, *Annals* 15.44:3–8**

As we look back on this whole episode of Paul in Rome, we have to acknowledge an unpleasant historical possibility: namely, that Nero's encounter with Paul (and perhaps also Peter, who was martyred in Rome around this time) may have played some part in prompting Nero later to blame the Christians for Rome's great fire in July AD 64.

Suetonius and Tacitus both make it clear that Christians in Rome suffered a severe outbreak of persecution on the orders of Nero after the fire. There is also the testimony of Clement. Listing examples of Christian heroes persecuted because of 'jealousy', he refers to Peter and then to Paul:

*Let us come to those who were athletes in the days nearest to our own. Through jealousy and envy the greatest and most righteous pillars of the church were persecuted...*

*Peter... made his way to his allotted place of glory. Paul, on account of jealousy and strife, showed the way to the prize of endurance; seven times he wore fetters, he was exiled, he was stoned, he was a herald both in the east and in the west... and, having reached the limit [*terma*] of the west, he bore testimony before the rulers, and so departed from the world and was taken up into the holy place – the greatest example of endurance...*

*To these men of holy life was gathered together a great multitude of the elect, who through their endurance amid many indignities and tortures because of jealousy presented to us a noble example.*

**1 Clement 5:1–7; 6:1**

*'Punishment was inflicted on the Christians, a class of men addicted to a novel and mischievous superstition.'*

**Suetonius, *Life of Nero* 16.2**

This last sentence seems to be a gentle, discreet way of referring to the 'indignities' of the Neronian persecution. Note, then, how Clement's order suggests that Peter and Paul were *precisely in the vanguard* of that significant persecution – some of the very first Christians to arouse Nero's anger. They went first and, tragically, others soon had to follow. No doubt Nero was learning about this new sect from other quarters too, but leading figures such as Peter and Paul may have attracted his attention more than most. In some senses, then, the fears triggered in Roman Christians by Paul's arrival proved to be well founded. He *did* play a part in bringing down the storm upon their heads.

Yet, when looked at from another perspective, the action of Peter and Paul can be seen for the brave thing that it was. For it was perhaps increasingly clear to all in Rome in the early 60s AD that persecution of Christians was imminent. All that was unclear was the 'when' and the 'how'. In these circumstances, as the wolves gathered around the sheep, it was only fitting that the two great shepherds of the flock offered to go ahead of the sheep, laying down their lives for them in advance.

Both men had long had a sense that such a death might one day be required of them. And seemingly, both sensed that if there was any one place where that death would symbolically be significant for the long-term life of the church, it was Rome. Sooner or later the fundamental clash between the good news of Jesus as King and the idolatry of the Roman state had to be brought into the light. It is remarkable that the young church had grown so fast that her leading apostles felt the time had come to force the issue so soon. But there was no doubting that, when it did come, there was only one place where the issue could be forced – and so they came to Rome. This was where the storm-clouds were gathering; Rome, not Jerusalem, would mark their journey's end.

## The developing church in Rome

The history of how the church developed in Rome in the centuries after the New Testament is a fascinating story. By the time of Constantine it was clearly the leading church within the western half of the empire, and numerous churches were built in Rome from the late third century through to the seventh century and beyond.

During the same period the 'papacy' developed apace, with the link back to Peter as the primary apostle and the first 'bishop' of Rome becoming firmly established. In the earliest tradition, however, Peter is not especially distinguished from Paul. The two apostles are frequently bracketed together (see, for example, Ignatius and Irenaeus), with *both* being seen as effectively the co-founders of the Roman church; though not the first to bring the gospel to Rome, they *had* led the way when it came to martyrdom.

So the stories of their deaths are often told together (possibly they *were* put to death at exactly the same time). This is paralleled in art and sculpture: in the catacombs, the graffiti expressly appeals to both Peter and Paul ('*Petre et Paule*'); and early sarcophagi (late fourth century AD) frequently have both apostles on either side of Christ. It was entirely fitting therefore that Constantine commissioned churches over *both* their tombs.

However, there were obvious ecclesiastical reasons (not least in the light of Jesus' words to Peter in Matthew 16) why the link with Peter would gain the upper hand – as expressed so powerfully now through the vast size and splendour of St Peter's Basilica, built over Peter's tomb on the Vatican Hill.

By the late Middle Ages Constantine's church was falling into disrepair, so Pope Julius II laid the foundation for a replacement, which ended up (over a century later) being far larger than he had ever anticipated. St Peter's today is the largest church in Europe and has become the visible centre for Roman Catholics throughout the world.

Even so, it is intriguing to note that from the early fourth century onwards the bishops of Rome used an alternative church (St John on the Lateran Hill) as their 'cathedral' – a practice that continued effectively until quite recent times. And, for those eager to espouse the cause of Paul, there is something appropriate about the way St Peter's Basilica is fronted on either side by large statues of *both* apostles. Despite those who would try to separate these two ancient figures, perhaps even seeing them as rivals and enemies, there was – in both their living and their dying – an incredible unity of purpose, focused on the good news of Jesus Christ.

# Rome today

Saving the best until last, our final Pauline site is Rome: the capital of Paul's world, still a capital of a modern state, and the centre of a major branch within the Christian church. Modern Rome is a great city, vibrant with life and full of history. Looking over the city (for example, from the roof of St Peter's or the promenade on the Janiculum Hill), you see the distinctive 'S-bend' of the Tiber, following its unchanged route since ancient times; you see a skyline littered with impressive buildings and monuments – including more than a dozen high-domed churches; and you can still see the distinctive features of several of the city's famous 'seven hills' (the Capitoline, Palatine and Aventine, in particular). Here you are in a place where history is all around you.



Finding Paul, however, in this large city is somewhat more difficult: being just one individual in the vast tide of humanity that has visited Rome, he requires of us some searching. We have to peel back so many layers of history (be it Mussolini in modern times or Bernini in the Baroque period, be it Michelangelo in the Renaissance period or the Popes of the Medieval world) – all in search of a man who was here in the early 60s AD for just three or four years. Moreover, as far as we know, he was here under continual 'house arrest' and so may never himself have got to see some of the key sites in Rome. There is also no knowing where he stayed during that period: some scholars (based on a variant reading of Acts 28:16) think Paul was handed over to an official based at a camp on the Caelian Hill, others to one based on the Viminal Hill; but in either case, Paul's house seems to have been elsewhere – outside these camps. Nor can we be sure where he came to trial, though there is some early evidence as to the place of his burial (see p. 202). So we need here to ask a slightly broader question: even though our focus is on Paul (not on the many other attractions within Rome today), is it possible to find traces of the Rome that existed when Paul visited in AD 60?

View along the *Via Sacra* (looking south-eastwards) with the three columns of the temple dedicated to Castor and Pollux; the white Arch of Titus can be seen in the distance.

## Rome in AD 60: the Forum

To gain a sense of first-century Rome, there is no avoiding a stroll through the **ancient Forum**. Since the 1600s some 50 feet (15 m) of rubbish has been cleared to return this to ground level in Paul's day. Originally a marshy spot between the nearby hills, the area had been drained out in the sixth century BC and became the city's commercial and civic centre. In this cramped space were located Rome's financial markets, its tax offices and administrative buildings, its law courts and many temples.

Running through the middle of the forum is the **'sacred way'** (*Via Sacra*): along this route marched all of Rome's returning armies, walking in triumphal procession towards the Capitoline Hill. Passing various key buildings on the north side (including the Basilica Aemilia, the city's central bank), the soldiers would then have passed the **curia** (or senate house). During the days of Rome's republic, this was the seat of government, the place where Cicero and others made their speeches; its restoration (in the 1930s) gives an idea of its original vast height, which was necessary for acoustics. Nearby, on the other side of the *Via Sacra*, is the **rostrum** from which speeches were made to the crowds (including, presumably, Mark Antony's address after Caesar's murder). Beyond it, close underneath the sheer face of the Capitoline escarpment, are the remains of the **Temple of Saturn**, the state treasury, which also housed a golden milestone recording the distances from Rome to the many cities in its empire.

*'Friends, Romans, countrymen, lend me your ears. I come to bury Caesar, not to praise him...'*

**Shakespeare, *Julius Caesar* III, ii**

Going back along the southern side of the Forum there are three columns in a straight line. This is all that remains of what may have been the most impressive building in Paul's day – a temple rebuilt by Tiberius in AD 6 and dedicated to Rome's twin patrons **Castor and Pollux**; these same gods, you may recall, were figureheads on the prow of the ship in which Paul had sailed from Malta (Acts 28:11). Nearby are three further columns, this time part of the small round **Temple of Vesta**, the goddess of the hearth; this was the building in which the city's 'eternal flame' was carefully guarded by the Vestal Virgins (who lived in the large three-storeyed 'convent' next door).

By Paul's day this ancient Forum, the tiny hub of the entire empire, was becoming more and more congested, almost claustrophobic: recent constructions included a large **Julian basilica** and a **temple in honour of Julius Caesar** (where wreaths are still laid in his honour). So Rome's rulers (from Julius Caesar onwards) had started a spate of buildings and other *fora* to the north; some parts of these are still visible but many parts now lie buried underneath Mussolini's unpopular but suitably named modern road, the *Via dei Fori Imperiali*.

Detail from the Arch of Titus: Roman troops plunder treasures from Jerusalem's Temple, including the seven-branched candelabra (*menorah*).

Many other buildings now visible in the original Forum therefore date to after Paul's day, not least the impressive **Arch of Septimius Severus** (c. AD 193–211) and the smaller **Arch of Titus** (built in AD 81 to mark Titus' victory in Judea). The reliefs under this arch show Roman soldiers carrying loot plundered from Jerusalem's Temple (including a seven-branched menorah). Standing underneath this arch, one wonders what Paul might have felt had he been able to stand here and look up at its decorations. For here was written in stone the sad end to all the dreams of his fellow-Jews, who longed for independence. Here was confirmation instead that Jesus had been a true prophet, warning his own nation of what the Roman armies would do, and seeing correctly the way in which God was fulfilling his promises – inaugurating a quite different kingdom. Perhaps too for Paul there was here a more personal sign that his life's work as an apostle to the Gentiles (establishing a Jew-cum-

## Visiting Rome today

There is so much to see in Rome. Visitors inevitably find themselves interacting simultaneously with the many different levels within the city's history. Some guidebooks divide up the material into chronological periods (for example, the ancient city, Christian Rome, the Renaissance and Baroque periods, more recent history); others divide up the city geographically into its many different areas (for example, Capitoline, Trastevere etc).

The following itinerary lists some of the main sites that all visitors might consider, suggesting a framework based around a long weekend:

**Thursday** Arrival in Rome; late afternoon view from Janiculum promenade; evening meal in Trastevere suburb, wandering towards Tiber Island.

**Friday** Walking tour: San Clemente, Colosseum, Forum (and Palatine?); Capitol musuems or Imperial forums; Pantheon and Piazza Navona (with shopping).

**Saturday** Vatican: Museums and St Peter's (including dome and crypt); St Paul outside the Walls; evening at Trevi Fountain.

**Sunday** Morning worship at local churches; afternoon of free exploration (for example, Villa Borghese, museums, St Maria Maggiore or smaller churches); evening at Spanish Steps.

**Monday** St John Lateran; catacombs; excursion either (eastwards) to Tivoli Gardens and Villa D'Este, or (southwards) walking along Appian Way (near Ciampino airport), or (westwards) to ancient Ostia (near Fiumicino airport).

There are major churches in Rome that attract countless visitors each year: St Peter's, St Paul's, St John Lateran (for many centuries the Popes' 'cathedral'), St Maria Maggiore, St Croce in Gerusalemme and San Sebastiano (in the catacombs). Those interested in early Christian art and architecture, however, might also consider some of the following: St Maria in Trastevere (perhaps the oldest official church in Rome, dating to the mid-third century, but now a twelfth-century gem with fine mosaics in the apse and over the western facade); St Pudenziana (fifth-century mosaics); St Sabina (a spacious fifth-century church with carving on the doors containing the oldest depiction of the crucifixion); St Maria in Cosmedin (sixth century with some Romanesque touches); St Agnes Outside the Walls (seventh-century apse mosaics); St Prassede (ninth-century mosaics); St Pietro in Vincoli (supposedly housing Peter's chains from prison; also Michaelangelo's figure of Moses).

The following churches contain important depictions of Paul in art (in addition to those found in musuems): St Maria del Popolo (Caravaggio's *Conversion*); St Pietro in Montorio (Vasari's *Conversion*); Sts Cosmias and Damian (sixth-century mosaic); the Scala Santa (thirteenth-century fresco). The depiction of Paul in the mosaics of St Prassede is particularly fine.

NB Papal audiences are on Wednesday mornings (tickets for seats are available in advance from the 'bronze door' next to St Peter's). Some museums and churches are closed on Mondays.

BELOW LEFT: Mosaics in the roof of St Prassede's (ninth century); the four Evangelists point up to the figure of Christ, the Pantokrator; on the side-wall are the figures of Paul (LEFT) and Peter (RIGHT).
BELOW RIGHT: the fifth-century mosaics over the apse in St Pudenziana's.

Gentile church, no longer centred on Jerusalem nor indebted to its Temple) had been worthwhile: in God's providence he had built a work that could survive the shockwaves of Jerusalem's calamitous fall. What he could not know was that he had also built a work that, 400 years later, would equally survive the shockwaves of the fall of Rome herself. He had built on rock, not sand.

## Rome in AD 60: other places

Other places too give an idea of Rome in Paul's day, but note again how many sites date to shortly *after* his death. This is true even of the impressive **Colosseum** (commissioned by Vespasian in AD 72, possibly with funding derived from Jerusalem's capture). This area had been an artificial lake within the gardens of Nero's vast golden palace, itself begun after the great fire of AD 64. Nero's Rome, however, was one that people, including Vespasian, very soon wanted to forget. It had been a decade of decadence and brutality, and Paul had arrived in Rome at its outset.

Climbing up the steep **Palatine Hill**, with its fresh breezes and great views, one senses the 'palatial' living enjoyed by Rome's aristocracy. Although there are some remains of the **home of Emperor Augustus**, the chief site to be explored, complete with its own small sports stadium, is the vast **Palace of Domitian** (c. AD 85). Though again built after Paul's day, we can sense the emperors' sheer power in the New Testament era – that same power that Paul had come to Rome to challenge.

Finally, there would have been good views from Domitian's balcony over the **Circus Maximus**. Walking its length today, one can try to sense what it was like to compete in a race surrounded by a crowd of spectators numbering up to 300,000. Such race-tracks had already inspired Paul's references to the Christian life as a race (see p. 134) but conceivably this Circus Maximus was in his mind when he now spoke of himself as having 'finished the race' (2 Timothy 4:7); it may have also inspired the famous words in Hebrews 12, written by a colleague to the fearful Christians in Rome.

*'Since we are surrounded by such a great cloud of witnesses, let us throw off everything that hinders… and let us run with perseverance the race that is set out for us. Let us fix our eyes on Jesus…'*
**Hebrews 12:1–2**

Other parts of Pauline Rome still visible today can be listed more briefly: the **Ponte Fabricio**, a bridge across the Tiber to the Tiber island; the two temples of the **Forum Boarium**; the foundations of the **Jupiter Temple** (the key shrine on the Capitol), now visible at the back of the Capitoline Museum; the **Mithraeum** (first century BC) under the Church of San Clemente; and the vast dome of the **Pantheon** (originally built in 27 BC, but rebuilt after a severe lightning strike in AD 120).

## Ostia: the unvisited gem

The best way to imagine Rome in Paul's day, however, may be to go to a place nearby, which he may never have visited – the ruins of **Ostia**, Rome's ancient harbour, some 16 miles (25 km) to the south-west. Few sites give such a clear outline of a Roman city. Right on the first-century coastline, there are the remains of a synagogue, orientated towards Jerusalem – conceivably the place where news about Jesus first hit the Italian shores, as Jewish traders returned from the east (Acts 2:10).

But did Paul ever visit Ostia? Intriguingly, if the boat on which Paul had left Malta had been somewhat smaller, then the answer would have been 'yes'. For this was where the vital grain fleet was offloaded onto barges. However, the very largest vessels had to dock instead at Puteoli (where the cargo was reloaded onto smaller vessels). This is precisely what happened with the large 'Alexandrian' ship on which Paul travelled (Acts 28:11–13): it docked at Puteoli, so Paul eventually arrived in Rome not by sea (via Ostia) but overland.

However, we know that Paul would have *liked* at some point to pass through Ostia. For this was the port he would have used if he had survived to set out on his planned expedition to Spain (Romans 15:24). Though some think this dream was fulfilled, most scholars now think it was not. So Ostia, for all the help it gives us in imagining life in Paul's time, must probably remain on the list of places Paul would *like* to have visited but *never did*.



## The Appian Way

Instead Paul arrived in Rome overland along the Appian Way – a journey of around a week (Puteoli to Rome was roughly 120 miles or 190 km). When they still had over 40 miles (70 km) to go, they were met by some Roman Christians near the 'Forum of Appius'; some more believers met them 10 miles (16 km) nearer to Rome at another staging post known as the 'Three Taverns' (both mentioned by Cicero in one of his letters: *ad Atticum* 2:10). Neither of these places has survived, but one can still walk major sections of this old Roman road.

When you pass the Alban hills on your right, you know the end is in sight (just four to five hours more walking). From here on, apart from one tiny incline at a point where the road makes a slight bend, it is downhill all the way, heading straight for the walls of Rome. In late March the air is thick with the smell of wild flowers coming into bloom; the sun is on your back, but there can still be an icy breeze

The grey basalt slabs of the Appian Way have survived for 2,000 years. Paul walked along these self-same stones in the spring of AD 60, under guard but talking with the Roman Christians who had come out to greet him. 'And so we came to Rome' (Acts 28:14).

blowing into your face from the north. In places the grey basalt slabs, some with clear Roman ruts, are still there. With 90 minutes to go before reaching the city gate, the remains of one of Rome's aqueducts comes close on the right-hand side, but the side of the road itself becomes littered with tombs. Many of these Paul would have walked past on that spring morning in AD 60 – including the large, drum-shaped **tomb of Cecilia Metella** on his right. The final approach thus gains a slightly macabre feeling: you are approaching a city full of life, yet the first evidence of that life is its tombs. Did Paul sense something of this too? Did he start wondering if he would ever get out of this city alive? And, if not, would anyone be bothered to build a tomb like one of these for *him*?

You then pass the area of the 'catacombs' (now named after **San Callisto**, **San Sebastiano** and **Domitilla**), one of which centuries later may have been used for a while to house the bones of Paul; next is the church called **Domine Quo Vadis** (commemorating Peter's attempted flight from persecution). Eventually you reach the city walls built (much later) by the emperor Aurelian, and any attempt to emulate Paul's arrival in Rome evaporates amid the noise of Rome's polluting traffic. Yet approaching Rome in this way, on foot along the Appian Way, casts a lasting impression. Just as the disciples sensed something of Jesus' destiny as he approached Jerusalem, so you sense something of Paul's destiny as he entered this city that he had wanted to visit for so long. This was *his* 'Jerusalem', his place of arrival, and his 'point of no return'.



*'Then both Peter and Paul were led away from the presence of Nero. And Paul was beheaded on the Ostian road... And some devout men wished to carry off the relics of the saints, and immediately there was a great earthquake in the city... But the Romans put them in a place three miles from the city, and there they were guarded a year and seven months, until they had built the place in which they intended to put them... And the consummation of the holy glorious Apostles Peter and Paul was on the 29th of the month of June.'*

***Acts of Peter and Paul***

## St Paul outside the walls

Like Jesus, there came a time when Paul too was led outside the city and put to death by Roman soldiers. It is argued above (pp. 192–95) that this took place in AD 63 or AD 64 after a period of continued confinement in Rome; others, however, have argued for a later date (c. AD 65–67), presuming that Paul escaped Rome for a season. Either way the general vicinity for his death seems agreed, being somewhere south-west of the city, along or near the **Ostian Way**.

The evidence for this is two-fold. First, the *Acts of Peter and Paul* (dated commonly to the fourth century AD) speaks of Paul being killed near the 'third milestone' on the Ostian Way. The story clearly has apocryphal elements within it, but may reflect some accurate Christian memory. This site is now commonly identified with **Tre Fontane**, where a church was built in the fifth century. The present **Church of St Paul** (now kept by Benedictines) was built over this in the sixteenth century and contains a column to which Paul was supposedly tied at the time of his execution. For many years the area was a malaria-ridden swamp (though now drained through the planting of eucalyptus trees), so it is not impossible that it was used as a place of discreet execution; yet one wonders why the soldiers came quite so far into the countryside before doing the deed.

Statue of St Paul in the courtyard of St Paul Outside the Walls.

More reliable is the tradition that locates the place of Paul's *burial* 1 mile (1.6 km) nearer the city – at the site now marked by the vast **Church of St Paul Outside the Walls**. This is close by the

Tiber and on the route of the ancient Ostian Way. In the late second century a Christian presbyter in Rome, called Gaius, when discussing Peter and Paul, confidently asserted:

*I can point out the trophies [*memoriae*] of the apostles: for if you will go to the Vatican Hill or the Ostian Way, you will find the trophies of those who founded this church.*

**Gaius' letter to Proclus (preserved in Eusebius, *Church History* 2.25:7)**

By this date memorial monuments of some kind seem to have been placed over the tombs of both Peter (on the Vatican) and Paul (here, by the Ostian Way) – both of them located in ordinary pagan cemeteries. Later, however, when Constantine came to power, he commissioned two churches to be built over these sites. That over Peter's tomb would last until the fifteenth century (when it was replaced by the present Church of St Peter's). That over Paul's tomb, however, was soon replaced by a vast church, commissioned by Emperor Theodosius and consecrated in AD 390. Its nave had five aisles, created by four rows of twenty columns. For the next thousand years (until the building of St Peter's) it would be the largest church in Christendom. And it survived right through to the night of 15 July 1823, when it was destroyed by a fire caused by some careless workmen repairing the roof. Though some engravings survive, it is hard now to imagine what it might have been like to walk inside this church that had stood for nearly *one and half millennia*.

A rare view of the sarcophagus under the main altar in the church of Saint Paul Outside the Walls, understood to contain Paul's remains.

To go inside the present church (though restored to the same dimensions as the original) cannot quite evoke the same sense of sheer antiquity. The **mosaics** above the central arch (fifth century) and in the apse (thirteenth century) were not totally destroyed by the fire and have been restored; and one of the west doors has silver and bronze carvings going back to the eleventh century. Yet most things, inevitably, speak of the nineteenth century. At the heart of the church, however, is the place of **Paul's tomb**. Those rebuilding the church in the nineteenth century found two slabs, on which were inscribed (in script dated to the time of Constantine) the simple words: PAULO APOSTOLO MART ('to Paul, apostle and martyr'). With a high degree of certainty, we can assume that this is the place where Paul's body was finally laid to rest.

It is a fitting place, then, to stop and reflect – perhaps pausing at the rail in front of the tomb, perhaps going out into the beautiful medieval cloister adjacent to the south transept – to ponder the apostle's death and, more especially, to evaluate something of what he achieved through his life.

*'I have fought the fight, I have finished the race, I have kept the faith. Now there is in store for me the crown of righteousness, which the Lord will award to me on that day – and not only me, but also all who have longed for his appearing.'*

**2 Timothy 4:7–8**

## Paul: his influence on Rome and beyond

It is also a fitting place to bring to an end our journey in the steps of Saint Paul. Looking back on the phenomenon of Paul in Rome, one realizes that, of course, this man has left his mark on this city far more than the above account allows. We have been searching for pointers to him in the streets of first-century Rome. Yet Paul left no physical tracks and, even in the more important categories of *personal* influence, Paul's effect *at that time* on the city was perhaps not that great.

In the centuries that followed, however, his influence would extend far, far wider: the Christian church, which he sought to build, would come eventually to a place of prominence throughout the empire; and his strategy of targeting Rome itself with the message of another king, called Jesus, would lead in due course to the conversion of Rome's own rulers. After that, with the consequent building of Rome's many churches, and then through the regular reading of Paul's words as contained in the New Testament (Sunday by Sunday), the influence of Paul on this city would grow exponentially.



Ironically, however, in the era of the Reformation the very letter that he wrote to the church in Rome (his 'epistle to the Romans') would play its part in spawning some churches that broke away from Rome's leadership. Yet this only served to catapult Paul's influence yet further afield – quite beyond the boundaries of the Roman empire that Paul himself had known.

For people discovered in the gospel preached by Paul a depth and clarity of insight into the human condition that was without parallel. He spoke of a God of great faithfulness who in Jesus his Son had come radically close – to reveal himself, to rescue a broken and fallen world, to touch individuals with an assurance of God's grace, mercy and love. He spoke of new life lived with the help of God's Spirit; he wrestled with the forces of darkness; and he offered hope for the renewal of all creation through his message of Jesus' death and resurrection. His was a theology that cut so truly to the depths of human need that it also scaled the heights of heaven's hope.

*'For we do not preach ourselves, but Jesus Christ as Lord, and ourselves merely as servants for Jesus' sake.'*
**2 Corinthians 4:4**

People hearing that message found themselves transported into Paul's mental world – a place where God was ceaselessly at work to bring good out of evil. And, as they were drawn into this new world, they came face to face with the Jesus whom Paul knew. Somehow, through the words of his frail servant, the voice of the Master himself was heard, and lives were reborn.

Such has been Paul's effect on countless millions from his own day through to the present. We have been following 'in the steps of Saint Paul', but in a strange sense we find (so close was the relationship between this servant and his Master) that we have all the while been following, unknowingly, 'in the steps of Jesus'.

Paul would have it no other way. And, if the above pages have done anything to increase your admiration for Paul or somehow created a desire to follow his lead, Paul himself would be the first to say: 'do not be a follower of me, Paul, but follow Christ' (1 Corinthians 1:12–13). Yes, by all means follow in the steps of Paul, but above all, he would insist, follow in the steps of Jesus.

# Epilogue

## Luke: in the steps of Jesus, in the steps of Saint Paul

Our journey is done. We have travelled with Paul from Damascus to Rome or, as Luke would have said, from Jerusalem to the 'ends of the earth'. In conclusion, however, it is worth pausing to consider how Paul's journey *from* Jerusalem relates to the earlier journey of Jesus *to* Jerusalem. For, as pointed out in the Introduction (p. 14), Luke deliberately set these two journeys in parallel. Thus in his Gospel Luke had given particular emphasis to the theme of Jesus being on the road, travelling from Galilee up to Jerusalem (Luke 9–18); now in his sequel, the book of Acts, his narrative structure deliberately takes us on a journey in the reverse direction – from Jerusalem, through Judea and Samaria, to the 'ends of the earth' (Acts 1:8). Thus, when we put these two books together, we realize that Luke wants his readers to travel on a journey *through Jerusalem* and then *out to the world*.

In constructing this great, two-part narrative, Luke inevitably hit upon some interesting parallels between the life of Jesus and the lives of his apostles: they alike set out on risky journeys and proclaimed good news; they alike met opposition but were vindicated by God; they alike were empowered by God's Spirit. Some more specific examples are intriguing. We noticed above (p. 177) how the violent storm that Paul experienced en route to Rome may have formed a parallel in Luke's mind with the crucifixion of Jesus, which he had to endure en route to the resurrection. Another telling example comes from the 'book-ends' of these two stories. In other words, Luke has Jesus *begin* his public ministry in Nazareth, proclaiming the kingdom of God based on a reading of Isaiah (Luke 4:16–21). Then he *finishes* his narrative showing Paul doing exactly the same thing in Rome thirty years later – speaking to synagogue rulers based on a passage in Isaiah and proclaiming the kingdom of God (Acts 28:17–31). What the Master did, his servants are now doing.

More intriguing still, this whole motif of two journeys (to and from Jerusalem) may have been lodged in Luke's mind *because of his own experience*: he himself had made both these journeys – literally. For, despite some scholarly doubts, Luke clearly went up to Jerusalem himself, travelling with Paul in the spring of AD 57 – '*we* went up to Jerusalem' (Acts 21:15); he also left Palestine with Paul, bound for Rome, two years later in the autumn of AD 59 (Acts 27). Quite probably, then, this experience of travelling to and from Palestine was precisely what inspired and supplied him with the structure for his two-volume work. If so, the two years he spent there in Palestine would almost certainly have been spent gathering materials for his first volume; meanwhile, after eventually arriving in Rome he would have a further 'two whole years' (Acts 28:30) to draw together the material for his second volume.

And Luke's own journeys had been costly and difficult. The journey up to Jerusalem had been fraught with danger: first, the plot to kill Paul on the vessel they were due to board (Acts 20:3); then, the dire warnings received in Caesarea confirming that great hardship awaited Paul in Jerusalem (Acts 21:11). Would he, Luke, survive? Would his fellow Gentile companions be hounded out of Jerusalem? Going up to Jerusalem (as for Jesus, so now for Luke himself) had been a risky business. And leaving Jerusalem for Rome had proved even more hazardous: fifteen days adrift on the Mediterranean in a violent storm. There seemed to be a pattern here, woven into his own life, which he now wove into the fine tapestry of his writing. This author was not far removed from his text, but was speaking out of his own live engagement with the issues and the places of his narrative.



It was suggested above that Luke may have died shortly after completing Acts around AD 62/63. This must remain conjecture. Many would date the composition of Luke's Gospel to the 70s or even 80s AD; and it is not impossible that Luke survived and brought out a definitive version of the Gospel after the fall of Jerusalem in AD 70 (reflected, some suggest, in his wording in Luke 21:20–24). Yet, on closer inspection, there is little in the Gospel that demands this later date, and the otherwise puzzling ending of Acts (with no account of Paul's long-expected trial before Caesar) is more easily explained by Luke's completing his narrative in AD 62 and then not being able to update it. After all, both Luke and Paul were advanced in years (perhaps now in their late fifties or early sixties?), and we must not underestimate the physical and emotional consequences of a traumatic experience like their shipwreck off Malta. Luke's travels thus seem to have ended in Rome, quite possibly before Paul's.

His legacy, however, is remarkable. In this and my previous book (*In the Steps of Jesus*) the focus has, rightly, been on Jesus himself and Paul – the two 'heroes' of Luke's account. Yet, as we close, we should give due credit to the one who was their biographer. What knowledge of the early church would we have if we did not have Acts? Without Luke and Acts, the New Testament would have a gaping hole. Many find Luke's portrait of Jesus the most humane, the most touching, the most accessible. Where would we be had Luke not recorded Jesus' parables (such as that of the Good Samaritan or the Prodigal Son)? So, even if Luke died in Rome in the early 60s AD, he manifestly left the world a much richer place.

For Luke's two volumes are a remarkable achievement, a priceless bequest. Through 2,000 years they have given inspiration to thousands upon thousands, being read now each day by someone somewhere around the globe. Truly his own message has gone out 'to the ends of the earth'. And people throughout the world have followed Luke's own example and heard his call: to travel, at least in their spirits, to Jerusalem with Jesus and then out to the world with his Spirit – in the steps of Jesus and in the steps of his apostle, Saint Paul.

# Further Reading


## Primary texts quoted or discussed in this book

For extracts of many texts, see Stephenson, J. (ed.), *A New Eusebius* (London: SPCK, 1957).

### Acts of Paul (and Thecla)

See James, M.R., *The Apocryphal New Testament* (Oxford: Clarendon Press, 1924), pp. 272–81.

### Clement of Rome

See Roberts, A. and Donaldson, J., *Ante-Nicene Fathers*, Vol. 1 (original, 1866; reprinted by Eerdmans in 1981), pp. 5–121.

### Eusebius of Caesarea

See Williamson, G.A., *The Ecclesiastical History* (Harmondsworth: Penguin, 1965).

### Irenaeus

See Roberts, A. and Donaldson, J., *Ante-Nicene Fathers*, Vol. 1 (original, 1866; reprinted by Eerdmans in 1981), pp. 309–577.

## Archaeological and Historical Issues

Akurgal, E., *Ancient Civilizations and Ruins of Turkey* (Istanbul: Haset Kitabevi, 4th edn, 1978).

Bauckham, R.J., (ed.), *The Book of Acts in its First Century Setting*, Vol. 4: Palestinian Setting (Carlisle/Grand Rapids: Paternoster/Eerdmans, 1995).

Fant, C.E. and Reddish, M.G., *A Guide to Biblical Sites in Greece and Turkey* (Oxford: OUP, 2003).

Gill, D.W.J. and Gempf, C. (eds), *The Book of Acts in its First Century Setting*, Vol. 2: Graeco-Roman Setting (Carlisle/Grand Rapids: Paternoster/Eerdmans, 1994).

Levinskaya, I. (ed.), *The Book of Acts in its First Century Setting*, Vol. 5: Diaspora Setting (Carlisle/Grand Rapids: Paternoster/Eerdmans, 1996).

McRay, J., *Archaeology and the New Testament* (Grand Rapids: Baker, 1991).

Murphy O'Connor, J., *St. Paul's Corinth* (Collegeville: The Liturgical Press, 1983 and 2002).

Ramsay, W.M., *St Paul the Traveller and the Roman Citizen* (London: Hodder & Stoughton, 1898).

Ramsay, W.M., *Luke the Physician* (London: Hodder & Stoughton, 1908).

Ramsay, W.M., *Pauline and Other Studies* (London: Hodder & Stoughton, 1908).

## Pauline Theology and New Testament Issues

Barrett, C.K., *Paul: an introduction to his thought* (Louisville: Westminster John Knox, 1994).

Bruce, F.F., *Paul: Apostle of the Free Spirit* (Exeter: Paternoster Press, 5th edn, 1988).

Green, G. L., *The Letters to the Thessalonians*, Pillar New Testament Commentary (Grand Rapids/Leicester: Eerdmans/IVP, 2002).

Ladd, G.E., *A Theology of the New Testament* (Grand Rapids: Eerdmans, revised edn, 1993).

Longenecker, R.N., *Galatians*, Word Biblical Commentary 41 (Dallas: Word Books, 1990).

Wenham, D., *Paul: Follower of Jesus or Founder of Christianity?* (Grand Rapids & Cambridge: Eerdmans, 1995).

Wenham, D. and Walton, S., *Exploring the New Testament*, 2 vols (London: SPCK, 2001/2002).

Witherington, B., *The Paul Quest: the Renewed Search for the Jew of Tarsus* (Leicester and Downers Grove: IVP, 1998).

Wright, N.T., *What Saint Paul Really Said* (Oxford: Lion Hudson, 1997).

## Travel Guides and Narratives

Brownrigg, R., *Pauline Places* (Sevenoaks: Hodder & Stoughton, 1978).

Cimak, F., *Journeys of Paul: from Tarsus 'to the ends of the earth'* (Istanbul: A Turizm Yayinlan, 2004).

Dalrymple, W., *From the Holy Mountain: a journey among the Christians of the Middle East* (London: HarperCollins, 1997).

Morton. H.V., *In the Steps of St Paul* (London: Rich & Cowan, 1936; reprinted by Methuen in 2002).

Richards, H., *Pilgrim to Rome: a practical guide* (Great Wakering: McCrimmon Publishing, 1994).

# Index

*Bold entries indicate main section on topic.*

## *Scripture References*

### Old Testament



### New Testament

# General references

# Picture Acknowledgments

All maps and diagrams by Richard Watts of Total Media Services unless credited otherwise below.

p. 3 Bettman/Corbis; p. 10 Todd Bolen/Bibleland Images; p. 13 Peter Walker; p. 14 Terry Harris Just Greece photo library/Alamy; p. 19 NASA; p. 25 Todd Bolen/Bibleland Images (both images); p. 26 David Alexander; p. 28 Peter Walker (bottom left), David Alexander (centre left); pp. 28–29 Geoffrey Morgan/Alamy; p. 29 mediacolors/Alamy; p. 30 Hemis/Alamy; p. 31 Lion Hudson; pp. 32–33 Images & Stories/Alamy; p. 34 www.HolyLandPhotos.org; p. 35 Peter Walker; p. 37 Images & Stories/Alamy; p. 39 dk/Alamy; p. 40 Peter Adams/jonarnoldimages.com; p. 44 The Print Collector/Alamy; p. 49 Peter Walker; p. 51 AFP/Getty Images (both images); p. 52 Rex Allen/Alamy (bottom left), Peter Walker (top left); p. 56 nagelestock.com/Alamy; p. 60 David Robertson/Alamy; pp. 60–61 Doug Pearson/jonarnoldimages.com; p. 63 DEA/G.DAGLI ORTI (bottom left), Todd Bolen/Bibleland Images (bottom right), Peter Walker (centre right); pp. 64–65 MERVYN REES/Alamy; p. 67 Eddie Gerald/Alamy; p. 68 David Alexander (bottom left), Demetrio Carrasco/jonarnoldimages.com (top); p. 72 Demetrio Carrasco/jonarnoldimages.com; p. 74 Jon Arnold/jonarnoldimages.com (bottom), Demetrio Carrasco/jonarnoldimages.com (top); p. 75 Travel Pix Collection/jonarnoldimages.com (bottom), Peter Walker (centre left and centre right); p. 76 INTERFOTO Pressebildagentur/Alamy; p. 79 David Alexander; p. 80 Peter Walker (both images); p. 83 Images & Stories/Alamy; p. 87 Todd Bolen/Bibleland Images; p. 88 Jon Arnold/jonarnoldimages.com; p. 90 Earl & Nazima Kowall/CORBIS; p. 91 Used by permission of the H V Morton Literary Estate; p. 94 ALIKI SAPOUNTZI/aliki image library/Alamy; p. 97 Jon Arnold/jonarnoldimages.com; p. 100 www.HolyLandPhotos.org; p. 103 DEA/A.GAROZZO; p. 104 ALIKI SAPOUNTZI/aliki image library/Alamy; p. 105 Jon Arnold/jonarnoldimages.com; p. 106 Werner Otto / Alamy; p. 109 Todd Bolen/Bibleland Images; p. 110 Jon Arnold/jonarnoldimages.com; p. 114 Travel Pix Collection/ jonarnoldimages.com; p. 115 Jon Arnold/jonarnoldimages.com (both images); p. 117 Pictu Ltd; p. 118 Jon Arnold/jonarnoldimages.com; p. 119 Jon Arnold/jonarnoldimages.com; p. 120 Peter Walker; p. 121 Pixida/Alamy; pp. 122–23 De Agostini/Getty Images; pp. 124–25 ACE STOCK LIMITED/Alamy; p. 125 Peter Walker; p. 127 Peter Walker; p. 129 Jon Arnold/jonarnoldimages.com; pp. 130–31 Rainer Hackenberg/zefa/Corbis; p. 132 Jon Arnold/jonarnoldimages.com; p. 134 Peter Walker; pp. 136–37 David Alexander; p. 137 Erich Lessing/ AKG Images/Zooid Pictures Ltd; pp. 138–39 Jonathan Adams; p. 142 Peter Walker (centre right), Peter Adams/ jonarnoldimages.com (top right); p. 145 Peter Walker; p. 146 Peter Walker; p. 147 Peter Walker (both images); p. 148 K. & H. Benser/zefa/Corbis; p. 150 David Alexander; p. 151 Peter Walker (centre left), David Alexander (centre right); p. 153 Peter Walker (both images); p. 154 Hanan Isachar; p. 157 David Alexander; pp. 158–59 Leen Ritmeyer; p. 159 David Alexander; pp. 160–61 Jon Arnold/jonarnoldimages.com; p. 163 Peter Walker; p. 164 Peter Walker (both images); p167 Hanan Isachar (bottom right), Jonathan Adams (top); p. 168 Peter Walker; p. 171 Travel Pix Collection/ jonarnoldimages.com; p. 172 Hanan Isachar; p. 173 David Alexander; p. 174 Peter Walker; p. 176 Peter Walker; p. 180 Todd Bolen/Bibleland Images; p. 183 Peter Walker; p. 188 © 1990 Photo SCALA, Florence – courtesy of the Ministero Beni e Att. Culturali; p. 195 imagebroker/Alamy; p. 196 Jon Arnold/jonarnoldimages.com; p. 197 Jon Arnold/jonarnoldimages.com; p. 198 AEP/Alamy (bottom left), Rough Guides/Alamy (bottom right); p. 200 Marco Cristofori; p. 201 Peter Walker; p. 202 AFP/Getty Images; p. 204 Hemis/Alamy.